D1450110

# THE BOSTON CHEF'S TABLE

## THE BEST IN CONTEMPORARY CUISINE

### CLARA SILVERSTEIN

**ThreeForks™**

GUILFORD, CONNECTICUT
HELENA, MONTANA
AN IMPRINT OF THE GLOBE PEQUOT PRESS

To buy books in quantity for corporate use
or incentives, call **(800) 962–0973**
or e-mail **premiums@GlobePequot.com.**

While we make every effort to obtain current information from
chefs and restaurants, some closings and changes in personnel are
inevitable. For the most current information about restaurants,
call or check the Web sites.

Copyright © 2008 by Clara Silverstein

All rights reserved. No part of this book may be reproduced or transmitted in any form by any means,
electronic or mechanical, including photocopying and recording, or by any information storage and re-
trieval system, except as may be expressly permitted by the 1976 Copyright Act or by the publisher.
Requests for permission should be made in writing to The Globe Pequot Press, P.O. Box 480, Guilford,
Connecticut 06437.

Three Forks is a trademark of Morris Book Publishing, LLC.

Cover design by Georgiana Goodwin
Cover photographs © Jane Booth
Photographs © Jane Booth except p. 113 © Photos.com/Index Open; p. 123 © Index Open; and p. 175 ©
photolibrary.com/Index Open
Text design by Nancy Freeborn

**Library of Congress Cataloging-in-Publication Data is available.**
ISBN 978-0-7627-4514-2

Manufactured in China
First Edition/First Printing

In memory of Murray David Schnee, 1924–2005: My father-in-law, who always appreciated a good meal.

# Contents

# Acknowledgments

This book would not have been possible without the generosity of the chefs whose recipes appear within it. I thank all who opened their kitchens and their recipe files, especially those who demonstrated their recipes for me while I furiously scribbled notes, clumsily trying to balance a fork and a pen. Many chefs also patiently answered my endless queries so I could adapt their recipes for the home cook. Behind the scenes, the publicists, assistants, and general managers who helped put me in touch with the chefs, and kept reminding them to send in their recipes, deserve plenty of recognition.

Many friends stepped up to help test recipes. I could always count on Esther Muhlfelder for her food expertise, especially in baking, her helpful suggestions about recipe revisions, and her interest in accompanying me on tasting missions. Bonnie Katz, Fran Newton, Lisa Shames, and Jane Walsh also cheerfully tested recipes. My neighbor and fellow foodie, Susan Katcher, answered cooking questions at all hours and tasted many recipes in progress. Cindy Ryan was willing to meet me anywhere, even on short notice, to sample dishes for the book.

Outside of the kitchen, I am grateful for the friendship and professional support of my fellow food writers, also known as the Ladies Who Lunch: Ali Berlow, Carolyn Faye Fox, Andrea Pyenson, Lisë Stern, Rachel Travers, Cathy Walthers, and Lisa Zwirn. Also supportive from the outset were Kay Cahill Allison, Laurie Burgess, Marjorie Druker, Jody Feinberg, Judy Gelman, Rosemary Herbert, Bernice and Murray Schnee, and Ann Silverstein. My writing always benefits from my affiliations with The Workshop for Publishing Poets, led by Barbara Helfgott Hyett, and the Writers' Center at Chautauqua. For legal counsel, I thank David Herlihy. For stress relief, few groups could surpass the CLG or the Crying Shames.

David Emblidge, my editor at Globe Pequot Press, took the proposal I sent in and helped me shape it into a book. His appreciation of food, thoughtful comments, and experienced hand kept me organized and focused. I also thank Heather Carreiro and the rest of the team at Globe Pequot—photographer Jane Booth, designers Georgiana Goodwin and Nancy Freeborn, production manager Melissa Evarts, and copy editor Laura Jorstad.

From the beginning, my husband, George, encouraged me to take on this project. Our adventures in eating have continued since our first date at the Thai buffet. He and our children, Jordan and Martha, endured endless recipe tests—but also enjoyed the results. Their love, support, and humor helped see me through.

# Introduction

Boston used to be the capital of clam chowder, baked beans, and brown bread. You can still find ample helpings of these old favorites around "Beantown," but many of the city's chefs have moved past them. Instead they use regional ingredients—scallops, lobsters, corn, winter squash, cranberries, and maple syrup—in more contemporary ways. Their cooking also reflects Boston's transformation from a provincial capital into an international city. Despite its stern Puritan roots, Boston has a long tradition of openness to outside influences, perhaps because of its role as a busy port. Once-exotic ingredients such as fresh mangoes, pickled ginger, and truffle oil have become readily available, challenging chefs to find ways to use them. The result—an energetic, Boston-based approach to cooking—deserves a closer look. *The Boston Chef's Table* takes you into some of the top restaurant kitchens in the city and offers a collection of recipes you can try at home.

Restaurants have become a vibrant part of Boston's cultural life, regularly earning national accolades. Certain dining rooms have become must-go destinations for the city's trendsetters, politicians, and power brokers. Chefs, more visible than ever through their public appearances on television cooking shows and at charity fund-raisers, personally greet customers. Dishes are designed to wow diners with color and complexity. Instead of the basic American broiled steak and baked potato, you might find spice-rubbed grilled pork chops with sweet potato fries, or seared steak with blue cheese mashed potatoes. Nowhere is this more obvious than on dessert menus, where sweets now come in elaborate pairs or trilogies—the better to offer cinnamon ice cream with warm chocolate cake and crisp tuile cookies.

Many culinary influences converge in Boston, still sometimes called "the Hub of the Universe" (a reference coined by nineteenth-century Boston writer Oliver Wendell Holmes). With a cleaned-up Boston Harbor and miles of Atlantic coastline nearby, there is always plenty of fresh seafood for chowder (never red—that's from Manhattan), steamed mussels, fried clams, and lobster rolls. There is newfound pride in native crops such as Macomber turnips and Concord grapes, sold seasonally at dozens of farmers' markets in the city or on its edges. Some neighborhoods have retained their ethnic markets and eateries, including Chinatown, the North End (Italian), South Boston (Irish), and East Cambridge (Portuguese). Newer immigrants from the Caribbean, Central and South America, and Southeast Asia have brought their own food traditions to liven up markets and menus.

A crossroads like Massachusetts Avenue in Central Square illustrates this kind of dining diversity. Within a square mile you can find an espresso bar, cutting-edge contemporary fare, American comfort food, gourmet ice cream, and Middle Eastern, Chinese, Indian, and Mexican cheap eats.

The Greater Boston area's cosmopolitan atmosphere, with about three and a half million residents, has helped fuel the restaurant boom. Since the city is home to so many universities and medical centers, its population tends to be young and well educated. Add to that all the high-tech and financial services businesses with headquarters here, and you have a lot of people with money to spend on eating out. So what if the Puritans set a dour tone that still lingers at bars, where the 2:00 A.M. closing time is shockingly early by big-city standards.

For most of the twentieth century, frugal Bostonians reserved eating out for special occasions. The choices usually came down to New England fare such as Yankee pot roast and Indian pudding (Durgin-Park, the Union Oyster House), Old World European (Locke-Ober, the Ritz-Carlton), Italian, or Chinese. Families splurged for hot fudge sundaes at Brigham's, an old-style ice cream parlor that's now a chain. The oversize blueberry muffins from the Jordan Marsh department store downtown were a favorite snack for shoppers.

Julia Child, who started broadcasting *The French Chef* on Boston's WGBH public television station in 1962, helped raise everyone's appreciation for fine dining. Nouvelle cuisine, health food restaurants, and food co-ops arrived in the 1970s.

In the 1980s, across America and in Boston as well, a new, energetic generation of chefs started to put creativity ahead of tradition. Some of the new wave of Boston chefs had been trained at the Culinary Institute of America in Hyde Park, New York, or Johnson & Wales College in Providence, Rhode Island; others learned on the job or during their travels. In Boston, chefs Jasper White, Lydia Shire, Chris Douglass, Gordon Hamersley, and Paul O'Connell were among the pioneers in reinterpreting New England cooking. At the East Coast Grill in Cambridge, Chris Schlesinger turned grilling into an art form. Using Italian food as a springboard for new ideas were Todd English, Barbara Lynch, and Jody Adams. All of these groundbreaking chefs are still cooking at Boston restaurants, where they continue to define and redefine eating out. They have trained and inspired dozens of other chefs, some of whom have gone on to open their own restaurants. Since so many Boston chefs have worked for one another, the professional community often seems more collegial than competitive—quite a different atmosphere than in other cities.

As a newcomer to Boston in 1983, and a professional food writer since 1990, I have worked closely with these chefs, sometimes scrambling to keep pace as the dining scene seemed to explode. Over time I realized that this remarkable group of chefs needed a collection of recipes that could represent how they have defined the best in contemporary dining in Boston.

*The Boston Chef's Table* introduces you to chefs who have built careers out of innovation, as well as to promising newcomers. Their thoughtfully prepared dishes can be found in candlelit, silk-curtained dining rooms or in casual cafes and take-out places. What they have in common is their creativity, especially with New England ingredients. You can find lobster in everything from Grill 23's chilled gazpacho with avocado ice cream to Radius's fried rice. The custard at Prose embellishes plain maple syrup, and a chocolate cranberry tart from Casablanca puts a sweet spin on another signature New England crop. The recipes in this book range in difficulty from Aquitaine's endive salad, which can be tossed together in fifteen minutes, to Olives' lasagna, which takes more than an hour to assemble and bake—*inside a pumpkin!* For contrast with these new approaches to New England cooking, and for a sense of history, there are also a few classics no visitor to Boston and no local food enthusiast would want to miss, including baked beans from the Union Oyster House and Boston cream pie from the Omni Parker House Hotel, where it was created in the 1850s. Woven into the book, also, is information about noteworthy local neighborhoods and food traditions with the occasional anecdote about who these Boston food purveyors and chefs really are.

For the most part, the restaurants in *The Boston Chef's Table* are located within 10 miles of downtown Boston, though there are a few suburban standouts, such as Ming Tsai's Blue Ginger in Wellesley, worth a drive out of the city. The focus here on culinary innovation put most of the city's taquerias, trattorias, pubs, and other ethnic restaurants—wonderful as they can be—beyond the scope of this book. There are other worthy restaurants we certainly could have presented here, but then you'd be carrying a much heavier book.

As you explore Boston and *The Boston Chef's Table*, remember that chefs thrive on new ideas; some of these recipes will disappear from restaurant menus to be replaced by the chef's latest—equally interesting—whimsy. And chefs rely on a retinue of helpers to chop vegetables, make stock, and scrub dirty pots. You probably won't have all that help at home. As needed, professional cooking methods have been modified so you can realistically reproduce the recipes at home, relying on ordinary stoves, pots, and pans. In many cases you'll need a food processor (or blender) and electric mixer—preferably a stand mixer, but a handheld will usually do. Find a well-stocked market to supply you with the herbs, spices, and fresh ingredients that the chefs like to use.

By following the recipes of chefs who introduced more sophisticated modern, varied tastes to Boston, you can step up to the challenge of re-creating some of these great meals in your own kitchen. Your family and friends will no doubt applaud, and you will become part of a grand cooking tradition from one of America's most colorful cities. Enjoy your journey through these new twists on regional New England ingredients and recipes. As Julia Child, the city's grande dame of cooking, would warble in her inimitable voice: *"Bon appétit!"*

# APPETIZERS

A well-designed appetizer menu gives each chef a chance to make a strong first impression that carries right through the meal. Inspired by Spanish tapas, some chefs are even re-labeling their appetizers "small plates" and serving them in any order, anytime, to match the flexible mealtimes of customers. Many people end up making a meal of these small portions, forgoing the entree altogether. This mix-and-match approach to dining clashes with the classic progression of appetizer-salad-entree-dessert but suits the current generation of busy Bostonians just fine.

In these recipes chefs like to reinterpret the old standbys. Tuna tartare at Pigalle gets a major overhaul with Asian ingredients including seaweed salad and fish roe, served in a martini glass with chopsticks on the side. Steamed mussels are taken out of the shell at Mistral for a creamy stew with smoked tomatoes. Seared scallops at blu gain renewed appeal when served on a puree of an obscure but much-lauded native Massachusetts vegetable, the Macomber turnip. Ever-inventive chefs have even found new ways to present carrot sticks, a dip for potato chips, and a cheese plate.

## UMBRIA RISTORANTE

295 Franklin Street
Boston (Financial District)
(617) 338–1000, www.umbriaristorante.com

**Former chef | Marisa Iocco**

In a five-story entertainment villa with a nightclub and a lounge, a regional Italian restaurant might seem like an afterthought. But owner and longtime Boston restaurateur Frank De Pasquale specializes in exuberantly re-creating the foods of his native Italy. His other restaurants include Bricco (see page xx), Mare, and the Gelateria ice cream cafe. Named after the Umbria region in central Italy (halfway between Florence and Rome), this restaurant explores ingredients that are largely unfamiliar to Americans. The so-called green heart of Italy is known for its black truffles, green lentils, sausages, and meat from the wild boars that roam the mountains.

The latter is put to good use in this restaurant's bitter cocoa pasta with wild boar sauce. With filet mignon comes a side of potatoes pureed with cicerchia, a fava bean–chickpea hybrid. After customers are seated, this dip, made with cannellini beans, is presented with the bread. "It's like a welcome. It stimulates the appetite," says former chef Marisa Iocco. It is ideal for a party, as it can be served with many kinds of snack food. Cut the recipe in half to serve a smaller group. Don't use canned beans: The vegetables and prosciutto need to simmer with the beans to infuse them with flavor.

### BEAN DIP FOR BRUSCHETTA

[MAKES ABOUT 4 CUPS]

1 pound dried cannellini beans
1 carrot, peeled and sliced thick
1 small yellow onion, roughly chopped
2 stalks celery, roughly chopped
½ pound prosciutto (preferably end cut), cubed
4 bay leaves
Pinch of kosher salt
Pinch of freshly ground black pepper
1 tablespoon extra-virgin olive oil

1. Place the beans in a large pot. Add enough water to completely submerge them. Soak overnight.

2. The next day, preserving the liquid in the same pot, add the carrot, onion, celery, prosciutto, bay leaves, and salt. Bring to a boil, then cook over medium heat until the beans become tender (1 to 2 hours).

3. Strain and reserve the excess liquid. In a food processor or using an immersion beater, puree the beans, adding a little liquid at a time, until they reach the consistency of mashed potatoes.

4. Place the mixture into a bowl and sprinkle with the black pepper and olive oil. Serve as a dip with crusty bread or raw vegetables.

## BRASSERIE JO

Colonnade Hotel
120 Huntington Avenue, Boston
(617) 425-3240, www.brasseriejoboston.com

**Executive chef and founder | Jean Joho**

**Chef de cuisine | Olivier Rigaud**

Founder Jean Joho modeled Brasserie JO after the brasseries in his native France—casual, neighborhood restaurants that serve simple, hearty food. Since Joho operates several restaurants (Brasserie JO's original location is in Chicago), the French-trained Olivier Rigaud runs day-to-day operations in Boston. A giant wall clock keeps time behind the bar, where you can order the way you might in Paris. A croque monsieur (a grilled ham-and-cheese sandwich that's a staple in any brasserie) goes well with the Alsatian-style house beer. The rest of the menu reads like a French culinary hall of fame, with onion soup, escargots, salade niçoise, steak frites, and coq au vin. At the end of the meal, a pushcart comes around with a selection of cheeses. Another offers profiteroles with homemade chocolate sauce poured until you say, "Stop!"

These carrots, spiced with horseradish and dressed with a light vinaigrette, are brought to every table with the bread. The horseradish gives them a distinct bite but doesn't overpower their flavor. Most people end up bypassing a plate and fork, picking them up with their fingers. These carrot sticks for grown-ups are irresistible.

## HORSERADISH CARROTS

[SERVES 4-6]

**HOUSE DRESSING:**

1 tablespoon Dijon mustard
5 tablespoons champagne vinegar
1 tablespoon freshly squeezed lemon juice
6 tablespoons olive oil
½ cup plus 1 tablespoon corn oil
½ teaspoon sugar
Salt and pepper, to taste

In a large bowl, whisk together all the ingredients. Set aside until ready to use. Cover and refrigerate any leftover dressing to use with a salad or another vegetable dish.

**CARROTS:**

2½ pounds carrots, cut into bite-size sticks
    about ¼ inch wide (see note)
1½ teaspoons bottled horseradish
2 tablespoons chopped fresh parsley
Salt and pepper, to taste
⅓ cup House Dressing (from recipe above)

Gently toss all ingredients together in a large bowl. Serve as an appetizer with crusty bread.

:: **Note:** Do not be tempted to substitute prewashed, precut carrots in this recipe. Sticks cut from whole carrots taste fresher and retain their crunch when tossed with the dressing.

## VOX POPULI

755 Boylston Street
Boston (Back Bay)
(617) 424–8300, www.voxboston.com

**Former chef | Eric Bogardus**

Only a Latin scholar could understand the speech by Cicero that is printed here on the bar top and lamp shades, but Vox Populi's name is not meant to be esoteric: It translates as "voice of the people." A mostly young, fashionably dressed crowd comes here to socialize. On a busy night, pink and blue martinis dot the restaurant's two dining rooms, creating a kaleidoscopic effect in the mirrors along the exposed-brick walls. Eric Bogardus designs nearly a dozen small, intensely flavored appetizers to go with the drinks—fried polenta batons with house-made ketchup, and whipped feta cheese with chile peppers are two. There is also a full menu for anyone who wants a meal.

In this eggplant caviar Bogardus remakes Middle Eastern baba ghanoush (eggplant spread) with Italian ingredients. "I like to travel a lot, so I start with a local ingredient and bring in influences from everywhere," he says. Charring the eggplant is important because it brings out a smokiness that will stand up to the basil, garlic, and onions. Cheese smooths out the texture and binds everything into a vegetarian dip that is packed with flavor. Though it's served with potato chips, it's in a whole different league from that predictable party standby, sour cream onion dip.

### EGGPLANT CAVIAR

[SERVES 8]

½ cup olive oil, plus more as needed for rubbing eggplants

2 large purple eggplants (approximately 1–1¼ pounds each)

4 cloves garlic, left whole

1 large Spanish onion, quartered

1 bunch basil leaves, stems removed

4 plum tomatoes, each cut in half

1 teaspoon salt

½ teaspoon pepper

1 cup grated Pecorino or Parmesan cheese, plus more for garnish

1. Preheat a broiler to high. Rub the exterior of each eggplant with olive oil. Place the eggplants on a baking sheet. Broil until the skin begins to blacken and char, using tongs to rotate frequently so they char on all sides. (The eggplants can also be charred on a grill at medium-high heat, rotating with tongs.) Place them in a mixing bowl and cover the bowl with plastic wrap. Let cool for 30 minutes.

2. Carefully remove the skin from the eggplants, and discard it. (You can do this by peeling the skin, which should slip right off, or by scooping out the pulp with a spoon.) Place

the pulp in a medium skillet or stockpot. Add the garlic, onion, basil, tomatoes, 1/2 cup olive oil, salt, and pepper. Cook over medium-low heat for 30 minutes, or until all the vegetables are completely soft.

3. Place the eggplant mixture into the bowl of a food processor, add the cheese, and process until pureed. Serve warm or cold with any type of chips. Garnish with a drizzle of extra-virgin olive oil and a sprinkle of cheese.

## MERITAGE

Boston Harbor Hotel
70 Rowes Wharf, Boston
(617) 439–3995, www.meritagetherestaurant.com

**Executive chef | Daniel Bruce**

After more than a decade of masterminding dinners for the annual Boston Wine Festival, chef Daniel Bruce decided to put wine–food pairings to work all year long at Meritage restaurant. The menu is organized by style of wine: Sparklers, full-bodied whites, and fruity reds are some of the categories. For wine alone, you have your choice of 12,000 bottles from all over the world. You won't find bacchanalian murals here. The restaurant looks like a museum of modern art, with a tabletop slab of marble lit from underneath, sprigs of overhead lights on wire cylinders, and a dramatic centerpiece of orchids. Setting it all off is one of the most sweeping views of the Boston waterfront in town. A window seat takes in the ferries, sailboats, water taxis, and barges that ply the Inner Harbor, as well as the runways of Logan Airport and the dramatically curved glass wall of the Federal J. Joseph Moakley Courthouse. In warm weather the patio at the hotel's casual Intrigue cafe (also overseen by Bruce) offers a surfside seat to the bustle at Rowes Wharf.

Because Bruce likes the constant challenge of matching food and wine, he wouldn't just settle for a cheese course of two or three wedges and a few crackers. In this recipe he combines five kinds of cheese—preferably all made in New England, but any high-quality cheese will work fine—in one pie shell. Slices are served over salad greens tossed in cider vinaigrette. There's not a cracker or a bunch of grapes in sight.

# NEW ENGLAND CHEESE PIE

[ SERVES 12 ]

**CHEESE PIE:**

4 ounces Gouda

4 ounces cheddar cheese

1 prebaked, 9-inch deep-dish pie shell

2½ ounces (½ log) goat cheese

4 ounces Brie

4 ounces mascarpone cheese

2 cups heavy cream

3 eggs

½ teaspoon white pepper

¼ cup chopped chives

1.  Preheat the oven to 350 degrees.

2.  In a bowl or on a sheet of waxed paper, grate the Gouda and cheddar cheeses. Place in the prebaked pie shell. Crumble the goat cheese and Brie and sprinkle around the shell. Spoon in the mascarpone.

3.  In a mixing bowl, beat together the cream, eggs, and pepper. Pour over the cheeses, then sprinkle with the chives.

4.  Bake for 45 to 55 minutes, until the top is golden brown and the custard has set.

5.  Let cool to room temperature, and then refrigerate overnight to set.

**CIDER VINAIGRETTE:**

¼ cup apple cider

¼ cup cider vinegar

½ cup olive oil

¼ cup chopped shallots

Salt and pepper, to taste

Combine all the ingredients in a bowl.

**GREEN SALAD:**

6 cups mixed baby greens

In a mixing bowl, toss the greens with the Cider Vinaigrette (from the recipe above).

**FINAL PREPARATION AND SERVING:**

½ cup toasted walnuts

2 green apples (such as Granny Smith), diced

Slice the cheese pie into small wedges and reheat at 250 to 300 degrees. Place the salad on individual plates, with a wedge of cheese pie beside it on each. Garnish each serving with toasted walnuts and diced green apples.

## New England Cheeses

New Englanders have been making their own cheeses since the Pilgrims established their colony in the 1620s. Now artisanal cheesemakers around the region keep the tradition going with more modern methods. Since 2000 the number of small-scale cheesemakers in Vermont has doubled, according to the Vermont Institute for Artisan Cheese. Chefs appreciate the distinctive flavor of these cheeses, which are often made with milk from the cheese-maker's own herds or local dairy farms. In his recipe Daniel Bruce specifically recommends Smith's Country Gouda from Winchendon, Massachusetts (800-700-9974, www.smithscountrycheese.com), and the Hubbardston Blue Rind goat cheese from Westfield Farm in Hubbardston (877-777-3900, www.chevre.com). He suggests looking for cheddar and Brie from Vermont. Also from Vermont is mascarpone from the Vermont Butter and Cheese Company (800-884-6287, www.vtbutterand cheeseco.com). An extensive list of New England cheese-makers can be found from the Great Cheeses of New England trade group (www.newenglandcheese.com).

## NED DEVINE'S

Faneuil Hall Marketplace
Quincy Market, Boston
(617) 248-9900, www.neddevinesboston.com

**Chef | Sean Ryan**

Tucked into a two-story space at one end of Quincy Market, Ned Devine's is an Irish pub where you can also find nachos, a pulled pork sandwich, and coconut chicken curry—eclectic choices guaranteed to appeal to the vast range of visitors to Faneuil Hall Marketplace (see the sidebar on page 106). It's part of the Brighton-based Briar Group, which owns five other Irish pubs in Boston, including the Green Briar and The Harp.

Sean Ryan responded to the high-energy summer crowds at Faneuil Hall—"It's like a playground around here," he says—by developing this recipe for lobster sweet potato cakes. "It's a creative way to use what we have in the summertime. A lot of tourists like them because they feature some of New England's most famous summer fare—sweet native corn, tomatoes, and lobster." The mashed sweet potato, best known for its supporting role at the Thanksgiving table, is the surprise in this dish. Somehow it all works—the potatoes complement that natural sweetness in the lobster, and the warm cakes served over greens with salsa on top make an appealing contrast of colors and temperatures. Because the salsa is mixed with oil and vinegar, it tastes more like a salad than a Mexican condiment. As an alternative, use flavored mayonnaise or guacamole as the accompaniment. The recipe can be adapted for a cocktail party by using the same batter to make smaller, bite-size cakes. Their bright orange hue is eye catching no matter where they are served.

# LOBSTER AND SWEET POTATO CAKES
## WITH SUMMER CORN AND TOMATO SALSA

[MAKES 6 CAKES (3 OUNCES EACH)]

**SUMMER CORN AND TOMATO SALSA:**

3 ears sweet corn, cooked (see page 112 for directions),
    kernels cut from the cob (reserve ¼ cup kernels
    for lobster cakes)
2 ripe tomatoes, seeded and diced
1 small red onion, finely diced
¼ fresh jalapeño pepper, finely diced
1 tablespoon chopped fresh flat-leaf parsley
2 tablespoons olive oil
1 tablespoon red wine vinegar
1 teaspoon granulated garlic or 1 clove garlic, minced
1½ teaspoons sugar
Salt, to taste

In a nonreactive bowl, combine all the ingredients and
chill for 1 hour.

**LOBSTER AND SWEET POTATO CAKES:**

1 large sweet potato (approximately 1½ pounds)
Kosher salt, to taste
2 tablespoons (¼ stick) unsalted butter
½ teaspoon ground white pepper
Meat from a 1½-pound steamed or boiled lobster,
    cut into ¼-inch pieces (about ¾ cup)
1½ teaspoons snipped fresh chives
¼ cup cooked sweet corn kernels (from recipe above)
Salt and pepper, to taste
Flour for dredging
3–4 eggs, beaten
Panko bread crumbs, to coat the lobster cakes
Olive oil, as needed

1. Peel and dice the potato into large pieces. Rinse under cold running water until the water runs clear. Place the potato pieces in a pot, adding cold water to cover them, plus a dash of kosher salt. Bring to a gentle boil and cook for 10 minutes, or until they're tender when pierced with a fork. Drain well, mash with a fork, and place in a mixing bowl. Stir in the butter and pepper. Do not overmix. Cover, place in the refrigerator, and chill for at least an hour.

2. When the potato mixture is well chilled, mix in the lobster meat, chives, and corn. Season with salt and pepper. Form the mixture into 6 cakes—3 ounces each, about the size of a golf ball. Cover and chill in the refrigerator again for 30 minutes.

3. Put the flour, beaten eggs, and panko into three separate, shallow bowls (aluminum pie tins work well for this). Dredge each lobster cake in the flour and dip it in the egg, then in the bread crumbs, turning to coat well on all sides.

4. In a large nonstick pan, add enough olive oil to cover the bottom. Heat until the oil is shimmering but not smoking. Add the cakes, browning them for 2 to 3 minutes per side. Be sure to brown the edges by tilting the skillet and letting the cakes reach the corners of the pan. Remove the cakes to paper towels to blot off any excess oil; keep warm until ready to serve. Serve with salsa (from the recipe above) over any baby greens or a mesclun mix.

## MISTRAL

223 Columbus Avenue
Boston (South End)
(617) 867–9300, www.mistralbistro.com

### Chef-owner | Jamie Mammano

Don't confuse French marinière sauce with the ubiquitous Italian marinara sauce. Marinière, which comes from the French word *marin* (sailor), is based on seafood stock, far more delicate than the garlic-and-onion-laden tomato sauce, which comes from the Italian word *marinare* (to pickle). In Jamie Mammano's capable hands, the seafood sauce becomes the creamy base for a mussels appetizer. By adding smoked tomatoes, the meat from steamed mussels, and fresh thyme to this sauce, he creates a dish that combines the best of both France and New England. The texture is almost like a stew, and it could be called a lazy man's mussels, because there are no shells to sort. When making this recipe, the most convenient method for preparing the tomatoes is grilling (use a grill rack designed for vegetables to keep the tomatoes from falling through). For the best flavor, put your oven to use by roasting and then smoking the tomatoes.

Mammano's personal touch appears in many aspects of Mistral, named after the dry northerly winds that sweep through the Mediterranean region of France. He picked out the terra-cotta tableware, some of which is on display near the front door. His menu ranges from classic escargots and rack of lamb to the more inventive pizza topped with mashed potato and beef tenderloin—not to mention roast Cornish game hen with maple cumin glaze. Wrought-iron chandeliers and banquettes upholstered in marigold yellow warm up a cavernous room with floor-to-ceiling windows. A line of potted cypress trees separates the bar from the dining room. This is the kind of place where the well-dressed crowd comes to celebrate birthdays and business deals.

After Mistral opened in 1997, Mammano and his business partners went on to open two Italian-themed restaurants—Teatro in the Theater District and Sorellina in the Back Bay. All give him room to practice his expertise—combining modern techniques and local ingredients with traditional Mediterranean flavors, working both sides of the French–Italian border.

# STEAMED MUSSELS WITH MARINIÈRE SAUCE

[SERVES 4 AS AN APPETIZER]

**ONION MARINIÈRE SAUCE:**

2 tablespoons butter
½ large onion
1 teaspoon minced garlic
¼ teaspoon crushed red pepper flakes
2 cups white wine, Sauvignon Blanc or Fumé Blanc preferred
2 cups heavy cream

In a saucepan, melt the butter. Add the onion, garlic, and red pepper flakes. Sauté over low heat until the onion is translucent. Add the white wine and bring to a simmer. Reduce until the wine is almost all evaporated. Add the cream and simmer over low heat for 15 minutes.

**TOMATOES:**

4 plum tomatoes, cut in half lengthwise
Olive oil, to coat
Salt and pepper, to taste

The tomatoes can be either grilled or smoked.

**For grilling:**

1. Preheat a grill to medium high. If possible, use cherrywood chips as part of the grilling fuel to add flavor.

2. Place the tomatoes in a shallow bowl and add olive oil, salt, and pepper. Toss to coat with oil.

3. Grill the tomatoes until they soften and the exterior begins to blacken, 2 to 3 minutes per side.

4. Roughly chop and set aside until ready to assemble the dish.

**For smoking:**

1. Place about 2 cups of cherrywood chips in a deep container and add water to cover. Soak while preparing the tomatoes.

2. Place the tomatoes in a shallow bowl and add olive oil, salt, and pepper. Toss to coat with oil. Place the tomatoes on a baking sheet and roast in a 275-degree oven for 2 to 3 hours, or until the tomatoes are tender but firm.

3. Turn the oven temperature up to 350 degrees. Add enough cherrywood chips to cover the bottom of an ovenproof sauté pan with a tight-fitting lid. On the stove-top over low heat, toast the cherrywood chips until they start to smoke. Place the tomatoes on a metal rack or a vegetable steaming basket that fits inside the sauté pan. Cover the pan and put it in the oven. Smoke the tomatoes for 15 minutes.

4. Roughly chop and set aside until ready to assemble dish.

**MUSSELS:**

1–2 pounds mussels
½ cup white wine
Salt and pepper, to taste
Fresh thyme leaves, to taste

Clean the mussels (for directions, see the note below). In a large pot with a tight-fitting lid, combine the mussels and white wine. Cook, covered, over high heat until the mussels open. Remove the meat from the shells and set aside. Reserve the cooking liquid, strain, and set aside.

**FINAL PREPARATION AND SERVING:**

In a saucepan, combine the Onion Marinière Sauce, meat from the mussels, the smoked tomatoes (to taste; you may not want to use all of them), the cooking liquid from steaming the mussels, salt, pepper, and thyme leaves. Bring to a simmer over low heat. Pour into a bowl and serve immediately with grilled bread.

:: **Note:** To clean mussels, place the mussels in a colander in the sink. Rinse them under cold running water. The patch of what looks like seaweed attached to the shell is often called the "beard." This should be removed by scrubbing with a brush or a kitchen towel. Before steaming, throw away any mussels that are already open or have cracked shells. After steaming, throw away any that have remained closed.

# CHINATOWN

An arch with a two-level pagoda roof dramatically marks the entrance to Boston's Chinatown. At street level it's hard to miss the food that characterizes the neighborhood. Crates of fresh lychees, hard-fleshed Asian pears, and other fruits line the sidewalks in front of grocery stores. Whole roast ducks and chickens hang upside down in the windows of take-out shops. People walk down the streets sipping bubble tea through extra-wide straws that can accommodate the marble-size tapioca pearls floating in the beverage. The aroma of wok-fried noodles and crispy chicken drifts from restaurants. On weekends people line up on the sidewalks for dim sum, the Cantonese-style brunch.

For many Westerners the welter of unfamiliar sights and smells can be overwhelming. That's one reason why Frances Srulowitz, a Chinese cooking teacher who studied in Asia, leads food tours of Chinatown through the Cambridge Center for Adult Education. The talkative, high-energy Srulowitz likes to demystify the markets, fast-food stalls, and restaurants jammed into an area roughly bounded by the New England Medical Center, South Station, and the Theatre District. The first Chinese to arrive in Boston, in the 1870s, pitched tents in what stands today as Ping On Alley. By 1900 about 500 Chinese were living in more permanent quarters, mostly men whose families remained in their homeland. Now more than 78,500 ethnic Chinese live in the Boston area, according to the Institute for Asian American Studies at the University of Massachusetts–Boston. The total Asian American population in the Boston area is close to 250,000. Of that number, 20 percent were enrolled in college or graduate schools in the year 2000.

Chinese restaurants and markets opened almost as soon as Chinatown was settled, as they had a built-in group of customers. Almost all reflected the Cantonese background of the residents. The neighborhood maintained its ethnic character even as Boston grew around it. In recent years Southeast Asian immigrants have added their own Thai, Vietnamese, and Malaysian eateries, especially along Washington Street, which used to be a seedy neighborhood of strip clubs known as the Combat Zone. Boston's Chinatown is the third largest in the country, behind San Francisco and New York. Srulowitz, who has been leading tours here for more than a dozen years, says food is still an important presence in the area.

On a whirlwind tour Srulowitz strides confidently through the weekend crowd of mostly Asian shoppers at a typical Chinese market. She identifies exotic vegetables including lotus root, bitter melon, and Chinese celery. In the candy aisle, she points out, "Everything is extremely sweet—like the gummy candies—or salty, like the preserved plums." Many of the biscuits and cream crackers just down the aisle show the influence of the British in Hong Kong. Dehydrated foods in clear plastic wrappers show a bit of history. "For many years there was no refrigeration in China, so things had to be dried and salted."

Outside, Srulowitz leads visitors past bakeries selling buns stuffed with red bean paste and sesame lotus seed cookies, and into a mall where a vendor is frying batter on what looks like a waffle iron. She points out good places to buy take-out dumplings and fresh noodles. There is always a break in the tour for dim sum, where the servers wheel carts of food past your table and you pick what you want by pointing. Each restaurant has a slightly different dim sum menu, but you are likely to find steamed buns filled with barbecued pork, dumplings with shrimp filling, sticky rice wrapped in lotus leaves, and egg custard. To wash it all down is tea, poured into cups without handles.

Srulowitz is always glad to share her knowledge with Westerners who want to visit Chinatown. "One of the biggest problems is that people don't know where to go and what to order. It's good to see the hole-in-the-wall that makes the best noodles or the best dumplings and then go back there on your own."

# Frances Srulowitz, Culinary Tour Guide

Chinese cooking instructor and tour guide Frances Srulowitz has spent many years adapting Chinese recipes for Westerners. Here's a dish that might be served in one of the Cantonese restaurants in Boston's Chinatown. Made with mussels, it's called *hak kin* (black clams) in Cantonese. You can also interpret the name literally by substituting clams for the mussels. The salted black beans (see the note below) are likely to require a visit to an Asian market or a mail-order source, such as www.ming.com, operated by Ming Tsai of Blue Ginger (see page 180).

## MUSSELS IN BLACK BEAN SAUCE

[SERVES 4–6]

2 pounds fresh mussels
10 cups water
5 slices fresh gingerroot (each ⅛ inch thick), smashed
2 teaspoons white vinegar
2 tablespoons soy sauce
1 tablespoon rice wine (such as sake)
¾ cup chicken broth
1 teaspoon sugar
½ teaspoon toasted sesame oil
1 tablespoon cornstarch, mixed with 2 tablespoons water
2 tablespoons salted black beans (see note)
2 tablespoons peanut, soybean, or corn oil
2 cloves garlic, minced
2 tablespoons minced scallions, green part only, for garnish

1. Rinse the mussels and scrub to remove any beards (see the note on page 17).

2. In a large pot, combine the water, ginger, and vinegar. Bring to a boil. Add the mussels and stir. When the mussels open, remove them (in their shells) with a slotted spoon or tongs and set aside.

3. In a bowl, combine the soy sauce, rice wine, chicken broth, sugar, sesame oil, and cornstarch-water mixture. Rinse the black beans under cold running water to remove excess salt. Coarsely chop the beans and set aside.

4. Place a wok on the stove and turn the heat to high. When the wok is hot, add the oil. When thin tendrils of smoke appear, add the garlic and black beans and stir-fry until the garlic is fragrant.

5. Re-stir the soy sauce mixture and add it to the wok, along with the reserved mussels. Stir-fry over high heat until the sauce has thickened, making sure the mussels are re-heated and well coated with sauce. Garnish with the minced scallions and serve immediately.

:: **Note:** Salted black beans are also sometimes labeled fermented black beans. They usually come wrapped in plastic and look like shriveled-up raisins dotted with salt.

## CHEERS

84 Beacon Street, Boston (Beacon Hill), (617) 227–9605
Faneuil Hall Marketplace, Boston (Downtown), (617) 227–0150
www.cheersboston.com

**Bartender and manager | Brian Cawley**

One of the most famous places in Boston has nothing to do with patriots, U.S. presidents, or the Red Sox. It's Cheers, the Beacon Hill bar owned by Tom Kershaw that inspired a sitcom broadcast on NBC from 1982 until 1993. Originally called the Bull & Finch Pub, the dimly lit, brick-walled basement room became famous after producers scouting around Boston thought it looked like an ideal American bar. The replica of its dark-wood top and red-upholstered stools became the set for a cast that included Ted Danson, Shelley Long, Kelsey Grammer, George Wendt, John Ratzenberger, and Kirstie Alley.

The TV show has been relegated to reruns, but the memorabilia lives on at the original Beacon Hill bar and a second location at Faneuil Hall. A yellow flag directs visitors past a wrought-iron railing to the entrance. Dishes on the basic pub-grub menu are named after *Cheers* characters—Sam's Garlic Bread, Woody's Garden Goodies, Giant Norm Burgers. The upstairs gift shop does a brisk business in souvenir T-shirts, glasses, and a surprisingly snappy-tasting bottled Bloody Mary mix. The staircase also leads to the Hampshire House (see page 52), a stately town house from 1910 that serves brunch and can be rented for special occasions.

If you're a TV trivia buff, you might recognize the name of this drink from a *Cheers* episode. The cast was trying to stump a cocky bartender by making up a cocktail—the "Screaming Viking." Woody and Carla thought fast and came up with a concoction of lime juice and cucumber. Below is Brian Cawley's more palatable interpretation. You can order it and pretend, just for a moment, that Cliff will be bursting through the door any minute with a sack of mail.

## SCREAMING VIKING COCKTAIL

[SERVES 1]

½ ounce orange-infused rum, preferably Bacardi O
½ ounce dark rum, preferably Bacardi Select
½ ounce Amaretto
½ ounce cranberry juice
½ ounce pineapple juice

Mix all ingredients in a cocktail shaker and serve straight up
or over crushed ice.

## B&G OYSTERS

550 Tremont Street
Boston (South End)
(617) 423–0550, www.bandgoysters.com

**Executive chef-owner | Barbara Lynch**

Frustrated by the seasonal, picnic-table atmosphere at clam shacks around New England, Barbara Lynch decided to create a chic urban alternative. "I wanted a place to go where I could order a plate of fried clams with a glass of wine, and here we are," says Lynch, who also owns No. 9 Park (see page 72), and The Butcher Shop (see page 74).

Behind a white marble bar, workers deftly shuck oysters to order. More than a dozen types are usually available, from waters that range from Cape Cod to the Pacific Ocean, depending on the season. The rest of the menu is simple—salads, clam chowder, lobster rolls, half a dozen seafood entrees. The wine list emphasizes whites by the bottle and the glass. The sleek room, with blue and gray tiles and stainless-steel accents, is a neighborhood hot spot. Most nights it fills right up with a talkative, trendily dressed crowd. In warm weather, so does the tiny outdoor patio. With dishes like these crisp fried oysters, presented on a dollop of tangy tartar sauce in the half shell, you can see why.

## FRIED OYSTERS

[SERVES 1-2 AS AN APPETIZER]

6–8 medium oysters
1½ cups all-purpose flour
½ cup oyster crackers, crushed
Vegetable oil, for frying
Kosher salt, to taste

1. Shuck the oysters and clean the shells. Place the oyster meat in a bowl until ready to fry and reserve the shells.

2. In a pie plate or a shallow bowl, mix the flour and cracker crumbs. Coat each oyster in the flour-crumb mixture and place on a clean plate, taking care that they don't stick together.

3. In a deep skillet, add enough oil to come to a depth of about 1 inch. Heat the oil and fry the oysters for 3 to 4 minutes, turning so they cook evenly on all sides. Do not overcook. Drain on paper towels and season with salt. Serve each oyster in its shell, accompanied by tartar sauce.

## PIGALLE

75 South Charles Street
Boston (Theater District)
(617) 423–4944, www.pigalleboston.com

**Chef-owner | Marc Orfaly**

Not all appetizers are created for your fingers or a plate. The martini glass is the container that Marc Orfaly chose for his presentation of tuna. Think of it as a deconstructed sushi roll or a gussied-up tuna tartare. The glass is lined with seaweed salad, an Asian favorite marinated in a sesame vinaigrette, which makes it taste far better than you'd expect for something that washes up on the beach. On top is a layer of tuna tossed in a wasabi-spiked dressing, along with bright orange fish roe about the size of poppy seeds. Lightly placed on top is a spray of fried wonton strips, which look a bit like onion strings. Though served with dark wood chopsticks, you might also want a fork to dig out every last morsel.

This recipe illustrates how Pigalle approaches French food with more jauntiness than formality—but what would you expect from a restaurant named after a red-light neighborhood in Paris? Orfaly has a particular affinity for Asian ingredients. As consulting chef at Peking Tom's in Downtown Crossing, he made Chinese food into chic bar snacks. At Pigalle it's not unusual to find poached cod with parsley root foam alongside a traditional cassoulet or pan-fried foie gras. Low lighting, gauzy half curtains, and jazz on the soundtrack create the appropriately insouciant mood for whatever the menu brings. Any well-stocked Asian market should carry the wonton skins, sushi-grade tuna, seaweed salad, and wasabi paste needed for this recipe.

# TUNA MARTINI

[SERVES 1]

Vegetable oil, as needed, for frying
2–3 wonton skins, sliced into thin strips
⅛ teaspoon hot chili sauce, preferably Sriracha brand,
    or Tabasco sauce
1 tablespoon crème fraîche
4 ounces sushi-grade ahi tuna, diced small
1 teaspoon toasted sesame oil, or to taste
Dash of wasabi paste
Salt, to taste
1 tablespoon prepared seaweed salad (available at
    Asian markets)
½ teaspoon tobiko roe (available at fish or Asian markets)
    or other fish roe

1. Add vegetable oil to a skillet until it reaches a depth of about ½ inch. Heat the oil over high heat. Add the wonton skins and fry until crisp. Set aside to drain on paper towels.

2. In a small bowl, mix together the hot chili sauce and crème fraîche. In another bowl, mix the tuna, crème fraîche mixture, sesame oil, wasabi, and salt.

3. Place the seaweed salad in the bottom of a chilled martini glass. Top with the spicy tuna mixture, place the roe atop, and sprinkle with the crispy wontons. Eat with chopsticks or a fork.

## BLU

Millennium Complex, at the Sports Club/L.A.
4 Avery Street
Boston (Downtown)
(617) 375-8550, www.blurestaurant.com

**Former chef | Tom Fosnot**

If you think a sports club is no place for fine dining, you haven't visited blu. The Lycra-clad crowd works out in one part of the building. In another is a modern, glass-walled dining room perched above the retail clothing shops, department stores, and steady pedestrian traffic of Downtown Crossing. Here Tom Fosnot (now chef at Rocca, which has the same owners as blu) aimed for simplicity in assembling dishes from fresh, seasonal ingredients. A marinated tuna appetizer comes with nothing more than cucumbers, radishes, ginger, and basil. This scallop appetizer is also built from basic components, including the regional favorite Macomber turnip (see the sidebar on page 35). "What I like best about this recipe is how it takes two mundane ingredients, turnips and brussels sprouts, and pairs them with two luxury ingredients to create a dish that is simple while at the same time being something very special," says Fosnot, who earned a degree in geology before becoming a chef. The vinaigrette helps tie together the sweet turnip puree and the slightly bitter brussels sprout leaves. The artful presentation—scallops on a silky pool of puree, with leaves arranged on top—should impress company when you try this at home. The recipe has many different components, so allow enough time to make and assemble everything. The turnip puree can be made a day in advance.

Though blu has become a destination restaurant, its cafe attracts a lively mix of gymgoers, office workers, and shoppers. The cafe menu is built from sandwiches, salads, and smoothies, though you can also find muffins and cookies. Overseeing both dining areas is the Sapphire Restaurant Group, which also owns Rocca and Noir. One of the partners, Michela Larson, has been at the forefront of Boston dining since her eponymous Michela's was a trendsetter in Cambridge in the 1980s (Todd English and Jody Adams were both chefs there).

# SCALLOPS WITH MACOMBER TURNIP PUREE

[SERVES 4 AS AN APPETIZER]

**MACOMBER TURNIP PUREE:**

1 tablespoon butter

1 large leek, white part only, thinly sliced (see sidebar,
    page 35)

4 medium Macomber turnips, peeled and quartered

½ gallon (2 quarts) milk

Salt and pepper, to taste

1. Melt the butter in a large saucepan over medium heat.
   Add the leeks and sauté until tender, about 5 minutes.

2. Add the turnips and the milk. Warm gently and simmer
   until the turnips are tender, about 30 minutes.

3. With a slotted spoon, remove the turnips from the pot.
   Place in a blender or a food processor and puree until
   smooth. Season with salt and pepper and set aside until
   ready to use. (Cover and refrigerate if making a day
   ahead.) Discard the milk.

**TRUFFLE VINAIGRETTE:**

2 shallots, minced

1 tablespoon lemon juice

1 truffle, grated with a zester, or
    1 tablespoon canned truffles (see note)

Salt and pepper, to taste

¼ cup extra-virgin olive oil

¼ cup truffle oil

In a nonreactive bowl, combine the shallots, lemon juice,
truffles, salt, and pepper. Stir in the oils. Set aside until ready
to use. Stir before using.

:: **Note:** If you don't want to use truffles or truffle oil, you
can make a variation on the vinaigrette with apple cider and
butter. Pour ½ cup apple cider into a saucepan and bring to
a boil. Reduce the heat and simmer until you only have
2 tablespoons liquid left. Use it in place of the lemon juice.

In a separate saucepan, melt 1 cup (2 sticks) butter. Continue cooking over low heat, stirring, until it becomes brown
and aromatic (do not let it burn). Cool slightly. Use it in
place of the two oils.

**FINAL PREPARATION AND SERVING:**

2 cups Macomber Turnip Puree (from recipe above)

2 tablespoons (¼ stick) butter

1 cup brussels sprout leaves (cut from raw sprouts), blanched

12 large sea scallops

Salt and pepper, to taste

¼ cup vegetable oil

Truffle Vinaigrette (from recipe above)

¼ cup chervil or parsley sprigs

1. Reheat the turnip puree until warm.

2. In a sauté pan, melt the butter. Sauté the brussels sprout
   leaves until heated through.

3. Season the scallops with salt and pepper. In a sauté pan
   over high heat, heat the vegetable oil. Add the scallops
   and sear on both sides until the scallops are cooked but
   not rubbery, about 2 minutes per side.

4. Place about ½ cup puree on each serving plate. Place
   3 scallops on the puree. Arrange the brussels sprout
   leaves on top. Drizzle with vinaigrette and garnish with
   chervil or parsley sprigs.

# SOUPS

Soup is popular year-round in Boston, where June nights can be chilly enough for Polarfleece. Forget those delicate consommés that your grandmother sipped. Chefs like big flavors, especially from the vegetables that are hardy enough to thrive in this climate—pumpkin and butternut squash at Sandrine's and asparagus at Verrill Farm. On those rare August days when the mercury finally inches above eighty-five degrees, there is Mango Gazpacho from the New England Soup Factory, a shop devoted to gourmet soups (Boston's answer to the "Soup Nazi" made famous by the *Seinfeld* TV show).

If Boston ever designated an official soup, it would have to be clam chowder. This creamy combination of clams and diced potatoes is sold right at Logan Airport—as well as at clam shacks with greasy picnic tables, white-tablecloth dining rooms, and even Red Sox games at Fenway Park. In this chapter you'll find a traditional chowder recipe from seafood specialty restaurant Skipjack's. Not that every seafood soup is traditional, as the chilled lobster gazpacho—garnished with a scoop of avocado ice cream—from Grill 23 demonstrates.

## GRILL 23 & BAR

161 Berkley Street
Boston
(617) 542–2255, www.grill23.com

**Executive chef | Jay Murray**

Grill 23 specializes in prime, dry-aged beef and other steaks, but executive chef Jay Murray sees red meat as just a starting point for his menu. He changes the lineup every week, adding dishes like chèvre cheesecake, or seared scallops with red curry lobster broth, to challenge himself and keep things interesting. The side dishes reflect his dual role as an innovator and a guardian of tradition: Truffled "tater tots" and Szechuan green beans are offered alongside mashed potatoes and buttered asparagus.

Murray, the executive chef at Grill 23 since 1998, develops many of his recipes in the open kitchen at the back of the restaurant's mahogany-and-brass-accented dining room. The lobster gazpacho started out that way, when he had extra cooked lobster roe (the reddish clumps of eggs found inside a female lobster, visible after the lobster is opened) and a wine dinner coming up. "I wondered how I could build a dish from the roe," he explains.

The result—a smooth, tomato-based soup flavored with lobster stock and fresh herbs—is enhanced by chunks of lobster meat and a scoop of avocado ice cream. "It's a different variation on summer," says Murray.

# LOBSTER CORAL GAZPACHO

[SERVES 6]

## GAZPACHO BASE:

3–4 pounds ripe tomatoes, diced

1 small Vidalia onion, sliced (see notes, page 91)

1½ teaspoons salt

1 teaspoon sugar

½ teaspoon pepper

1 tablespoon cooked lobster roe (optional)

1 tablespoon chopped fresh chervil or parsley (see notes)

1 teaspoon chopped fresh tarragon

¼ cup lobster stock (see notes)

½ cup extra-virgin olive oil

2 tablespoons sherry vinegar

1. In a stainless-steel bowl, combine all ingredients except the stock, oil, and vinegar. Allow to rest 1 hour, tossing occasionally.

2. Add the lobster stock, oil, and vinegar and stir to combine. Let the mixture rest for half an hour, tossing occasionally. Transfer to a blender and process until smooth, working in batches if necessary. Strain through a fine strainer, such as a mesh chinois, to remove the solids. (You may have to stir the liquid and gently press with the back of a spoon for it to go through.) Chill until ready to serve.

:: **Notes:** Fresh cilantro or snipped fresh chives may be substituted for the chervil or parsley. In that case, omit the tarragon.

Lobster stock can sometimes be found at a seafood market. If it's not available, substitute clam juice.

## LOBSTER RELISH:

1 tablespoon crème fraîche or sour cream

1 tablespoon mayonnaise

1 tablespoon freshly squeezed orange juice

¼ teaspoon fresh vanilla bean seeds or a scant ¼ teaspoon pure vanilla extract

2 teaspoons honey

½ pound cooked lobster meat (preferably from the knuckles), cut into bite-size pieces

2 teaspoons minced fresh chervil or parsley

Salt and pepper, to taste

In a medium bowl, combine the crème fraîche, mayonnaise, orange juice, vanilla, and honey. Toss with the lobster and chervil or parsley. Season to taste with salt and pepper.

## AVOCADO ICE CREAM:

2 ripe avocadoes

½ cup milk

2 tablespoons sugar

⅓ cup heavy cream

2 teaspoons lemon juice

1. Cut each avocado in half and remove the pit. Using a spoon, scoop the flesh from the skin. In a blender, puree the avocado flesh with the milk and sugar.

2. Using an electric mixer or whisking by hand, whip the avocado puree with the cream and lemon juice for 2 minutes.

3. Freeze in an ice cream maker according to the manufacturer's instructions.

:: **Note:** This ice cream is an optional addition to the soup. Guacamole or finely chopped fresh avocado seasoned with lemon juice, salt, and pepper may be substituted.

## FINAL PREPARATION AND SERVING:

Fill a bowl with about ½ cup gazpacho. Add a scoop of ice cream and garnish with the lobster relish and a sprig of fresh herbs or snipped chives.

## NEW ENGLAND SOUP FACTORY

2–4 Brookline Place
Brookline
(617) 739–1695

244 Needham Street
Newton
(617) 558–9966
www.nesoupfactory.com

**Chef-owner | Marjorie Druker**

It's no wonder that a girl who liked to make "giggle" noodle soup for her family would grow up to start a soup company. Since 1995 Marjorie Druker has built her business on a rotating menu of soups, from her signature triple-strength chicken to the New England–inspired clam and corn chowder. She specializes in creative combinations, which might include pumpkin and white bean with nutmeg; curried crab and coconut; or chilled avocado and cucumber with lime juice. "Fragrance, color, and flavor are really important," says Druker, who has created more than 150 varieties of soup, which are served in bright purple, yellow, and green containers. Sandwiches, salads, and sweets complete the counter-service menu.

In summer traditional Spanish-style gazpacho is the best-selling cold soup at the Soup Factory. This fruity version veers into the tropics with mangoes, papayas, and guava juice. The marriage of fruits and vegetables succeeds because each brings out the best in the other. This is a fun appetizer at a summer party. Cut the recipe in half to serve a smaller group.

### MANGO GAZPACHO

[MAKES ABOUT 1 GALLON]

1 English cucumber, diced
2 yellow peppers, diced
1 red pepper, diced
1 large tomato, diced
6 tomatillos, diced
1 bunch scallions, sliced
1 papaya, peeled and diced
4 mangoes, peeled and diced
½ cup extra-virgin olive oil
3 cloves garlic, crushed
Juice of 4 limes
1 tablespoon key lime vinegar (if available) or
   white wine vinegar

1½ teaspoons kosher salt
2 tablespoons chopped fresh cilantro
1 quart guava juice
2 quarts tomato juice
2 teaspoons minced habañero chile peppers
½ cup plain bread crumbs

In a large bowl, add all the ingredients and mix together well. In a blender, puree 2 cups of the gazpacho and add back into the mixture. Stir again and chill.

## CRAIGIE STREET BISTROT

5 Craigie Circle
Cambridge (Harvard Square)
(617) 497–5511, www.craigiestreetbistrot.com

**Chef | Tony Maws**

On any particular night there's no predicting what you'll find at Craigie Street, which builds its menu from seasonal New England produce and organic meats shipped in by the truckload. "If it's on the menu tonight, it was the best of the market this morning," says Tony Maws, who seems to thrive on the frenetic pace of reinventing the menu each night. Though the kitchen may be a whirlwind, all is calm in the lamplit, basement-level dining room decorated with framed French travel posters.

This pale green, pureed soup typifies Maws's style of applying French techniques to fresh ingredients. He transforms the humble, Massachusetts-grown Macomber turnips (see the sidebar) into an elegant first course. The earthy sweetness of the turnips is offset by the tangy crème fraîche. The chives add bright green contrast as well as a slightly sharp finish.

# VELOUTÉ OF MACOMBER TURNIPS

[SERVES 6]

½ cup (1 stick) butter, divided
1 leek, cleaned and diced into small pieces (see sidebar)
Salt and pepper, to taste
3 pounds Macomber turnips, peeled and diced
1 quart chicken or vegetable stock (or water)
1 cup crème fraîche
Snipped fresh chives, for garnish

1. In a sauté pan, melt 2 tablespoons of the butter. Add the leek and season with salt and pepper. Sauté until the leek is soft, about 8 minutes. Set aside.

2. Place the diced turnips in a stockpot. Add the stock and enough water to cover the turnips by about 2 inches of liquid. (Press down the turnips with a spoon: They float.) Season with salt and pepper and bring to boil over high heat. Lower the heat to a simmer. When the turnips are thoroughly cooked (10 to 15 minutes), drain, reserving the liquid.

3. Return the turnips to the stockpot. Add the leeks, the remaining butter, and the crème fraîche. Add about 4 cups of cooking liquid from the turnips. Working in batches, put the soup in the blender and puree until smooth. For an extra-smooth texture, strain the soup through a fine strainer. Adjust the thickness with the remaining turnip liquid.

4. Serve hot, garnished with chives.

## How to Clean a Leek

A leek can be confounding because no matter how well you rinse it on the outside, it can still harbor dirt in its core. Clean a leek by laying it flat on a cutting board, taking a sharp knife, and cutting a slit from just above the roots all the way up the stem. Rotate the leek and make another slit or two, until the leek is open in the center but still held together by its root. Rinse under running water until all the dirt is removed. Cut off the root end and proceed with dicing. Alternatively, dice the leek, then soak the pieces in a bowl of cold water to remove the dirt. Rinse under running water and proceed.

## Macomber Turnips

The Macomber turnip is truly a made-in-Massachusetts vegetable. In the late 1870s brothers Adin and Elihu Macomber planted radishes next to rutabagas on their Westport farm. The cross-pollination yielded the first Macomber turnips. This new variety was sweeter than the turnips that the Pilgrims had brought to the Massachusetts Bay Colony in the 1630s.

The brothers sold their seeds to other local farmers, but there was nothing glamorous about their hybrid, as turnips at that time were disdained as food for the poor. Only in the last twenty years or so, as the public developed new appreciation for heirloom vegetables, has the Macomber become a darling of chefs. Now Macomber turnips are proudly named on many menus and used in everything from soups to pies. Who knew that a haphazard farming experiment could end up having such long-term appeal?

## VERRILL FARM

11 Wheeler Road
Concord
(978) 369–4494, www.verrillfarm.com

**Chef | Kevin Carey**

Many of Boston's chefs regularly rely on Verrill Farm in Concord to grow their corn, potatoes, and bushels of other fresh vegetables. Its rolling hills near the Sudbury River, about 20 miles northwest of downtown Boston, are so scenic that local artists often set up easels to capture the view. The family-owned business started as a dairy farm, but the Verrills turned exclusively to cultivating 140 acres of produce in 1990. Though much of the harvest is shipped off to restaurants, anyone can buy vegetables from the overflowing bins at the farm stand. It's even more fun if you come for a pancake breakfast, a cooking class, or the annual Corn & Tomato Festival, where you can sample thirty varieties of farm-grown tomatoes and eight varieties of corn.

This vegetarian, dairy-free soup comes from another annual festival celebrating asparagus. Chef Kevin Carey serves it right after a tour of the fields, during which you can pick your own asparagus. Inside the farm stand, owner Jennifer Verrill Faddoul oversees a busy take-out operation of soups and other prepared foods (see page 176). With ingredients that go right from field to kitchen, everything at Verrill Farm offers the ultimate in freshness. This soup—with leeks, potato, and parsley enriching the asparagus—is no exception.

## ASPARAGUS SOUP

[MAKES APPROXIMATELY 3 QUARTS]

3–4 tablespoons olive oil
2 leeks, sliced lengthwise, cleaned and chopped
    (see sidebar, page 35)
1 medium onion, chopped
1 large baking potato, such as Idaho
Salt and pepper, to taste
3 pounds asparagus, tough stalk ends trimmed,
    chopped in approximately 1-inch lengths
2 quarts chicken broth
½ cup chopped fresh flat-leaf (Italian) parsley

1. In a large saucepan, heat the olive oil. Add the leeks, onion, and potato. Season with salt and pepper and sauté until the onion becomes translucent.

2. Add the asparagus and sauté until coated with oil and mixed with the other vegetables.

3. Add the chicken broth and simmer until the potato and asparagus are cooked through.

4. In a food processor, working in batches if necessary, puree the soup. Alternatively, puree with an immersion beater.

5. Return the soup to the pot. Add the parsley and stir to mix in. Season to taste with additional salt and pepper, and serve.

## BRISTOL LOUNGE

Four Seasons Hotel Boston
200 Boylston Street, Boston
(617) 338-4400, www.fourseasons.com

**Former executive chef | David Blessing**

The Four Seasons Hotel Boston, which celebrated its twentieth anniversary in 2005, is best known for luxury, especially at its Aujourd'hui restaurant (see page 210). Less formal but still classy is the Bristol Lounge, where the burger—hardly high-end fare—has been acclaimed as one of the best in Boston. Former executive chef David Blessing, who grew up in Maine, used New England's seasonal and artisanal ingredients as the foundation for most of the dishes on the menu.

This white bean soup was inspired by Blessing's Italian grandmother, who often kept a pot of hearty bean or lentil soup on the stove so visiting family members could help themselves. Blessing made a huge batch of white bean soup one fall to give as gifts to family and friends. Their enthusiastic response prompted him to put the soup on the Bristol Lounge's cold-weather menus. This is not bean soup for wimps. Its rich, smoky broth, accented by beans as well as chicken, bacon, and smoked ham, has made it a popular item. This recipe can easily serve a crowd at a ski condo or a Super Bowl party, but leftovers can be frozen and reheated for comfort food on any cold night.

# HEARTY WHITE BEAN SOUP

[MAKES 1 GALLON]

1 pound small white navy beans
¼ cup extra-virgin olive oil
4 bone-in, skin-on chicken thighs
Salt and freshly ground black pepper, to taste
1 cup medium-diced smoked bacon
1 cup spicy Italian-style sausage, removed from casings
    and crumbled
1 small white onion, peeled and diced medium
1 small carrot, peeled and diced medium
1 stalk celery, diced medium
4 cloves garlic, roughly chopped
4 smoked ham hocks
2 bay leaves
3 quarts chicken stock
½ cup (1 stick) butter
1 head escarole, washed, trimmed, and roughly
    chopped (see note)
¼ cup grated Parmesan cheese
¼ bunch chopped fresh parsley

1. Place the beans in a large pot. Add enough cold water to
   cover. Soak overnight. Drain before using.

2. In a large, heavy-bottomed pot, heat the olive oil until
   hot. Season the chicken thighs with salt and pepper and
   place into the pot. Sear both sides until golden brown, remove, and set aside. In the same pot, add the bacon and
   sausage and continue to sauté slowly over medium heat
   until the bacon is almost crisp, but not fully. Remove the
   bacon and sausage and set aside.

3. Drain and discard all but about ¼ cup of drippings from
   the pot. Add the onion, carrot, celery, and garlic. Slowly
   sauté, stirring often, until they become very tender but
   do not change color.

4. To the pot, add the beans, reserved chicken, bacon,
   sausage, ham hocks, bay leaves, and chicken stock. Bring
   to a boil, then reduce the heat to a slow simmer. Skim the
   top and continue to simmer for approximately 1½ to 2
   hours, or until the white beans are tender (when they are
   not grainy in the middle). Remove the chicken thighs and
   ham hocks from soup. Set aside and let cool; pick the
   meat from both, roughly chop it, and add it back to
   the soup.

5. Heat the butter in a sauté pan until foamy. Add the escarole to the pan and sauté until wilted. Season to taste
   with salt and pepper and add to the soup. After adding
   the escarole, add the Parmesan cheese and parsley. Season again if necessary. Serve with crusty bread.

:: **Note:** You can put the escarole directly into the soup
without sautéing it first; it will wilt in the hot liquid. In that
case, chop it into small pieces first.

## SANDRINE'S BISTRO

8 Holyoke Street
Cambridge (Harvard Square)
(617) 497–5300, www.sandrines.com

**Chef-owner | Raymond Ost**

Though Raymond Ost has been a chef in Boston for more than a decade, he reaches back to his roots in France at Sandrine's Bistro. The front door, surrounded by art deco ironwork, is modeled after a Parisian subway station. Inside, on a typical day, the brick oven behind the bar turns out dozens of orders of flammekuche—a specialty pizza from Ost's native Alsace region. Ost, who carries the prestigious title of Master Chef in France, is equally adept at turning out classical French dishes such as foie gras terrine, crepes, and chicken cordon bleu. The atmosphere is fairly upscale, though dining at the bar can be fun and less formal.

This soup combines two New England fall vegetables in a creamy, French-style base. It turns out a lovely pale orange, spiced with cinnamon and nutmeg. The maple syrup balances the flavors, bringing out the sweetness in the squash. It makes a good first course for dinner—especially during the winter holidays. For a prep shortcut, buy peeled squash from the supermarket.

# PUMPKIN AND BUTTERNUT SQUASH SOUP
## WITH MAPLE SYRUP

[SERVES 6]

**SOUP:**

1 tablespoon vegetable oil, such as canola
1 clove garlic, crushed
1 small onion, peeled and sliced
1 leek, cleaned and sliced (see sidebar, page 35)
1 cinnamon stick
1 large Idaho potato, peeled and diced
1 pound butternut squash, peeled and diced
1 cup dry white wine
1 quart milk
1 cup heavy cream
Pinch of nutmeg
Salt and pepper, to taste
1 cup canned pureed pumpkin
¼ cup real (not imitation) pure maple syrup

1. In a soup pot, heat the oil. Add the garlic, onion, leek, and cinnamon stick. Sauté until the onion becomes translucent. Add the potato and squash. Add the wine, stirring to deglaze the pan.

2. Bring to a boil and continue boiling for 2 minutes. Add the milk, cream, nutmeg, salt, and pepper and return to a boil. Let simmer for 45 minutes.

3. Remove the pot from the heat. Remove and discard the cinnamon stick. Puree the soup in a food processor, working in batches if necessary. Return the soup to the pot and bring to a boil again. (Alternatively, use an immersion beater to puree the soup right in the pot.)

4. Add the pumpkin puree, whisking in a little at a time, until the soup thickens as much as you like. (The more pumpkin you add, the thicker it will be.) Stir in the maple syrup at the very end. Check the seasoning and adjust to taste, adding more maple syrup if you like.

**GARNISH:**

1 tablespoon vegetable oil, such as canola
¼ pound butternut squash, peeled and diced
1 tablespoon sugar

In a skillet, heat the oil. When it's very hot, add the squash. Sauté for 2 minutes and sprinkle with the sugar. Continue stirring for 2 to 3 minutes until the sugar caramelizes, turning brown.

**FINAL PREPARATION AND SERVING:**

Chopped fresh chives, to taste
Croutons, to taste (see note)

Place a small amount of caramelized squash in each serving bowl. Top with hot soup and garnish with chopped chives and croutons.

:: **Note:** You can easily make your own croutons with any kind of European-style bread, such as a French bread or focaccia. Stale bread works even better than fresh. Preheat the oven to 400 degrees. Using a serrated knife, cut the bread into bite-size cubes. Place them in a mixing bowl and drizzle olive oil over the top. Sprinkle with salt and pepper. Add a sprinkle of dried herbs such as rosemary or thyme if you like. Toss so the pieces are lightly coated with olive oil. Place the pieces in a single layer on a baking sheet. Bake until lightly toasted, stirring occasionally so the bread is toasted on all sides. Let cool before serving.

# CHOWDER HISTORY

Chowder has sustained New Englanders since the 1700s, when the settlers reported that they made stew from the plentiful seafood around them. The word might come from the French *chaudière*, which refers to a large cauldron (and contains the word *chaud,* which means "warm"). The recipe evolved over time—one early version called for red wine—but its basic ingredients now usually include salt pork, onions, potatoes, milk or cream, and fish. Though Rhode Islanders add tomatoes, northern New Englanders generally insist on keeping their chowder creamy and white as the winter snow. The Legal Sea Foods (see page 98) version of fish chowder became so famous that it was served in 1981 at the inauguration of President Ronald Reagan. Clam chowder became a Boston favorite in the nineteenth century and is still proudly served around the city.

Oyster crackers—crisp, coin-shaped wheat crackers sold in cellophane-wrapped individual servings—have become the standard garnish for chowder. Developed in the 1840s in Trenton, New Jersey, to accompany oyster stew, the crackers were prized because they could float in the hot stew without dissolving. They were sometimes called Trenton crackers. Common crackers, which look like oversize oyster crackers with a hollow middle, were a New England favorite, especially when split and topped with melted cheddar cheese. Now they have become more of a specialty item than a pantry standby.

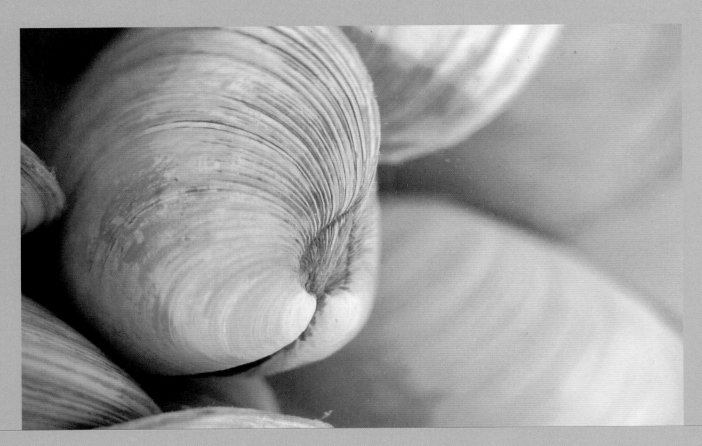

# Skipjack's Clam Chowder

(for restaurant details, see page 100)

Chowder offers the quintessential taste of Boston. This recipe from Skipjack's, adapted for home use by executive chef Andrew Wilkinson, sticks close to tradition, though bacon stands in for salt pork, which can be difficult to find in markets. Each serving contains a heady balance of clams, potatoes, and cream.

## CLAM CHOWDER

[SERVES 4 TO 6]

36 cherrystone clams, washed
2 cups water
½ pound bacon, cut into ¼-inch strips
6 tablespoons butter
2 cups diced onions
1 cup diced celery
1 tablespoon chopped garlic
½ teaspoon dried thyme
½ cup flour
2 bay leaves
Pinch of ground nutmeg
2 cups potatoes, peeled and diced
   into ½-inch pieces
2 cups light cream
Salt and pepper, to taste
Butter and oyster crackers, for garnish (optional)

1. In a large pot combine the water and clams. Cover with tight lid and bring to a boil. Continue to cook, stirring every 2 minutes. When most of the clam shells have opened and clams feel firm to the touch, remove from heat.

2. Strain the broth through a fine mesh strainer. Lining the strainer with paper towels works well so no sand gets into the chowder. You should have about 8 cups of broth. If you do not, add enough water to make it 8 cups.

3. When the clams are cool enough to handle, remove the clam meat from the shell and chop it into ½-inch pieces. Refrigerate until needed. Discard the clam shells.

4. In the same large pot, cook the bacon over medium heat until crisp. Remove the bacon and drain on paper towels, leaving about ¼ cup of drippings in the pan. Add the butter and heat over medium until it melts into the drippings. Add the onions, celery, and garlic. Cook over medium heat until soft, but not brown, about 10 minutes. Stir in the thyme and the flour. Cook over medium heat for 2 minutes. Once again, do not allow the mixture to brown.

5. Stir in the clam broth, mixing well, and return to a boil. Add the bay leaves and nutmeg. Add the potatoes and cooked bacon, lower the heat, and simmer until the potatoes are soft, 15 to 20 minutes.

6. Just before serving, add the cream and return to a boil. Add the chopped clams and season with salt and pepper. Garnish with a pat of butter and oyster crackers.

## EXCELSIOR

272 Boylston Street
Boston (Back Bay)
(617) 426–7878, www.excelsiorrestaurant.com

**Executive chef | Eric Brennan**

The dining room at Excelsior will make you feel like royalty, with its diamond motif, red and gold accents, and leather seats. So will the view of the Boston Public Garden. There is even an enchanted-looking glass tower in the middle of the dining room, which stores the 600 bottles for the wine list. But don't expect a formal banquet from chef Eric Brennan. He'd rather grill hearts of romaine lettuce for the Caesar salad, or fry lobster claws in ginger tempura.

After serving hundreds of oysters on the half shell at the Excelsior raw bar, Brennan decided to experiment with cooked oyster dishes. This recipe was inspired by the lunch counters at Grand Central Station in New York, where he grew up. "They served a stew that was like oyster-flavored milk with paprika on top," he recalls. Since chowder-loving New Englanders were unlikely to go for something that thin, he decided to add body—and sweetness—to his stew with pureed parsnips. A smoky undertone comes from finnan haddie (see the sidebar). Served over toast, this smooth, rich stew easily makes an entire meal when accompanied by a salad or green vegetable.

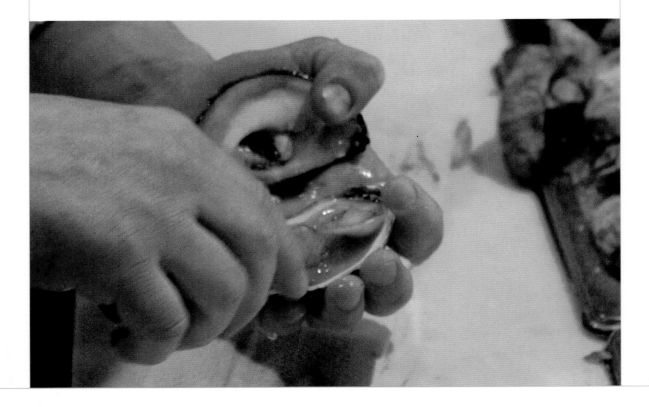

## EAST COAST OYSTER STEW

[SERVES 4]

2 tablespoons (¼ stick) unsalted butter, divided
2 medium parsnips, peeled and diced medium
½ onion, peeled and diced medium
Salt and pepper, to taste
1 cup chicken stock
½ cup small-diced finnan haddie (smoked haddock) or
 small-diced cooked bacon
4 shiitake mushrooms, stems removed, sliced thin
2 shallots, peeled and minced
4 slices white bread
2 cups heavy cream
12 shucked East Coast oysters (larger varieties preferred),
 liquid reserved
2 tablespoons chopped fresh chives

1. In a small saucepan, heat 1 tablespoon of the butter. Add the parsnips and onion. Sauté over low heat for 5 minutes, stirring occasionally. Season with salt and pepper, add the chicken stock, and simmer until the parsnips are soft, about 10 minutes more. In a food processor, or with an immersion beater, puree until smooth. Set aside.

2. In a large saucepan, heat the remaining tablespoon of butter over medium heat. Add the finnan haddie or bacon, shiitake mushrooms, and shallots. Sauté, stirring often, for 8 minutes, or until the shallots and mushrooms soften.

3. Place 4 slices of bread in a toaster.

4. Add the heavy cream and the reserved oyster juice to the soup. Turn the heat to high and bring to a boil. Reduce the heat to a slow simmer and whisk in the parsnip puree. Add the oysters and heat through.

5. Butter the slices of toast and place each in the bottom of a soup bowl. Ladle a portion of stew atop. Garnish with the chives.

## Finnan Haddie

Finnan haddie is smoked haddock. The name comes from Scotland, where people in the fishing village of Finnan smoked their haddock over a peat fire. Emigrants introduced this method of smoking to New England, where the supply of haddock (a type of cod) was plentiful. Finnan haddie baked in milk and butter, sometimes with sliced potatoes, was one of New England's early comfort foods. Some Boston-area eateries, including Captain Marden's Seafoods in Wellesley, still sell a creamed finnan haddie dinner. These days, however, "finnan haddie is mostly a thing of the past," says Kim Marden, owner of Captain Marden's. Finnan haddie was made from a whole fish, with the center bone and the head removed. "Now a smoked cod or haddock fillet is what people ask for." Today's method of smoking the haddock might be the same as what is used for the more popular smoked salmon, but the result is different. "You get a much smokier flavor with haddock or cod because it's a milder fish to begin with," explains Marden.

If you do want to try smoked haddock in this recipe, call ahead to a seafood store or specialty food market to see if it's available. (Sometimes it can be special-ordered.) You can also order it on line through a specialty seafood retailer like Stonington Sea Products in Maine (www .stoningtonseafood.com).

# SALADS

The concept of salad has come full circle in Boston. The early settlers picked an assortment of greens (such as lettuce, watercress, and spinach) from their kitchen gardens, supplementing them with wild plants like purslane and sorrel. Some planted Boston lettuce, a type of butterhead lettuce with soft, yellowish green leaves at its core, but the origin of the *Boston* in its name is a mystery. In the 1920s and '30s, crisp, sturdy (and flavorless) iceberg lettuce started to dominate the market. Packed in ice, it could be shipped by train to Boston from the California fields where it grew. In all but the city's European-style restaurants, *salad* quickly became synonymous with a bowl of iceberg lettuce topped by a few sliced carrots, tomatoes, and cucumbers.

Assorted seasonal greens are now popular once again, though these days they tend to be the French-inspired mesclun mix of baby lettuces (oak leaf, mâche, arugula, and frisée are popular components). Rare these days is the chef who builds a salad from iceberg lettuce. Spinach is the green of choice in a salad at Chez Henri, which is topped with a warm bacon dressing and a chile-spiked vinaigrette. At Henrietta's Table spinach is topped with goat cheese, raspberries, and maple pecan dressing. Also in this chapter, lobster migrates from its esteemed place at the center of a clambake to a chilled presentation with spring vegetables and edible flowers at UpStairs on the Square.

569 Tremont Street
Boston (South End)
(617) 424-8577, www.aquitaineboston.com

**AQUITAINE BIS**

11 Boylston Street
Chestnut Hill
(617) 734-8400, www.aquitainebis.com

**Executive chef-owner | Seth Woods**

Aquitaine is part of a French revolution in Boston—bringing French food out of its traditionally stuffy surroundings into a lively bistro lined with bottles of wine, mirrors, and a menu on a chalkboard. For many years French dining in Boston (and in most major American cities) translated as haute cuisine—a maître d' in a tuxedo, a menu with unpronounceable words in fancy

script, excruciatingly correct service. Aquitaine's menu re-creates a more casual French cooking style, with favorites including coq au vin, steak frites (steak with french fries), and steamed mussels. Specials give Seth Woods and his culinary team more latitude to work with ingredients like soft-shell crabs or hand-cut pasta. The Aquitaine Group's other restaurants—Union Bar and Grille (see page 224), and Metropolis—veer away from French into more contemporary American menus.

This endive salad "has been on the menu since day one," says Woods. "It's real fresh, real fast, and real simple." Yet simple does not mean dull. The dressing gains extra flavor from two kinds of oil and two kinds of vinegar. The Granny Smith apples balance the somewhat bitter endive. Because you toss the dressing with the ingredients as you go along, everything comes out perfectly coated and still crisp.

## ENDIVE SALAD

[SERVES 2]

2 teaspoons sherry vinegar
2 teaspoons cider vinegar
2 teaspoons walnut oil
2 teaspoons canola oil
3 turns of black pepper from a pepper mill
Pinch of salt
2 tablespoons Roquefort cheese
2 tablespoons toasted walnuts, crushed
½ Granny Smith apple
2 Belgian endives
Dash of chopped fresh parsley

1. Place both vinegars in a stainless-steel bowl. Slowly whisk in the oils. Season with salt and pepper.

2. Crumble the Roquefort cheese into the bowl and toss with the vinaigrette. Add the walnuts and toss again.

3. Slice the Granny Smith apple as thinly as possible (use a mandoline if you have one). Add to the bowl and toss with the dressing.

4. Remove 3 leaves from the outer part of each endive and reserve. Cut the remaining endive into thin, julienned pieces. Add the cut endive and parsley to the bowl and toss.

5. Adjust the seasoning with additional salt and pepper to taste. Place 3 endive leaves on each serving plate. Top with the tossed salad mixture and serve.

## TAMARIND BAY

75 Winthrop Street
Cambridge (Harvard Square)
(617) 491–4552, www.tamarind-bay.com

**Executive chef | Wali Ahmad**

Boston may be famous for its beans, but chickpeas (also known as garbanzo beans) are a relative newcomer. White navy or pea beans were the traditional choice for Yankee pots, largely because they were the most readily available. The Native Americans were already cultivating beans when the Pilgrims arrived in the 1620s. It took longer for chickpeas—which are native to Central Asia and the Mediterranean (they are an essential ingredient in hummus)—to arrive in the United States. Trade brought them first to Mexico, and they crossed the border through Tex-Mex dishes.

In India chickpeas have been a staple for hundreds of years. Tamarind Bay's executive chef, Wali Ahmad (whose television cooking show in India made him a national celebrity), accents mild-flavored chickpeas with chaat masala, a spicy mix that contains chili powder, coriander, and cumin. Three kinds of bell peppers add color and crunch. Since it contains no oil, this salad is a healthy option for a picnic or a summer meal.

The Tamarind Bay menu goes beyond the greatest hits of Indian food to delve into little-known regional foods, such as lamb cooked with fresh mustard greens, or fenugreek-spiced trout. Students in search of an interesting vegetarian meal, Indian families, and adventurous eaters all flock to this subterranean space in Harvard Square.

# CHANNA (CHICKPEA) SALAD

[SERVES 6]

**CHAAT MASALA SPICE MIX:**

2 tablespoons cumin seeds

1 tablespoon coriander seeds

1 tablespoon anise seeds

1½ teaspoons freshly ground black pepper

1½ teaspoons powdered ginger

1½ teaspoons red chili powder

1½ teaspoons lemon salt

1 teaspoon ground black salt (see notes)

1 teaspoon table salt or sea salt

Mix all the ingredients together until ready to use. Store leftovers in a covered container.

:: **Notes:** This spice mix can be found at many specialty grocers and other stores with a good spice selection. Of course, it can also be made by hand.

   Black salt is available at Indian markets. If you can't find it, substitute the same amount of table salt or sea salt.

**SALAD:**

1 pound dry chickpeas or 5 cups canned, cooked chickpeas

1 red onion, diced

1 yellow pepper, diced

1 green pepper, diced

1 red pepper, diced

1 bunch fresh cilantro, chopped

2 tablespoons lemon juice

1 tablespoon chaat masala (prepackaged or
   from recipe above)

Salt, to taste

1. If you're preparing dry chickpeas, place them in a mixing bowl and add enough water to completely cover them by about 2 inches. Soak overnight. Drain and place in a saucepan. Add more water to cover by about 2 inches. Bring to a boil, lower the heat, and slowly simmer until the chickpeas are tender but still hold their shape. Drain and cool. If you're using canned chickpeas, drain, place in a colander, and rinse thoroughly.

2. Place the chickpeas in a large mixing bowl. Add the chopped onion and peppers. Toss gently to mix. Add chopped cilantro and toss again. Add the lemon juice, chaat masala, and salt. Toss again until thoroughly mixed.

3. Serve in a large bowl or on individual plates, along with an Indian flat bread like nan or wedges of pita.

## HAMPSHIRE HOUSE

84 Beacon Street
Boston (Beacon Hill)
(617) 227–9600, www.hampshirehouse.com

### Corporate chef | Markus Ripperger

Upstairs from the showbiz glitz of Cheers (see page 21)—in the very same building—is a dining room that looks like it could be the setting of an Edith Wharton novel. The Hampshire House has retained the Italian marble, carved oak paneling, and Palladian windows from its heyday as a turn-of-the-twentieth-century residence for a wealthy family. The second-floor room that once housed their private library is still lined with books but is now also outfitted with tables for a weekly jazz brunch, holiday meals, and special-event dinners (one re-created the menu from the *Titanic*). Other parts of the mansion can be rented for weddings and private parties.

Swiss native Markus Ripperger uses his European training as a base for fanciful baked oysters with Chardonnay cranberry sauce, and melted chocolate soup with almonds. After arriving at the Hampshire House in 1992, he became the corporate chef, overseeing the menu at Cheers as well as 75 Chestnut, a third Beacon Hill restaurant owned by Tom Kershaw. This warm salad is built from pasta and contrasting green vegetables—asparagus, spinach, and endives. Dressed with raspberry vinaigrette, it bridges the transition from spring to summer. To turn it into an entree, serve it with a loaf of crusty bread.

# SPRING ASPARAGUS SALAD

[SERVES 4]

**DRESSING:**

½ cup chopped walnuts
¼ cup raspberry vinegar
½ cup olive oil or walnut oil
1 tablespoon grainy mustard, such as Pommery
¼ cup chopped fresh thyme, or to taste
Salt and freshly ground pepper, to taste

In a small, nonreactive bowl, mix all the ingredients together.

**SALAD:**

1 pound mushroom ravioli, cheese tortellini, or
    your favorite filled pasta (see note)
1 pound green asparagus, stem ends trimmed
    and discarded
3 Belgian endives, leaves pulled off stems, rinsed,
    and dried
1 pound fresh spinach leaves, chopped
1 cup crumbled feta cheese
1 small roasted red pepper, diced

1.  Bring a large pot of water to a boil. Add the pasta and
    cook according to the package directions. Drain and set
    aside.

2.  While the pasta is cooking, bring another pot of water to
    a boil. Add the asparagus and cook for 5 minutes. Drain
    and plunge into a bowl of cold water to stop the cooking.

3.  Line 4 plates with endive leaves. Toss the pasta and
    vegetables with the dressing (you may not need all of it),
    asparagus, spinach, cheese, and red pepper. Serve on top
    of the endive leaves.

:: **Note:** Smaller filled pastas, such as tortellini and ag-
nolotti, work better than larger shapes, as they can be
tossed more easily with the vegetables.

## HENRIETTA'S TABLE

Charles Hotel
1 Bennett Street
Cambridge (Harvard Square)
(617) 661–5005, www.henriettastable.com

**Chef | Peter Davis**

Henrietta's Table was named after a 1,000-pound pig, but don't be misled by the 4-foot-tall metal pig at the entrance, or by the pig puppets and dish towels in the gift shop. The restaurant is more than a paean to Charles Hotel owner Dick Friedman's mega-pet. Farm freshness is the theme, with each menu—and even trading cards—listing suppliers by name.

Peter Davis worked at hotels in Asia before returning to his native Boston and thinking locally. Nearly a dozen side dishes celebrate what's in season, from roasted root vegetables to sautéed mushrooms. The rest of the menu revisits New England classics, updating them with components like house-made chutney or sun-dried tomatoes. In this salad Davis wanted to use maple syrup in a way "that wouldn't end up too sweet." Pecans, spiced with a fragrant mix that includes cumin and cardamom, help balance the flavors. So does goat cheese.

## SPECIALTY COCKTAILS

- HT LOCAL MARTINI
- POMEGRANATE MANHATTAN
- CRANBERRY-GINGERLY
- WINTER RUM PUNCH
- SNOWBALL
- FIZZY'S FAVORITE

- HARVEST SKY
- HAPPY APPLE RUM TWIST
- ESPRESSO MARTINI
- PEAR MARTINI w/ROSEMARY + LEMON

- S'MORETINI

$9⁵⁰

### BAR MENU 3 PM TO 5 PM

- HOUSE-MADE YUKON POTATO CHIPS: VINEGAR, BBQ $6⁵⁰
  TRUFFLE & PARMESAN CHIPS $9⁵⁰
- PETE'S SPICY NUTS $6⁵⁰
- SOUP OF THE DAY $5⁷⁵
- MAINE CRAB & CORN CHOWDER w/SMOKED BACON $6²⁵
- ORGANIC FIELD GREENS, LEMON & FRESH HERB VINAIGRETTE $6⁰⁰
- SPINACH SALAD, FRESH BERRIES, GOAT CHEESE MAPLE PECAN VINAIGRETTE $9⁵⁰
- CHICKEN & ROMAINE SALAD, CREAMY GARLIC & PEPPERCORN DRESSING $12
- BLT WITH NEUSKE'S BACON $11⁰⁰
- ROTISSERIE ROASTED CHICKEN CLUB $11⁷⁵
- CHOCOLATE BREAD PUDDING & PIE OF THE DAY WITH HOMEMADE ICE C...
  SELECTION OF HOMEMADE ICE CREAM & SORBET $7⁰⁰

---

Pig Brew
RPOON IPA
MBRIDGE WINTER ALE
MBRIDGE AMBER ALE
FO
E

HEINEKEN, AMSTEL LIGHT
SAM ADAMS, SAM ADAMS LIGHT
CORONA, ANCHOR STEAM
BUD CLAUSTHALER,
BUD LIGHT,
SIERRA NEVADA PALE ALE,
AL...

# FRESH SPINACH SALAD WITH MAPLE PECAN VINAIGRETTE

[SERVES 4]

**SPICY PECANS:**

½ pound pecan halves

1 tablespoon cumin

1½ teaspoons chili powder

Dash of cayenne pepper

1½ teaspoons dried thyme

½ teaspoon ground cardamom

½ teaspoon ground cinnamon

1 tablespoon paprika

¼ teaspoon salt

2 tablespoons (¼ stick) butter

3 tablespoons maple syrup

1. Preheat the oven to 400 degrees. Line a baking sheet with foil. Spread the pecans in a single layer on the baking sheet. Place in the oven and toast, stirring once or twice, until the pecans become fragrant and begin to brown, 5 to 10 minutes. (Check frequently; pecans burn easily.) Place in a mixing bowl.

2. In a separate small bowl, mix together the dry ingredients.

3. In a saucepan, melt the butter. Add the maple syrup, bring to a boil, and remove from the heat. Alternatively, place the butter in a microwave-proof dish and melt—this will require about 1 minute on high power. Stir in the maple syrup and reheat for another 30 seconds on high power. Stir again.

4. Pour the butter-maple mixture over the pecans and toss. Then sprinkle the spice mixture over the pecans and toss again until well coated. Cool before using in the salad.

:: **Note:** The nuts can be made a day ahead. You can also toast the pecan pieces for the vinaigrette in the next step of this recipe. Set them aside after they're toasted.

**PECAN VINAIGRETTE:**

2 ounces pecan pieces

1 cup safflower oil or other light salad oil

⅓ cup rice wine vinegar

2 tablespoons maple syrup

Salt and pepper, to taste

1. Toast the pecans in the oven, using the directions above. (You can toast all the nuts at once; see the note above.)

2. In a bowl, whisk together the oil, vinegar, and maple syrup. Add the toasted pecans. Season with salt and pepper.

**SALAD:**

12 ounces fresh spinach, tough stems removed

2 ounces goat cheese

1 cup fresh berries, such as raspberries or strawberries

Wash the spinach and dry it in a salad spinner. Tear it into bite-size pieces. Toss the spinach with the Pecan Vinaigrette (from the recipe above), then top with the Spicy Pecans (above), goat cheese, and berries. Serve immediately.

:: **Note:** You may not use all the dressing or spicy pecans. Leftover dressing can be saved for another salad; leftover pecans can be eaten as a snack.

## CHEZ HENRI

1 Shepard Street
Cambridge (between Harvard and Porter Squares)
(617) 354–8980, www.chezhenri.com

### Chef-owner | Paul O'Connell

Imagine crepes doing the cha-cha: That's Chez Henri, a French bistro with Latin flair tucked away on a side street off Massachusetts Avenue. You can't miss the bright red sign, which matches the red trim inside. Though Paul O'Connell grew up in New England, he discovered the fun of Latin ingredients on his travels and in other restaurant kitchens. Now he is equally at home pressing Cuban-style sandwiches, brushing rum glaze on grilled pork—and stirring up French bouillabaisse.

This colorful spinach salad shows what O'Connell likes to do best: "Take a classic recipe and give it Latin flavors." The spinach salad with warm bacon dressing starts out in familiar bistro territory. Then it heads south—as in *south of the border*. The spicy vinaigrette that accompanies it gives your tongue a little pinch and tells it to go dancing.

## SPINACH SALAD AND CHIPOTLE CHILE PEPPER VINAIGRETTE

[SERVES 6]

**CHIPOTLE CHILE PEPPER VINAIGRETTE:**

1 can (7 ounces) chipotle peppers in adobo sauce
    (see sidebar)
2 cloves garlic
6 tablespoons red wine vinegar
¾ cup olive oil

1. Use a spoon to remove 2 chipotle peppers and ¼ cup sauce from the can. Place those in a blender, saving the rest of the can for another use. (Try not to handle the peppers directly with your hands, as they can irritate your skin.)

2. Place the garlic, vinegar, and oil in the blender. Puree until smooth. Place in a squeeze bottle (see the sidebar on page 124), or pour into a small container. Set aside.

**SPINACH SALAD:**

1 pound bacon
2 tablespoons grainy mustard, such as Pommery
½ cup red wine vinegar
Black pepper, to taste
4 bunches (1½ pounds) fresh spinach, washed, dried, and torn into bite-size pieces
2 cups julienne-cut radicchio, washed and dried

1. In a large skillet over medium-high heat, cook the bacon until crisp on both sides. Place on paper towels to drain. Cut into ¼-inch pieces. You should have about 1½ cups.

2. Reserve ¼ cup of the drippings from the skillet and discard the rest.

3. Add the bacon pieces back to the skillet and heat over a medium flame until the bacon is hot. Stir in the mustard, red wine vinegar, and black pepper.

4. Place the spinach in a large bowl along with the radicchio. Spoon the dressing over the salad and toss well.

5. To serve, divide the salad among 6 serving plates. Drizzle a little Chipotle Chile Pepper Vinaigrette around the plate and over the salad.

## Chipotles in Adobo

Almost any market with Hispanic specialty products carries small cans of chipotle peppers in adobo sauce. Puckered and dark brown, chipotle peppers look a bit like prunes. These peppers are a dried, smoked version of the more recognizable jalapeño pepper. Chipotles are typically packed in adobo sauce—a vinegary brew of tomatoes and spices. In Mexican cooking they are used to flavor sauces, soups, and stews. "They are slightly sweet along with the heat, which makes them appealing, and they are quick and ready to use," says O'Connell.

## THE FIREPLACE

1634 Beacon Street
Brookline
(617) 975–1900, www.fireplacerest.com

### Chef-owner | Jim Solomon

The Fireplace takes its name from the enormous stone hearth near its front door, but the restaurant's concept extends beyond coziness. The copper-topped tables, blond wood accents, and mustard-yellow walls look more slick than homey. The New England–inspired menu takes comfort food up a few notches by adding green apples to slaw for extra flavor, or accompanying ham with house-made sweet bourbon jam. "We like to go with what's fresh and what's in season, with a few early colonial influences," says chef-owner Jim Solomon. The latter shows up in hearth-roasted fish and baked beans with brown bread. Working within the limited growing season is a challenge that Solomon likes. He grew up in Brookline and worked in financial services before becoming a restaurateur.

In this recipe soft-shell crabs, a late-spring and early-summer treat in New England, are doused with classic, 1920s-era Green Goddess salad dressing. According to Solomon, "You get the crunch of fried crabs with the rich, sweet meat of the crab itself, and a nice tang from the dressing. This would be great to serve on a summer day, sitting on your deck with cold iced tea, lemonade, or a frosty beer." The Fireplace also uses this Green Goddess Dressing as dipping sauce for grilled vegetables.

# CRISPY SOFT-SHELL CRAB SALAD WITH GREEN GODDESS DRESSING

[SERVES 6]

**GREEN GODDESS DRESSING:**

2 egg yolks

1 tablespoon mustard

2 anchovy fillets

1 clove garlic

1 tablespoon salt

½ cup buttermilk, divided

1 tablespoon fresh tarragon leaves

¼ cup watercress leaves

1 tablespoon fresh parsley leaves

2 tablespoons roughly chopped scallions (green part only)

2 cups canola oil

2 tablespoons cider vinegar

2 tablespoons lemon juice

Put the egg yolks, mustard, anchovies, and garlic in the bowl of a food processor and puree until smooth. Add the salt and ¼ cup of the buttermilk, along with the tarragon, watercress, parsley, and scallions. Process until smooth. With the motor running, drizzle in the oil. Pour into a bowl and stir in the vinegar and lemon juice. Thin with more buttermilk, if necessary.

**CRAB SALAD:**

12 soft-shell crabs

1 cup buttermilk mixed with 1 teaspoon curry powder

6 ears corn, shucked

2 tablespoons olive oil, plus more as needed

3 red onions, cut into ¾-inch-thick slices

6 plum tomatoes

2 tablespoons lemon juice

1 tablespoon mint chiffonade (thinly sliced leaves)

Salt and pepper, to taste

1 cup cornmeal

2 cups canola oil

18 leaves Boston or Bibb lettuce, washed and dried

1 cup Green Goddess Dressing (from recipe above)

1. Clean the crabs, removing the faces. Place the buttermilk-curry mixture in a shallow bowl and add the crabs, pushing down gently with a spoon so they are submerged. Let the crabs marinate while you prepare the rest of the recipe.

2. Preheat a grill. Rub the ears of corn with olive oil. Drizzle more olive oil over the onion slices. Grill the corn and onions until soft, turning to cook on all sides, about 10 minutes total. Set aside until cool enough to handle.

3. Cut the corn kernels off the cob (see page 112 for technique). Dice the onions and tomatoes. Add the vegetables to a bowl and toss with the 2 tablespoons olive oil, lemon juice, mint, salt, and pepper. Refrigerate until ready to use.

4. Drain the crabs and roll them in the cornmeal. Heat the canola oil in a deep skillet and fry the crabs, a few at a time, until crispy. Season with salt and pepper. Drain on paper towels.

5. Distribute the lettuce leaves among 6 plates. Top each with the corn salad and 2 crabs. Drizzle with the dressing and serve.

## UPSTAIRS ON THE SQUARE

91 Winthrop Street
Cambridge (Harvard Square)
(617) 864–1933, www.upstairsonthesquare.com

**Executive chef and co-owner | Deborah Hughes**

When this restaurant opened in 1981—singer Ella Fitzgerald was one of the first customers—it was one flight up from the Hasty Pudding Club, a social and theater group at Harvard University. Originally named UpStairs at the Pudding, it became known for its innovative, fun food and the garden-party atmosphere of its roof terrace. Mary-Catherine Deibel and chef and business partner Deborah Hughes were among the first female restaurateurs in Boston. When UpStairs moved to Winthrop Street in 2003 (and became UpStairs on the Square), Hughes took her flair for interior decorating to unparalleled boldness. She installed red and purple floor tiles in one dining room, along with plaid wallpaper; you'll find lavender suede banquettes and leopard-print carpet in another.

On the menu you can't help but be entertained by Hot Dates (dates stuffed with almonds and wrapped in bacon), Flash-in-the-Pan Salmon, or pink champagne splits on the afternoon tea menu (see the sidebar on page 212).

Sprinkled with flower petals and vegetables, this lobster salad illustrates the whimsy—but also the freshness of the food—at UpStairs. "Lobster is a good way to show what you can do as a chef—when to push, when to hold back, when to self-edit. I love to serve this when beans are fresh. It looks beautiful with all the vegetables," says Hughes, ever the designer. For even more color, sprinkle on fresh edible flowers (such as pansies or nasturtiums from a farmers' market, a grocery store, or your own garden—but avoid flowers intended as decorations, as they might contain a lot of chemicals). Another variation is to use spring-dug potatoes, cooked with their skins on, sliced, and arranged on the plate. The recipe has lots of steps, but none is too complicated. An easy shortcut is to purchase cooked lobster meat.

# LOBSTER SALAD WITH ORANGE TRUFFLE AIOLI
# AND FRESH HARVEST BEANS

[SERVES 6–8]

**LOBSTERS:**

6 lobsters (1½ pounds each), or
    1½ pounds cooked lobster meat
Salt, to taste
Juice of 1 lemon
Juice of 1 lime

Bring a large pot of water to a boil. Add the lobsters and boil for 10 minutes. Drain and set aside until cool enough to handle. Remove all the lobster meat and discard the shells. Cut the meat into large (³/4- to 1-inch) pieces and place into a nonreactive bowl. Sprinkle with salt, then squeeze the lemon and lime juice over the top and toss gently. Set aside.

**AIOLI:**

1 cup good-quality mayonnaise
1 tablespoon truffle oil
2 tablespoons freshly squeezed orange juice
Finely chopped zest of 1 orange
About ½ teaspoon orange oil (available at gourmet
    markets), or to taste

Place the mayonnaise in a nonreactive bowl. Add the truffle oil, orange juice, chopped orange zest, and several drops of orange oil. Gently mix together. Fold in the lobster meat (from the recipe above), cover, and chill in the refrigerator until ready to use.

**CHIVE OIL:**

1 cup finely chopped fresh chives
1 cup canola oil
1 large clove garlic, finely chopped
Salt, to taste

Bring a large pot of water to a boil. Add the chives and blanch until slightly soft. Remove with a slotted spoon. Place the oil in the bowl of a food processor. Add the chives and garlic. Pulse to mix together. Add the salt and set aside.

**VEGETABLES:**

2 cups *haricots verts* (French string beans) or
    small green beans
1 cup fresh fava or cranberry beans (see note)
1 cup fresh corn kernels, cut from the cob
    (see page 112 for technique)
1 cup freshly shelled peas

Bring a large pot of water to a boil. Add the string beans and blanch until slightly soft. Remove with a slotted spoon and immediately plunge in cold water so they retain their color and do not overcook. Drain in a colander. Using the same technique, blanch the corn and peas.

:: **Note:** This salad is based on fresh beans and peas, available in spring and summer from farmers' markets and well-stocked gourmet markets. They are sold in their pods, which you need to strip off and discard to find the beans nestled inside. Cranberry beans (also known as shell beans and borlotti beans) are cream colored with distinctive red streaks and a slightly nutty flavor. (For another recipe using cranberry beans, see page 165.) Starchy-tasting fava beans look like giant white lima beans. Other varieties of beans can be substituted according to what's in season. If you can't find any fresh beans, just use fresh corn and peas. Canned or frozen varieties are too mushy to work well.

**FINAL PREPARATION AND SERVING:**

Segments of 2 oranges, trimmed of all white membrane
1 head frisée lettuce (see note)
Flower petals, for garnish (optional)

Place a few *haricots verts* in a crisscross pattern around the perimeter of each dinner plate. Place the frisée in the center of the plate and cover with the lobster-mayonnaise mixture.

Drizzle with Chive Oil. Strew a handful of beans and a small amount of corn kernels and peas over the top. Arrange the orange segments around the perimeter of the plate. Decorate with flower petals, if you're using these.

:: **Note:** Frisée is a sturdy variety of chicory with curly leaves that resemble a head of frizzy hair. If you can't find it, substitute a firm lettuce such as romaine.

# PASTA

The Prince company probably did more to promote pasta in Boston than any restaurant. The macaroni and spaghetti shop opened in 1912 in Boston's predominantly Italian North End, and eventually expanded to a factory in Lowell, about 30 miles to the north. In the 1950s a local radio commercial declared, "Wednesday is Prince Spaghetti Day"—and people listened. A television commercial that featured a mother calling her son, Anthony, off the streets of the North End for a Prince Spaghetti dinner promoted the brand even more in the 1970s. Prince is now part of Borden foods.

By the 1980s many Boston chefs, fresh from travels and training in Italy, were ready to look for pasta outside a factory-made box. Their interest in handmade tortellini, tagliatelle—even spaghetti—turned pasta into gourmet fare. The recipes in this chapter reflect the chefs' ongoing appreciation of pasta, low-carb diets be damned. What other food is versatile enough to be tossed with peaches and pistachio pesto at Restaurant Dante, or scallops and lobster-flavored bread crumbs at Sonsie? Barbara Lynch, who learned many of her recipes in Italy, tops pasta with cannellini beans and sausage at The Butcher Shop, and with meaty Bolognese sauce at No. 9 Park. Potato-based gnocchi are paired with delicate spring vegetables at Rialto, and hearty short ribs at Grotto. For traditionalists, spaghetti with clam sauce from Cantina Italiana brings it all back to Boston's most famous Italian neighborhood, the North End.

## RESTAURANT DANTE

Royal Sonesta Cambridge Hotel
40 Edwin H. Land Boulevard, Cambridge
(617) 497–4200, www.restaurantdante.com

**Chef-owner | Dante de Magistris**

The first dish that budding chef Dante de Magistris made, at age four—scrambled eggs in a Tupperware container on top of the stove—ended with town firefighters putting out the flames. Undiscouraged, the Boston-area native has since become much more proficient. He earned three Michelin stars at a restaurant on Italy's Amalfi coast before coming back home to be the inaugural chef at blu (see page 26). With his two brothers, he opened Dante in spring 2006. In a spot overlooking the Charles River, he reinvents classic Italian, French, and Spanish dishes with unusual ingredients and avant-garde presentations. Service goes through breakfast, lunch, and dinner, from blueberry pancakes with mascarpone ice cream to snack-size lobster and chorizo corn dogs with three sauces.

De Magistris draws on his family's Italian background in his handmade pasta menu, which includes potato gnocchi from his grandmother's recipe. The inspiration for this dish was not pasta, but a perfectly ripe white peach. "I started thinking of what I wanted to eat with the peach," he recounts. "First I thought of Gorgonzola cheese. Then pesto of some sort, and pistachio was the right nut for this job. I put it all together with gnocchi or ravioli, and it made sense." He rolls and fills his own ravioli dough, but you can use a good-quality, store-bought variety—or better yet, he says, come in and taste his version. This makes a nice variation on the standard cold pasta with basil pesto.

# RAVIOLI WITH ROASTED PEACHES AND PISTACHIO PESTO

[SERVES 4]

**ROASTED PEACHES:**

1 tablespoon unsalted butter

2 teaspoons extra-virgin olive oil

3 ripe peaches, pits removed, cut in quarters

Heat a large sauté pan over medium heat. Add the butter and olive oil. Sear the peaches on both sides until caramelized. Keep warm until ready to serve.

**PISTACHIO PESTO:**

10 large fresh basil leaves, 1 sprig fresh cilantro,
    and 5 large fresh mint leaves, all washed and dried

1 small clove garlic

1 tablespoon freshly grated Parmigiano Reggiano cheese

¼ cup shelled pistachios

¼ cup extra-virgin olive oil

Juice of ¼ lemon

Salt and pepper, to taste

Add all the ingredients to a blender or food processor and blend on high speed until smooth. Set aside.

**PASTA AND SAUCE:**

¼ pound Gorgonzola dolce (see notes)

2 teaspoons unsalted butter

1 pound fresh cheese ravioli

2 tablespoons freshly grated Parmigiano Reggiano
    cheese (see notes)

Salt and pepper, to taste

Shelled pistachios, for garnish

1.  Bring a large pot of salted water to a boil over high heat.

2.  While the water is coming to a boil, in a large sauté pan over medium heat, melt the Gorgonzola dolce and butter.

3.  Add the ravioli to the boiling water and cook for 3 to 4 minutes, or until 1 minute after they float to the top of the water. Gently scoop the pasta out of the water with a strainer or slotted spoon and transfer to the pan with the melted Gorgonzola. Add a little pasta water to the pan to thin the melted cheese into a sauce that coats the pasta and toss well. Pull the pan off the heat, add the Parmigiano Reggiano, and season with salt and pepper.

4.  Place the pasta on a serving plate. Garnish with the Roasted Peaches, a drizzle of the Pistachio Pesto, and shelled pistachios.

:: **Notes:** Gorgonzola dolce, also called Dolcelatte, is a creamy version of the Italian Gorgonzola blue cheese. If you cannot find it, substitute ½ cup crème fraîche or sour cream mixed with 1 tablespoon crumbled blue cheese.

Parmigiano Reggiano is an aged Parmesan cheese made in Italy. Another type of Parmesan can be substituted, but it will have less of a complex, nutty flavor.

Look for both these cheeses at a specialty cheese shop or an Italian market.

## JER-NE RESTAURANT & BAR

The Ritz-Carlton, Boston Common
12 Avery Street
Boston (Downtown)
(617) 574–7176, www.ritzcarlton.com

**Former executive chef | Scott Gambone**

When the original Ritz-Carlton, Boston, expanded, it didn't annex an adjoining space in the Back Bay. It built a new, thirty-nine-story tower all the way across the Boston Common, completed in 2001. If the old Ritz (now the Taj Boston hotel) defined tradition, the new hotel is decidedly twenty-first century, with its modern-art-filled lobby and its mixed use as a hotel, luxury condos (home to some Red Sox players), and a high-end gym, the Sports Club/L.A.

JER-NE, the restaurant in a narrow, glass box of a space at street level, also looks thoroughly contemporary. A glass sculpture custom-designed by artist Howard Ben Tré divides the bar from the dining area. On the wall, an abstract wood installation by Michael Beatty named *Blips,* would look at home in a gallery. An illuminated marble panel backs the bar, making the bottles glow. White plates even have a designer's touch, as they are shaped like triangles and decorated with swirls. Scott Gambone's menu works especially well for theatergoers, with brisk service and food

that starts a night out with more fun than fuss. For couples and groups of friends, dishes designed for sharing include a Boston lager and cheddar cheese fondue. For dessert, the fun continues with a flight of petits fours and cocktails matching the flavors of oatmeal cookies, crème brûlée, and apple tarte tatin.

This pasta dish puts together colorful vegetables with smoked chicken and a creamy sauce. "The flavors are their own story," says Gambone, who chose the smoked chicken for its assertive taste. To tone it down, use regular chicken; to make a vegetarian version, omit it altogether.

## GEMELLI PASTA WITH SMOKED CHICKEN BREAST

[SERVES 4]

4 quarts water
3 tablespoons salt, plus more to taste
2 tablespoons olive oil
1 teaspoon minced garlic
1 tablespoon small-diced yellow onion
1 cup button mushrooms, cut into quarters
½ pound smoked chicken breast, julienned
3 tablespoons Chardonnay
1 pound uncooked gemelli pasta (see note)
2½ cups heavy cream
2 tablespoons chopped flat-leaf parsley
½ cup shredded Asiago cheese
8 cherry tomatoes, each cut in half through the stem end
Pepper, to taste

1. In a large pot, bring the water and 3 tablespoons salt to a boil.

2. While the pasta water is heating, heat the olive oil in a large saucepan. Add the garlic, onion, mushrooms, and smoked chicken breast and sauté until the onion is translucent, approximately 5 minutes.

3. Deglaze the pan with the Chardonnay. Simmer until the wine has evaporated but the ingredients have not started to brown.

4. When the pasta water comes to a boil, cook the pasta according to the package directions. Once the pasta is cooked, drain and keep warm in a covered pan.

5. Add the heavy cream to the sauté pan and bring to a boil, sustaining the boil for 2 to 4 minutes until the sauce thickens slightly (enough to coat the back of a spoon).

6. Add the warm pasta to the sauce and toss in the parsley, Asiago cheese, and cherry tomatoes. Season with salt and pepper.

:: **Note:** Gemelli is a spiral-shaped pasta that looks like two strands twisted together. If you can't find it, substitute penne or rigatoni.

## NO. 9 PARK

9 Park Street
Boston (Beacon Hill)
(617) 742–9991, www.no9park.com

**Chef-owner | Barbara Lynch**

Raised Irish Catholic in South Boston's housing projects, chef Barbara Lynch learned to cook in home economics classes; one of her first jobs was in a rectory kitchen. She has since become a local legend not only for her food, but also for a local-gal-makes-good career that looks a lot like the female version of the movie *Good Will Hunting*. Equally talented and tenacious, Lynch went on to become a nationally recognized chef at some of Boston's most elite restaurants. *Amuse-Bouche,* a film by Boston filmmaker Maryanne Galvin, shows how Lynch beat the odds of succeeding in a male-dominated profession. The 2002 film is still being shown at schools and Boys & Girls Clubs; Lynch sometimes makes guest appearances to help inspire students.

What catapulted this aspiring young cook beyond her provincial background was a trip to Tuscany. "Before that, I had been no farther than from South Boston to Cambridge," she admits. Even

after more than twenty years, Lynch vividly recalls some of the meals that the local grandmothers made for her in Italy. Ever since, she has been making this recipe for meat sauce at No. 9 Park and The Butcher Shop (see page 74). "I remember the cook telling me, 'You have to use lots of chicken livers and lots of sage.' That is the key."

Barbara Lynch became an expert in Italian cooking, working her way up at restaurants including Boston's Olives (see page 148). No. 9 Park, the first restaurant that Lynch owned, gave her a chance to add French food to her repertoire. "I like challenges," she deadpans about her audacity in opening a new eatery *and* learning French cooking at the same time.

In the shadow of the Massachusetts State House atop Beacon Hill, No. 9 Park attracts politicians as well as neighbors and suburbanites who are fans of Lynch's food. The restaurant makes fresh pasta every day, including the chef's popular prune-stuffed gnocchi. One of Lynch's favorite ingredients is shellfish, which led her to open still another Boston establishment, B&G Oysters (see page 22). With three restaurants, a growing catering business, and a daughter born in 2002, Lynch still seems fueled by the prodigious ambition and energy that helped launch her career in the first place.

## TAGLIATELLE WITH TUSCAN MEAT SAUCE

[SERVES 8]

1 tablespoon extra-virgin olive oil
1 medium onion, diced
1 stalk celery, diced
1 medium carrot, diced
5 ounces chicken livers, diced
¼ cup chopped fresh sage
Salt and pepper, to taste
1½ pounds ground meat, preferably ½ pound each veal, pork, and lamb
1½ cups red table wine
2½ cups veal or chicken stock
1½ cups chopped canned tomatoes
½ cup chopped fresh basil
1 cup heavy cream (optional)
Freshly grated Parmesan cheese, to taste

1. In a deep skillet, heat the olive oil over medium high. Add the onion, celery, and carrot; cook, stirring occasionally, until the vegetables begin to get tender. Add the chicken livers and sage, sprinkle with salt and pepper, and cook, stirring, until the liver pieces lose their red color.

2. Add the ground meat in bits, along with more salt and pepper. Cook, stirring occasionally, again until the meat loses its red color. Add the wine, raise the heat to high, and cook until the wine is almost evaporated, about 15 minutes.

3. Add the stock, tomatoes, and basil. Bring to a boil, then adjust the heat so the mixture simmers gently. Cook for about 45 minutes, until the mixture is dark and rich.

4. Just before serving, stir in the cream (optional). Serve over cooked tagliatelle or other pasta, topped with freshly ground black pepper and Parmesan cheese.

## THE BUTCHER SHOP

552 Tremont Street
Boston (South End)
(617) 423–4800, www.thebutchershopboston.com

**Executive chef-owner | Barbara Lynch**

As a companion to the seafood-specific B&G Oysters (see page 22), Barbara Lynch designed The Butcher Shop, located just across the street, to focus on meats. (Both of these eateries are different from her fine-dining restaurant, No. 9 Park; see page 72.) Hanging strings of sausages and giant rolls of brown meat-wrapping paper give The Butcher Shop an Old World feeling. The selection of specialty meats includes Kobe beef pastrami, and even a whole suckling pig (ordered in advance).

House-made hot dogs, pâtés, soups, and sauces can be picked up from the refrigerator case to take home. A butcher-block table displays almonds, olives, and other snacks to accompany the meat dishes.

Unlike other butcher shops, this one morphs into a wine bar in the evening, serving light bites including plates of charcuterie, duck tacos with house-made tortillas, salads, and pasta dishes. Lynch recalls that she has been making this sausage and cannellini bean sauce since she lived in South Boston in the early 1980s and had to trek into the North End for fresh sausages. "I'm a huge bean and pasta fan," she enthuses. "This is an easy weeknight meal, since it relies on pantry staples. But it's important to use real cheese, real garlic, fresh herbs, and good-quality sausage here, since that's what gives this dish its flavor." For less spice, substitute sweet Italian sausage and omit the red pepper. No matter which sausage you choose, the sauce that Lynch recommends has just the right consistency to coat pasta, and a balance of hearty flavors.

## RIGATONI WITH SPICY SAUSAGE AND CANNELLINI BEANS

[SERVES 6]

2 tablespoons extra-virgin olive oil

4 cloves garlic, minced

1 large onion, coarsely chopped

1 pound hot Italian sausage, casings removed (see note)

1 cup dry red wine

1 can (28 ounces) peeled Italian tomatoes, drained and coarsely chopped, liquid reserved

½ teaspoon crushed red pepper

Salt and pepper, to taste

1 pound rigatoni

1 can (19 ounces) cannellini (Italian white) beans, drained and rinsed

½ cup freshly grated Parmesan cheese

2 tablespoons coarsely chopped fresh basil

2 tablespoons (¼ stick) unsalted butter, cut into small pieces

1. In a large sauté pan over medium heat, heat the olive oil until it shimmers. Add the garlic and cook, stirring, until it becomes light golden. Add the onion and sausage; break up the meat with a wooden spoon and cook until it's no longer pink, about 5 minutes.

2. Add the wine, increase the heat to high, and cook until the wine is reduced by half, about 10 minutes. Add the tomatoes, the reserved tomato liquid, and the red pepper. Season to taste with salt and pepper.

3. Reduce the heat to medium and cook the mixture until it is slightly thickened, about 30 minutes.

4. Meanwhile, bring a large pot of water to a boil and salt it generously. When it's boiling, add the rigatoni and cook until al dente. Drain, reserving ½ cup of the cooking water.

5. Add the rigatoni to the sauce and gently stir in the beans, Parmesan, basil, and butter. Cook until heated through, about 3 minutes. If the pasta looks dry, add some of the reserved pasta cooking water.

6. Serve each portion with extra Parmesan and chopped basil, if desired.

:: **Note:** An easy way to remove uncooked sausage from its casing is to cut a small hole in one end of the casing, squeeze out the meat, and discard the casing. (Wash your hands well afterward, as you have been handling raw meat.)

## CANTINA ITALIANA

346 Hanover Street
Boston (North End)
(617) 723–4577, www.cantinaitaliana.com

**Chef | Charles Colella**

An upside-down, neon-edged wine bottle pouring into a giant glass makes it hard to miss the entrance to Cantina Italiana. Since 1931 this landmark restaurant has been dishing out hearty portions of lasagna, veal Parmesan, and homemade bombolotti pasta with lobster, shrimp, and tomato sauce. Autographed pictures of Bruins and Celtics players show the celebrity appeal of the place. In one room is a hand-painted mural of Venice; in another are barrels stamped with the names CHIANTI and VALPOLICELLA, two Italian styles of wine.

Despite the influx of more contemporary restaurants in the neighborhood, Cantina Italiana has remained faithful to the old North End cooking style. The chef, Italian native Charles Colella, upholds tradition with this made-to-order version of the classic *spaghetti alla vongole*. Note that the pasta is tossed with the sauce before serving—just the way your *nonna* (Italian grandmother) would make it, too.

### SPAGHETTI ALLA VONGOLE
### (SPAGHETTI WITH CLAM SAUCE)

[SERVES 1]

7 fresh littleneck clams
2 tablespoons olive oil, divided
2 cloves garlic, chopped
½ cup clam juice
2 tablespoons dry white wine
4 ounces uncooked spaghetti
Chopped fresh parsley, to taste

1. Bring 2 quarts of salted water to a boil. Wash the clams in cold water.

2. In a sauté pan with a tight-fitting lid, heat 1 tablespoon of the olive oil. Add the garlic and sauté until it turns slightly brown. Add the clams, clam juice, and white wine. Cover and continue to cook.

3. Add the spaghetti to the boiling water. Cook until al dente (slightly firm), about 10 minutes.

4. When the clams open, remove the pan from the heat. Drain the spaghetti, adding it to the pan and tossing together. Sprinkle with parsley and drizzle with the remaining tablespoon of olive oil.

## BOSTON PARK PLAZA HOTEL

64 Arlington Street
Boston
(617) 426-2000, www.bostonparkplaza.com

**Executive chef | J. J. Fernandes**

Park Plaza has long been a busy intersection between the South End, the Back Bay, and Downtown. A 1932 menu from the old Hotel Statler, posted inside the current Boston Park Plaza Hotel, shows the area's long history as a dining destination. The "luncheon" lists an "alligator pear" (an avocado), lamb kidney, and lime Jell-O for dessert. Culinary choices have expanded considerably since then. The Boston Park Plaza now houses eight restaurants and lounges, including McCormick & Schmick's (see page 104), and Finale (see page 202).

The hotel itself runs the Swans Café at one end of the lobby, set apart by a mirrored wall, tables with a single rose on each, and a player piano. J. J. Fernandes, a native of the Cape Verde Islands off the coast of Africa (once a colony of Portugal), has worked at the Park Plaza since 1992. During his tenure he has cooked for four U.S. presidents who were visiting Boston, including Bill Clinton and George W. Bush. Aside from afternoon tea (see page 214), one menu is served from lunch through late night. This recipe, a combination of three winning components—lobster, pasta, and white wine sauce—is popular at all hours.

### LOBSTER LINGUINE

[SERVES 4]

1½ pounds fresh or 1 pound dried linguine
3 ounces (6 tablespoons) olive oil
2 shallots, peeled and finely chopped
4 cloves garlic, finely chopped
1 medium tomato, diced
1½ cups dry white wine
¼ cup (½ stick) butter
2 tablespoons chopped fresh parsley, plus
  more for garnish
12 ounces (¾ pound) lobster meat, preferably
  knuckle and claw meat (from 2–3 lobsters)
Salt and pepper, to taste
Grilled focaccia, for garnish (optional)

1. Bring a large pot of water to a boil. Cook the linguine according to the package directions. Drain and set aside.

2. Heat the olive oil in a sauté pan. Sauté the shallots and garlic until the shallots are translucent. Add the tomato and wine. Simmer until the liquid is reduced by half.

3. Add the butter, parsley, and lobster meat. Cook very briefly, just until the lobster meat is heated through.

4. Toss with the linguine. Season with salt and pepper. Garnish with focaccia cubes (optional) and a sprinkle of fresh parsley.

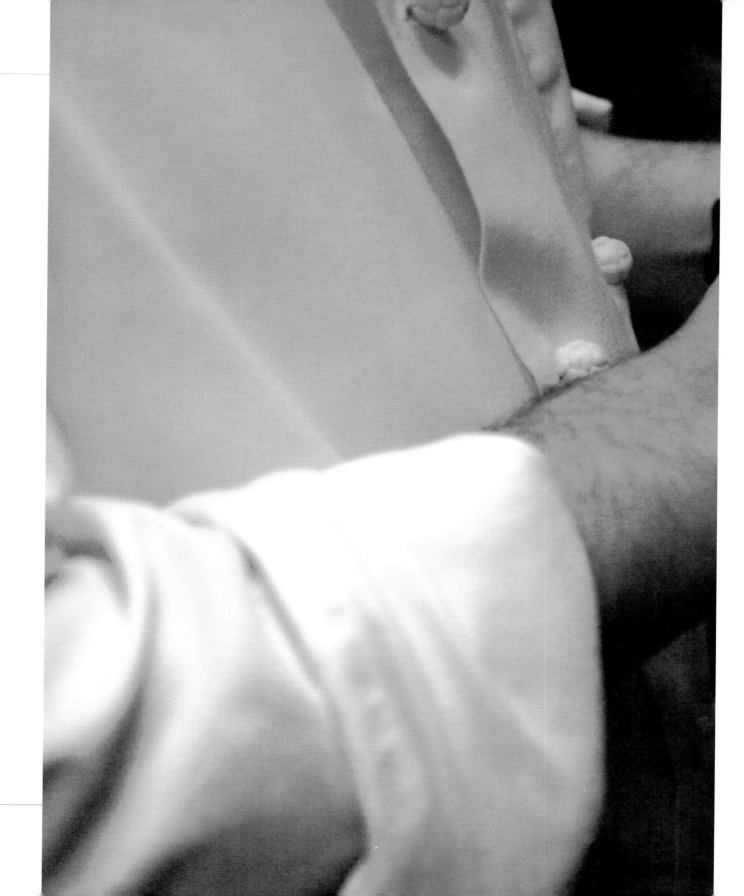

## SONSIE

327 Newbury Street
Boston (Back Bay)
(617) 351-2500, www.sonsieboston.com

**Chef | Bill Poirier**

Sonsie looks about as much like a European cafe as you can find in Boston. Wicker chairs at round tables face Newbury Street. The front windows turn into open doors in warm weather, giving an unobstructed view of the multiply pierced Newbury Comics shoppers across the street, as well as pocketbook-swinging fashionistas. There is plenty of strutting inside Sonsie, too, as the throngs of young regulars gravitate to the long, mahogany bar for mango mojitos and red apple martinis. In this lively scene, you might expect food to be an afterthought, but Bill Poirier has kept a steady hand in the kitchen since 1993. He balances crowd-pleasing steamed mussels and pizzas with well-executed entrees like grilled pork tenderloin with wild mushroom cream and braised sweet onions.

Poirier's menus also offer about half a dozen choices of pasta, from angel hair with veal meatballs to crispy Thai noodles advertised as "spicy, spicy, spicy!" This recipe for pappardelle (flat, wide noodles) updates the Italian classic of spaghetti with bread crumbs. "I gave thought to making the basic idea more upscale with a New England twist," Poirier says. "The lobster-and-bread-crumb combo came to mind to add richness." Seared scallops, spinach, and mushrooms turn this into a one-dish meal with a satisfyingly salty-crunchy topping from the lobster bread crumbs. For the best flavor, avoid using prepackaged bread crumbs; instead, toast your own.

# PAPPARDELLE WITH PAN-ROASTED SCALLOPS AND LOBSTER BREAD CRUMBS

[SERVES 2]

## LOBSTER BREAD CRUMBS:

2 slices white bread
2 tablespoons (¼ stick) butter
½ cup finely diced cooked lobster meat
½ teaspoon lemon juice
⅛ teaspoon grated lemon zest
Salt and pepper, to taste

1. Use a food processor with a metal blade to turn the fresh bread slices into crumbs; you should have 1 cup. Preheat the oven to 350 degrees. Spread the bread crumbs in a single layer on a baking sheet. Toast until completely golden. Remove from the oven and set aside.

2. In a sauté pan, melt the butter. Sauté the lobster meat until hot.

3. In a large mixing bowl, toss together the bread crumbs, lobster meat, lemon juice, lemon zest, salt, and pepper. Mix thoroughly. Keep warm until ready to use.

## PAPPARDELLE:

8 ounces uncooked pappardelle (see notes)
8 large sea scallops
Salt and pepper, to taste
¼ cup olive oil, divided
2 cloves garlic, thinly sliced
8 ounces mushrooms, thinly sliced
2 cups raw spinach leaves
2 tablespoons (¼ stick) butter
1 teaspoon lemon juice
1 cup lobster broth, heated through (see notes)
½ cup Lobster Bread Crumbs (from recipe above)

1. Bring a large pot of salted water to a boil. Add the pasta and cook according to the package directions.

2. Sprinkle the scallops with salt and pepper. In a sauté pan over high heat, heat 2 tablespoons of the olive oil. Sear the scallops for 2 to 3 minutes on each side. Remove from the pan and set aside.

3. In a clean sauté pan, heat the remaining 2 tablespoons of olive oil. Add the garlic and mushrooms and sauté until the garlic is golden.

4. Drain the pasta and toss it with the sautéed mushrooms, raw spinach, butter, lemon juice, salt, and pepper.

5. Divide the pasta mixture between 2 plates. Spoon lobster broth around the pasta. Place 4 scallops on top of each serving of pasta. Spoon Lobster Bread Crumbs over the top. Serve immediately.

:: **Notes:** If you can't find pappardelle, substitute spaghetti or linguine.

For a lobster broth substitute, use a simple pureed tomato sauce made with basil. The texture should be somewhat thin.

## THE GRAPEVINE

26 Congress Street
Salem
(978) 745-9335, www.grapevinesalem.com

### Chef-owner | Kate Hammond

There's more to Salem than witches and the home that inspired Nathaniel Hawthorne's *House of Seven Gables*. When residents of this North Shore waterfront town want a night out, the Grapevine delivers contemporary, Italian-accented food. From the twig-laced window blinds to the grape-leaf-patterned tablecloths and purple walls, the restaurant's decor matches its name. In winter, silver Christmas ornaments hang from the ceiling, making the dining room more festive.

In the eighteen years Kate Hammond has been in business, she has seen the Salem waterfront come back to life with new shops and a hotel at Pickering Wharf. Her menu has evolved over time, too, though it doesn't stray far from risotto, pasta, and hearty fare like roast lamb with Swiss chard and mashed potatoes. "We've been through everything you can imagine with our pasta dishes," she confides. This dish proved to be a winning combination of corn, bacon, scallops, and cream sauce. "People ask for this pasta even when it's not on the menu." Some go so far as to bring in their own ears of corn just in case the kitchen doesn't have any on hand. When corn is out of season, use cooked asparagus or artichoke hearts, chopped into small pieces. You can also substitute shrimp for the scallops.

# FETTUCCINE WITH BACON, CORN, AND SCALLOPS

[SERVES 4]

2 cups diced uncooked bacon
3 cups heavy cream
2 tablespoons (¼ stick) butter
1 cup diced Spanish onion
2 large ears corn, shucked
½ cup Parmesan cheese, plus more to pass at the table
1 pound fettuccine
1 cup chicken stock
1–2 tablespoons olive oil
16 large sea scallops (see note)
Salt and freshly ground black pepper, to taste
Chopped fresh chives, for garnish

1. In a large sauté pan, cook the bacon over medium-high heat until crispy. Drain on paper towels and set aside.

2. Pour the heavy cream into a saucepan. Bring it to a simmer over low heat and continue simmering until the liquid has reduced by one-third.

3. Wipe out the sauté pan. Add the butter and melt over low heat. Add the onion and sauté over low heat until soft, 7 to 8 minutes. Remove the pan from the heat and add the cooked bacon pieces.

4. Bring a large pot of salted water to a boil. Add the corn and cook for 7 minutes. Using tongs, remove the corn from the water. (Reserve the water to cook the pasta.) Plunge the corn into a bowl of ice water to stop the cooking. Use a sharp knife to scrape the kernels off the cob (see the instructions on page 112). Put the kernels into the sauté pan with the bacon and onion.

5. Pour the reduced cream into the sauté pan. Add the Parmesan cheese. Turn the heat to low; you just want to keep the sauce warm.

6. In the boiling water left from the corn, cook the fettuccine according to the package directions.

7. In a saucepan or in a microwave oven, heat the chicken stock just to boiling.

8. Heat a large, nonstick pan over high heat. Add enough olive oil just to coat the bottom. Add the scallops and sprinkle with salt and pepper. Sear until the scallops are golden brown on one side, about 4 minutes. Flip the scallops and sear for 2 or 3 minutes on the other side.

9. Drain the fettuccine and place it in a large bowl. Add the sauce from the sauté pan and toss well. Add ½ cup of the hot chicken stock, plus more if the pasta seems too dry. Season with salt and pepper and toss again.

10. Divide the pasta among 4 large bowls. Place 4 scallops on top of each serving, sprinkling each with chives. Pass more Parmesan cheese at the table.

:: **Note:** For appetizer portions, use 18 sea scallops; divide the pasta among 6 plates, using 3 scallops per serving.

## RIALTO

Charles Hotel
1 Bennett Street
Cambridge (Harvard Square)
(617) 661–5050, www.rialto-restaurant.com

**Chef-owner | Jody Adams**

At the forefront of Boston dining for the past twenty years is Jody Adams, who began her career by working for another local legend—Lydia Shire (see page 184). In the early 1990s Adams became the executive chef at Michela's, the Cambridge restaurant started by Michela Larson, famous for turning out some of the most inventive Italian food in Boston. Rialto opened in 1994.

Adams still focuses on Italian food at Rialto, frequently using the New England ingredients that are freshest. She is known for stuffed pastas and for entrees with a whimsical touch. A green onyx bar, lit from underneath, dramatically leads the way into a terra cotta and gold dining room with S-shaped banquettes. Unlike a chef who prefers to stay cloistered in the kitchen, Adams regularly teaches classes at Rialto. She gathered many of the recipes she makes for family and friends in her cookbook *In the Hands of a Chef*, co-authored with husband Ken Rivard.

The inspiration for this recipe came from rustic Italian dishes based on broth, greens, pasta, and cheese. "This simple combination of ingredients is really comforting," explains Adams. Her dish has a foundation of handmade spinach gnocchi, with the vegetables more like a garnish than a sauce. The broth coats everything and ties it together. "What you want when you take a bite is the crunchy vegetables, the soft gnocchi, and the warm broth," she enthuses. Sounds like satisfaction in a bowl.

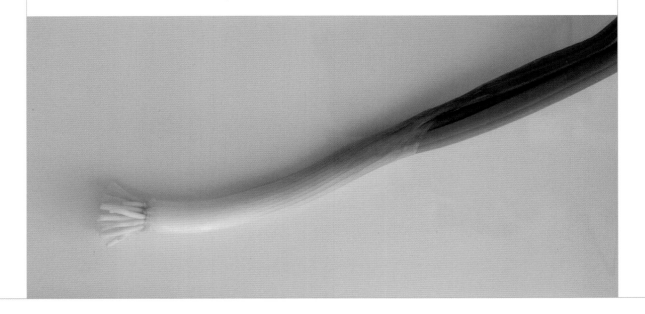

# TINY GREEN GNOCCHI WITH SPRING VEGETABLES

[SERVES 4 AS AN APPETIZER]

**GNOCCHI:**

1 pound baking (Russet or Idaho) potatoes, scrubbed
    but not peeled
1 pound fresh spinach, washed and trimmed of stems
    (baby spinach works well)
Salt, to taste
½ cup ricotta cheese
1 extra-large egg, beaten
½ cup grated Parmesan cheese, divided
Freshly ground black pepper
¾ cup all-purpose flour
¼ cup melted unsalted butter

1. Preheat the oven to 400 degrees. Prick the potatoes in several places with a fork so the steam can escape. Bake the potatoes for 1 hour, or until tender. While the potatoes are still warm, cut them in half, scoop the meat out of the skin, and push it through a ricer, a strainer with small holes, or a fine grater. If you wait until the potatoes are cool, they will be gummy.

2. Meanwhile, put the spinach into a large pot, sprinkle it with salt, cover, and cook over medium-high heat in just the water that clings to the leaves until the spinach has wilted. Drain in a colander, and when it's cool enough to handle, use your hands to squeeze out all the water. (An easy way to do this is to press the spinach against the sides of the colander. You can also put the spinach in a clean towel, then wring out the towel.) Chop the leaves as finely as possible with a knife—do not put in food processor or the spinach will become too soggy from its own moisture.

3. In a large bowl, mix the spinach with the ricotta and egg. Add the potato meat and ¼ cup of the Parmesan cheese; season with salt and pepper. Fold in the flour. Turn the mixture onto a floured counter and knead until it's smooth and slightly elastic, 1 to 2 minutes.

4. Roll the dough into a log about ½ inch in diameter. (You may need to divide the dough into 2 or 3 logs, depending on the length of your countertop.) Cut the logs into ½-inch pieces. Dust with flour so the gnocchi don't stick together. Using your finger, form a depression in the center of each piece.

5. Bring a large pot of water to a boil. Season with salt. Add the gnocchi and cook at a gentle boil until the gnocchi float to the top, 5 minutes or less. With a slotted spoon, scoop out the gnocchi, tossing them with the melted butter and the remaining ¼ cup Parmesan. Serve immediately with spring vegetables (below).

**SPRING VEGETABLES:**

½ cup diagonally cut asparagus
¼ cup sliced scallions
¾ cup fresh peas
1 cup chicken stock
¼ cup (½ stick) unsalted butter
2 tablespoons chopped fresh herbs, such as parsley, mint,
    basil, chervil, and/or savory
1 teaspoon lemon juice
Salt and freshly ground black pepper
2 ounces freshly shaved Parmesan cheese

1. Bring a large pot of water to a boil. Blanch the asparagus, scallions, and peas. Drain, rinse with cold water, and set aside until ready to use.

2. Bring the chicken stock to a simmer and let it reduce by half. Whisk in the butter, a little at a time, until well incorporated. Add the blanched vegetables, herbs, and lemon juice and heat through. Season with salt and pepper.

3. To serve, place about 12 gnocchi in each serving bowl, cover with sauce, and top with shaved cheese.

## GROTTO RESTAURANT

37 Bowdoin Street
Boston (Beacon Hill)
(617) 227–3434, www.grottorestaurant.com

**Chef-owner | Scott Herritt**

Grotto's exterior, set in a row of nineteenth-century, Federalist-style redbrick buildings, looks like the Beacon Hill made famous in Robert McCloskey's *Make Way for Ducklings*. Inside, it looks more like a jazz club, with a ceiling painted red and a framed portrait of Wynton Marsalis on the exposed-brick wall. Lamp shades sport hanging beads, and red satin drapes from the ceiling. Scott Herritt added these details to decorate the forty-six-seat, basement-level space. It's a cozy hangout in a political neighborhood dominated by the Massachusetts State House, the McCormack State Office Building, and take-out shops that serve perpetually hurrying officials. Herritt started his career in Oklahoma until the allure of a big city brought him to Boston. He was a chef in the North End before opening Grotto in 2003.

The theme of Herritt's menu is Northern Italian, but he cheerfully upends tradition with his lobster macaroni and cheese, and immodestly describes his tomato sauce as "insanely fabulous." His "Big Night" dinners, banquets modeled after the movie of the same name, routinely sell out. This pasta recipe combines two favorite comfort foods—gnocchi and braised short ribs. The mushrooms add chewiness, and the Gorgonzola finishes the dish with a burst of flavor.

### POTATO GNOCCHI, BRAISED SHORT RIBS, AND MUSHROOMS

[SERVES 4]

**SHORT RIBS:**

¼ cup extra-virgin olive oil
1 pound boneless beef short ribs
2 carrots, peeled and diced medium
1 bunch celery, diced medium
1 onion, diced medium
1 tablespoon finely diced garlic
4 strips bacon (preferably applewood smoked), chopped
Salt and pepper, to taste
1 bottle (750 ml) inexpensive red wine
2 tablespoons tomato paste
1 gallon veal or beef stock

1. In a large braising pan, heat the olive oil until smoking. Add the short ribs, turning them to brown on all sides, then remove to a plate. Add the carrots, celery, onion, garlic, and bacon. Sauté until the vegetables begin to brown. Season with salt and pepper and add the bottle of red wine. Simmer until the wine has almost all evaporated. Add the tomato paste and cook until the sauce thickens.

2. Return the short ribs to the pot, add the stock, and bring to a boil. Cover the pan (use foil if it doesn't have a lid) and bake at 375 degrees for 4 hours. Remove and allow the liquid to cool. Remove the short ribs,

cover them, and refrigerate overnight. Strain and discard the solids from the sauce. Cover and refrigerate the sauce.

3. The next day, dice the short ribs into ½-inch-thick pieces and remove any fat from the top of the sauce.

## GNOCCHI:

4 Idaho potatoes, peeled and diced medium
1 egg
2 egg yolks
2 pinches of ground nutmeg
¾ cup finely grated Parmesan cheese (preferably Parmigiano Reggiano; see notes, page 69)
Salt and pepper, to taste
1¼ cups sifted all-purpose flour, divided

1. In a large pot, boil the potatoes in salted water until cooked through. Drain. Place the potatoes on a baking sheet and bake in a 500-degree oven for 5 minutes to dry.

2. Working quickly, push the potatoes through a ricer or fine grater, then let them cool. Place the potatoes in a mixing bowl and push down the center to form a well.

3. In a separate bowl, whisk together the egg and egg yolks. Into the well of the potatoes, add the egg mixture, nutmeg, Parmesan, salt, and pepper. Mix together by hand until all the ingredients are incorporated.

4. Add 1 cup flour and continue to mix together. If the dough is still sticky, add more flour until it can be easily handled. Sprinkle a bit of flour on a countertop or another flat surface. Roll the dough with your hands to form long snakes or ropes about ½ inch thick (you may need several pieces, depending on the length of your countertop). Cut the ropes on the bias into about ½-inch pieces. (You can freeze the gnocchi at this point. Sprinkle a sheet pan with flour,

arrange the gnocchi so they are not touching, and cover with plastic wrap.)

## FINAL PREPARATION AND SERVING:

1 tablespoon olive oil
½ pound cremini mushrooms, quartered (see sidebar, page 122)
Crumbled Gorgonzola cheese or grated Parmesan cheese, for garnish

1. Bring a large pot of salted water to a boil.

2. In a large sauté pan, heat the olive oil. Add the mushrooms and sauté until lightly brown. Add the short ribs and sauce. Simmer until the short ribs are heated through and the sauce has thickened.

3. Add the gnocchi to the boiling water and cook until they float (usually less than 5 minutes). Lift the gnocchi from the pot with a strainer or slotted spoon and add them to the short rib mixture. Toss to coat the gnocchi with sauce and spoon into bowls. Top with Gorgonzola or Parmesan cheese.

# ENTREES

Boston area residents have been feasting on local seafood ever since the Pilgrims dangled their fishing poles into Plymouth Bay. At first, however, lobsters were considered more of a creepy nuisance than a luxury. Plimouth Plantation governor William Bradford once apologized for serving such lowly fare to newcomers. The clambake had no cachet then, either.

Now, of course, clambakes, steamed lobsters, and many other seafood dishes define Boston fare, though overfishing has diminished supplies since colonial days. Despite the long tradition, not all chefs faithfully re-create old recipes. In this chapter, chef Todd English retools the classic lobster roll by adding truffles and serving it on a bed of slaw. At Legal Sea Foods, chef Rich Vellante bakes a plain fillet of cod in a savory sauce of tomatoes, chopped almonds, and capers. Condiments that the Pilgrims never could have imagined accompany other dishes—apple caponata at Oleana, pineapple salsa at the East Coast Grill.

Though a good selection of seafood is almost essential to any Boston restaurant that specializes in regional cooking, chefs also like to transform basic cuts of meat into impressive entrees. You can find lamb with espresso vinaigrette at EVOO, and grilled pork chops with a maple-mustard glaze at Icarus. Vegetarians can find the recipe for Julia Child's favorite egg salad from Darwin's, as well as ratatouille Napoleons from a native French chef, Jacky Robert of Petit Robert Bistro.

## CAFÉ FLEURI AND JULIEN BAR & LOUNGE

Langham Hotel
250 Franklin Street
Boston (Financial District)
(617) 451–1900, www.langhamhotels.com

**Executive chef | Mark Sapienza**

With its wingback chairs and burgundy carpet, Café Fleuri and the adjoining Julien will make you want to lower your voice, fold your napkin in your lap, and be on your best behavior. Named after the very first French restaurant to open in Boston, in 1794, this former headquarters of the Federal Reserve Bank (the pastry chefs toil in what used to be the gold vault) is unabashedly elegant. Its coffered ceiling is decorated with gold paint. At either end of the bar hang original Andrew Wyeth paintings of George Washington and Abraham Lincoln. Super-attentive service assures that your most difficult task is raising the fork to your mouth.

You might expect the food to be as heavy as the elaborate, cut-glass chandeliers in the dining room, but Mark Sapienza likes "clean, simple" flavors. A Boston-area native, Sapienza was the first American chef hired to oversee the previously all-French restaurant. He found a way to use fiddlehead ferns, Vermont-farm-raised pheasant, Maine shrimp, and other typical New England ingredients on the menu—sometimes in French preparations, sometimes not. These crab cakes use local Jonah crabs, once considered a nuisance in lobster traps but now appreciated for their sweet meat. "I don't use a lot of herbs and spices to mask the flavors in this dish. I want the crab flavor to really stand forward," says Sapienza. In this recipe, it does, with lightly dressed, heirloom tomatoes (see the sidebar) as the fresh underpinning.

Seafood

## JONAH CRAB CAKES WITH LEMON CAPER TARTAR
## AND HEIRLOOM TOMATO SALAD

[ SERVES 6 ]

**TARTAR SAUCE:**

½ cup mayonnaise

2 teaspoons lemon juice

1 teaspoon minced onion

2 tablespoons capers, chopped

Tabasco sauce, to taste

Salt and pepper, to taste

In a small bowl, mix all the ingredients. Cover and refrigerate until ready to use.

**HEIRLOOM TOMATO SALAD:**

1 pound assorted heirloom tomatoes

3 tablespoons minced Vidalia onion (see notes)

Salt and pepper, to taste

2 tablespoons chopped fresh chives

3 tablespoons olive oil

Slice and arrange the tomatoes on 6 plates. Sprinkle each portion with minced onion, salt, pepper, and chives. Drizzle with olive oil and set aside.

**CRAB CAKES:**

1 pound Jonah crabmeat (see notes)

¼ cup mayonnaise

1 tablespoon chopped fresh chives

Salt and pepper, to taste

2 cups panko bread crumbs

¼ cup vegetable oil or clarified butter

1. Preheat the oven to 350 degrees.

2. In a mixing bowl, gently combine the crabmeat, mayonnaise, chives, salt, and pepper, trying not to break up the crabmeat. Divide the mixture into 6 portions of equal size. Roll each one in bread crumbs and use your hands to form into cakes approximately 3 inches in diameter and 1 inch thick. Refrigerate for 30 minutes to allow the cakes to become firm.

3. In a sauté pan, heat the oil over medium-high heat. Add the cakes and brown on both sides, turning only once, 2 to 3 minutes per side. Place the cakes on a baking sheet. Place in the oven to heat through, 3 to 4 minutes. Place each crab cake on top of a plate prepared with Heirloom Tomato Salad. Garnish with tartar sauce and serve immediately.

:: **Notes:** Vidalia onions are sweet onions specifically grown in southeast Georgia. They typically arrive in the market in spring. If you can't find them, substitute another variety of sweet onions.

If you can't find the Jonah crabs called for in this recipe, any good-quality, fresh crabmeat will do.

## Heirloom Vegetables

When commercial growers began cultivating tomatoes that tasted bland but could ship well and ripen quickly, consumers answered back by popularizing heirloom tomatoes. The heirloom seeds come from great-tasting varieties originally grown for gardens and small-scale farms. Heirloom preservationists have been at work since the 1970s rescuing all-but-forgotten varieties of tomatoes, as well as other vegetables and fruits. Heirloom seeds can now be ordered from dozens of catalogs. Chefs, always after peak flavor, are some of the best customers for heirloom harvests. Verrill Farm (see pages 36 and 176) and other local growers are generally happy to oblige. A good resource for finding growers and ordering seeds is the nonprofit Seed Savers Exchange in Iowa, (563) 382–5990, www.seedsavers.org.

## KINGFISH HALL

188 Faneuil Hall Marketplace
Boston
(617) 523–8862, www.toddenglish.com

**Owner | Todd English**

This busy Faneuil Hall restaurant gives owner Todd English (see Olives, page 148) a showcase for seafood. New England classics like chilled lobster tail and wood-grilled calamari are served alongside Thai mussels with lemongrass and miso-marinated cod with sushi rice. You can watch a special fire pit outfitted with a rotisserie making "Dancing Fish," and a giant kettle boiling up New England feasts of lobster, steamers, sausage, corn, and red potatoes.

Leave it to a risk-taking chef like Todd English to reinterpret the almost sacred New England lobster roll (see the sidebar). His recipe inverts the normal procedure for toasting a roll and then stuffing it with lobster salad. To his lobster filling, he adds truffle oil and truffle peelings for a jolt of aromatic, earthy flavor (and luxury). Instead of serving a side of coleslaw, he cuts the rolls into individual portions and places them on a bed of slaw. Voilà, he has transformed a staple of paper-napkin clam shacks into elegant party food.

# MEXICAN-STYLE MAHIMAHI WITH HEARTS OF PALM SLAW AND PINEAPPLE SALSA

[SERVES 4]

## HEARTS OF PALM SLAW:

½ cup fresh lime juice (about 4 limes)
¼ cup orange juice
¼ cup red wine vinegar
½ cup roughly chopped fresh cilantro
8 dashes of Tabasco sauce, or to taste
Kosher salt and freshly cracked black pepper, to taste
1 cup thinly sliced green cabbage
1 cup thinly sliced red cabbage
½ cup shredded carrots
5 hearts of palm, cut into long strips

In a large bowl, whisk together the lime juice, orange juice, vinegar, cilantro, Tabasco, salt, and pepper until blended. Add the cabbages, carrots, and hearts of palm. Toss to coat with the dressing. Cover and refrigerate until serving time.

## PINEAPPLE SALSA:

1 cup fresh pineapple, diced small
½ cup red pepper, diced small
½ cup green pepper, diced small
⅓ cup fresh orange juice
2 tablespoons pureed chipotle peppers in adobo sauce
    (see sidebar, page 59)
2 tablespoons red wine vinegar
¼ cup chopped fresh cilantro
Kosher salt and freshly cracked black pepper, to taste

Mix all ingredients in a nonreactive bowl. Set aside until ready to use.

## MEXICAN-STYLE MAHIMAHI:

2 tablespoons ground paprika
2 tablespoons ground cumin
2 tablespoons minced garlic
Kosher salt and freshly cracked black pepper, to taste
4 mahimahi fillets (8 ounces each)
3 tablespoons olive oil
Cilantro sprigs, for garnish (optional)
1 lime, thinly sliced, for garnish (optional)

1. Build a fire in your grill, banking the coals so there are about three times as many on one side as on the other. Bring the temperature to medium hot: You can hold your hand about 5 inches above the grill grid for about 5 seconds.

2. In a small bowl, combine the paprika, cumin, garlic, salt, and pepper and mix well. Brush the fillets with the olive oil, then rub all over with the spice mixture. Grill over the coals until just opaque all the way through, about 5 to 6 minutes per side (see the note).

3. Place 1 fillet on each of 4 plates, along with a small mound of slaw. Garnish with cilantro sprigs and thin lime wedges. Pass the Pineapple Salsa on the side.

:: **Note:** In just a minute or two, a fish fillet can change from cooked through to tough, dry, and overcooked. To tell if fish is properly done, Schlesinger recommends poking it with your finger to check its firmness level. If you're still unsure, nick, peek, and cheat: Cut into one of the fillets at its thickest point and peek to be sure it is opaque all the way through. If so, immediately remove from the grill.

## TRYST

689 Massachusetts Avenue
Arlington
(781) 641–2227, www.trystrestaurant.com

**Former chef de cuisine | Mark Usewicz**

Growing up with one Polish and one Italian grandmother, Mark Usewicz developed an early appreciation for cooking with fresh ingredients. "The menu is often driven by what the farmers bring in," he explains.

Usewicz built this seafood dish around two Massachusetts summer staples: fresh bluefish and Japanese-style eggplant from local farms. Charmoula, the marinade for the fish, uses North African spices (some of which have also migrated to Sicily). The eggplant can accompany the fish, or can be part of an antipasto platter. The salsa verde is a condiment "kind of like ketchup," and can be used with a variety of other seafood, braised red meats, or chicken. When fresh bluefish is not available, you can substitute another firm-fleshed fish such as mahimahi, escolar, red snapper, sardine, king mackerel, or grouper.

For a quick variation on this recipe, use the salsa verde as a marinade for the bluefish and omit the eggplant. Place the bluefish in a nonreactive dish, pour in the salsa verde to coat it on both sides, and let it marinate at room temperature for approximately 15 minutes. Remove from the marinade and grill. Discard any unused marinade. To streamline prep time for the entire recipe, make the fish marinade, eggplant marinade, and salsa verde in a single blender session. Store each in the refrigerator until you're ready to use it.

# GRILLED BLUEFISH WITH MARINATED EGGPLANT AND SALSA VERDE

[SERVES 4]

**BLUEFISH AND CHARMOULA MARINADE:**

1 cup extra-virgin olive oil

6 cloves garlic, peeled

Zest of 1 lemon

1 teaspoon whole black peppercorns

2 teaspoons cumin seeds, toasted lightly in a dry,
  nonstick skillet

½ cup chopped fresh parsley

½ cup chopped fresh cilantro

1 jalapeño pepper (optional)

4 bluefish fillets (6 ounces each), skin on

Salt

1. Place all the ingredients, except the bluefish and salt, in a blender, combining until smooth. Place in a sealed container and refrigerate until ready to use. This can be stored for up to 2 weeks.

2. Place the bluefish in a nonreactive dish and pour in the marinade, making sure the fillets are fully coated on both sides. Cover with plastic wrap and refrigerate for at least 4 hours or overnight.

3. When ready to cook, remove the bluefish from the marinade and wipe off any excess to avoid flare-ups on the grill. Season with salt and place skin-side down on a hot grill (or skin-side up under a broiler). Grill or broil until the skin becomes crispy and slightly charred. Flip the bluefish and continue to grill or broil until firm to the touch and cooked through, 8 to 14 minutes depending on the thickness of the fillets.

**EGGPLANTS:**

8–10 Japanese eggplants (see note)

2 cups extra-virgin olive oil

1 cup red wine vinegar

3 cloves garlic, minced fine

1 teaspoon dried oregano

1 teaspoon chopped fresh marjoram or 1 teaspoon
  chopped fresh mint

Salt and pepper, to taste

1. Cut off the stem end of each eggplant. Slice the eggplants in half lengthwise and score the flesh side about ¼ inch deep in a crisscross pattern. Combine the olive oil, vinegar, garlic, oregano, marjoram, salt, and pepper. Stir until combined. Add the eggplants to this mixture and let sit for 30 minutes.

2. When ready to cook, preheat a grill or broiler to medium-high heat. Remove the eggplants from the marinade, reserving the marinade. Place the eggplants, flesh-side down, on the grill or under the broiler. Cook for 7 minutes, then flip and continue cooking until the eggplants begin to soften, 4 to 7 minutes. Remove the eggplants, put them back in the marinade, and cool to room temperature. The eggplants can be stored in the marinade, covered and refrigerated, for up to a week.

:: **Note:** Japanese eggplants are long and thin, with more tender flesh than the more familiar pear-shaped variety with dark purple skin.

**SALSA VERDE:**

½ cup chopped fresh mint leaves

1 cup chopped fresh parsley

1½ cups extra-virgin olive oil

4 anchovy fillets, rinsed

2 tablespoons capers, rinsed

½ cup red wine vinegar

1 teaspoon red pepper flakes

1 teaspoon fresh marjoram leaves or 1 teaspoon
  chopped fresh mint

3 cloves garlic, peeled

Combine all the ingredients in a blender and blend until smooth.

**FINAL PREPARATION AND SERVING:**

Lemon wedges

Serve each fillet with 3 eggplant halves, drizzle with Salsa Verde, and place lemon wedges on the side.

## LEGAL SEA FOODS

26 Park Place
Boston
(617) 426–4444 (plus more than thirty locations in Greater Boston and
along the East Coast), www.legalseafoods.com

**Executive chef and vice president of food operations | Rich Vellante**

In 1950, when George Berkowitz opened a seafood market next to his father's Legal Cash Market grocery in Cambridge, he had no intention of building a restaurant empire. He was simply selling fresh fish. (The *Legal* in the name came from the type of trading stamps once handed out.) In the 1960s he and his wife, Harriet, began serving broiled or fried fish on paper plates at picnic tables. The storefront sign advertised THAT FISHY PLACE: TO TAKE OUT OR EAT HERE.

From these modest beginnings, Legal Sea Foods managed to continue thriving as food trends swept into the city. Though Bostonians began to embrace sushi and seviche, Legal Sea Foods never lost its appeal to the quahog-and-chowder crowd.

Now run by George's son, Roger Berkowitz, Legal Sea Foods has expanded into several locations in the Boston area and dozens more along the East Coast. The menu sticks to many of the basics that made it famous, including the fish chowder that was served at President Ronald Reagan's inauguration in 1981. More recently Berkowitz and executive chef Rich Vellante have added Asian-influenced entrees, including spicy selections that they developed with chefs from India in 2002.

An avid runner, Vellante has finished marathons in Boston, New York, and Chicago. He says running helps him withstand the stress of a restaurant kitchen and keeps him focused. This recipe takes advantage of two New England seafood favorites—cod and littleneck clams. Potatoes are the suggested accompaniment, but you can also serve this dish with crusty white bread. Add a salad for a complete meal.

## COD AND LITTLENECK CLAMS IN ALMOND TOMATO SAUCE
## WITH SMASHED POTATOES

[SERVES 4]

**COD:**

½ cup olive oil, plus more as needed

1 tablespoon chopped garlic

Pinch of hot pepper flakes

1 cup sliced Spanish onion

1 teaspoon chopped fresh thyme

½ cup sliced fresh basil leaves

10–12 tomatoes, skinned and seeded, or
    1 can (16 ounces) peeled tomatoes, drained

1 teaspoon sugar

½ cup capers

½ cup roughly chopped almonds

1½ pounds cod

Salt and pepper, to taste

12 littleneck clams

1. Place ½ cup of the olive oil along with the garlic and hot pepper flakes in a large saucepan and sauté over medium heat until lightly brown. Add the onion and continue sautéing until soft, about 10 to 12 minutes. Add the thyme, basil, tomatoes, sugar, capers, and almonds. Cook at a low simmer for about 10 minutes. Let cool and reserve. (The sauce can be made a day ahead, covered, and refrigerated until you're ready to use it.)

2. Preheat the oven to 350 degrees. Place the almond-tomato mixture in the bottom of an ovenproof casserole dish (9x13 inches works well). Lightly brush the cod with olive oil and season with salt and pepper. Place the cod on top of the sauce in the center of the casserole dish. Distribute the clams around the outer edge. Bake, uncovered, for 15 to 20 minutes. Serve with Smashed Potatoes (recipe follows).

**SMASHED POTATOES:**

1 pound small new potatoes (preferably Yukon Gold),
    scrubbed

Salt and pepper, to taste

Lemon zest, to taste

Chopped flat-leaf parsley, to taste

2 tablespoons olive oil, or to taste

Place the whole potatoes in a saucepan and add water to cover. Bring to a boil and let boil gently until soft, 15 to 20 minutes. Drain. Place the potatoes in a serving dish and slightly smash each with a fork to flatten it out. Sprinkle with salt and pepper. Garnish with lemon zest, chopped parsley, and olive oil.

## SKIPJACK'S

199 Clarendon Street, Boston (Back Bay)
(617) 536-3500

55 Needham Street, Newton
(617) 964-4244

1400 Worcester Road (Route 9), Natick
(508) 628-9900
www.skipjacks.com

**Executive chef | Andrew Wilkinson**

You can certainly find New England clam chowder and baked stuffed lobster at Skipjack's, which specializes in seafood—and is appropriately decorated with antique nautical maps and blue accents. But owner Jeff Senior and chef Andrew Wilkinson have wide-ranging tastes, which might include blackened tuna sashimi, or mahimahi with Jamaican jerk spices. Two of the locations even have in-house sushi bars with their own chefs, and a surprisingly extensive list of French and American wines. The mix of basics and more international dishes attracts couples on dates, as well as families who appreciate a children's menu that offers popcorn shrimp and grilled fish.

Wilkinson was experimenting with Asian ingredients when he came up with this ginger marinade, which uses two kinds of Japanese rice wine—regular sake and sweet mirin. He tried it on sea bass, and the dish is now the most popular entree at Skipjack's. "The marinade lets the fish steam and bake at the same time," explains Wilkinson. The sweetness in the mirin creates a glaze on top of the bass. The result is a moist fish with an intensely concentrated ginger and soy flavor—and no added fat. When served with stir-fried vegetables and steamed rice, this is about as healthy a meal as you can get. Use the marinade on any other firm-fleshed fish, or on chicken.

For Skipjack's clam chowder recipe, see page 43.

# GINGERED SEA BASS

[SERVES 4]

**MARINADE:**

1 cup sugar

2 cups soy sauce

½ cup sake (Japanese rice wine, available at liquor stores)

¼ cup mirin (sweet Japanese rice wine, available at liquor stores)

¼ cup chopped fresh garlic

¼ cup roughly chopped fresh gingerroot

Combine all the ingredients in a saucepan. Turn the heat to low and let the mixture simmer for 1 hour. Strain through a mesh strainer, let cool, and chill in the refrigerator until you're ready to use it.

**SEA BASS:**

1 cup base marinade (from recipe above)

1 tablespoon coarsely grated fresh gingerroot

4 sea bass fillets (6 ounces each)

½ cup water

1. In a nonreactive bowl, stir together the base marinade and ginger. Add the fish, cover, and let the fish marinate in the refrigerator overnight, or no more than 24 hours.

2. Preheat the oven to 400 degrees.

3. Remove the fish from the marinade, discarding any excess marinade. Place the fillets in a glass baking dish, adding the water to the bottom. Bake for 15 to 18 minutes. Test with a skewer for doneness: The fish should be opaque and flake easily when the skewer is pulled out.

4. Serve with steamed rice and your favorite stir-fried vegetables.

## SUMMER SHACK

50 Dalton Street, Boston
(617) 867-9955

149 Alewife Brook Parkway, Cambridge
(617) 520-9500,

Additional locations at Logan Airport and Mohegan Sun
www.summershackrestaurant.com

### Executive chef-owner | Jasper White

In the 1980s Jasper White was one of the first Boston chefs to branch out from the provincial formula of chowder and cod, making Jasper's restaurant a pioneer in contemporary New England cooking. Jasper's closed in 1995, but White now reproduces his ideas on a larger scale at four Summer Shack locations. The atmosphere is more fun than fine dining, with picnic tables, metal buckets for discarded seafood shells, and the menu posted on a chalkboard. The Boston location is affiliated with the Kings Bowling Alley. Lobster rolls, cod cakes, and corn dogs are as much a part of the concept as pan-roasted lobster and Bermuda fish and crab chowder.

White's expertise with seafood is reflected in this recipe for whole fish with onion and fennel stuffing. "When I catch a striped bass, this is my favorite way to cook one for friends and family," he says. He suggests serving it with simple accompaniments like fresh green vegetables, salad, rice, or home-fried potatoes.

# SLOW-ROASTED WHOLE FISH
## WITH ONION AND FENNEL STUFFING

[SERVES 6-8]

1 fresh whole striped bass (6–8 pounds) or other whole fish
   (see note), scaled and gutted
6 tablespoons olive oil or vegetable oil, divided, plus more
   as needed
3 medium cloves garlic, minced
2 small onions (8 ounces), thinly sliced
1 bulb fennel (8–10 ounces), thinly sliced after branches
   and tough outer sections are removed; fronds reserved
1 tablespoon minced fresh thyme (leaves from 4–6 sprigs)
6 ounces Portuguese chorizo, linguica, or other spicy,
   dry sausage, casings removed, cut into ⅓-inch dice, or
   2 tablespoons (¼ stick) butter
2 tablespoons minced fresh chives or scallions
½ bunch flat-leaf parsley, chopped (½ cup)
2 ounces hard dry crackers (such as oyster crackers),
   coarsely crumbled or chopped—about ¾ cup crumbled
Kosher or sea salt, to taste
Freshly ground black pepper
1 lemon, cut into wedges

1. Run the back of your knife over the fish to be sure all the
   scales have been removed. Using kitchen scissors or a
   sharp knife, cut off all the fins. Remove the gills, creating
   a large pocket that extends from the head to the tail.
   Rinse the fish inside and out to remove any blood. Dry it
   on paper towels, wrap it in plastic, and refrigerate until
   ready to cook.

2. In a 10-inch skillet, heat 3 tablespoons of the oil over
   medium heat. Add the garlic, onions, fennel, and thyme.
   Sauté, stirring frequently, until the mixture is tender and
   beginning to brown, about 10 minutes. Add the diced
   sausage, if you're using it, and sauté until it's fragrant,
   about 1 minute more. (If you're making the stuffing without the sausage, add the butter now, stirring to melt.)
   Remove the skillet from the heat and cool slightly. Add
   the chives, parsley, and cracker crumbs; season to taste
   with salt and pepper and mix to combine. The stuffing
   will be fairly loose. Set aside.

3. Adjust the oven rack to the lower position and preheat
   the oven to 325 degrees. Rub the bottom of a large
   roasting pan with 1 tablespoon of the oil. Remove the fish
   from the refrigerator, rub the outside with the remaining
   oil, and season it generously with salt and pepper. Spoon
   the filling into the fish's cavity and place the fish in the
   roasting pan. Drizzle it with a little more oil, cover the
   roasting pan loosely with aluminum foil, and place in the
   oven. Roast for 45 minutes. Remove the aluminum foil
   and baste the fish with its pan drippings. Continue to
   bake, uncovered, for 15 minutes, then baste again with
   pan drippings. Bake 15 minutes more, remove from the
   oven, and check for doneness; the flesh should be
   opaque. (A 6-pound fish will usually take about 1¼ hours
   to cook; an 8-pound fish, about 1½ hours.)

4. When the fish is cooked, turn the heat up to 450 degrees
   and return the fish to the oven for 5 minutes to crisp the
   skin. Remove the fish from the oven and let it rest for
   5 minutes. Turn off the oven and place a platter inside
   to warm. Transfer the fish to the warm platter with two
   spatulas, garnishing with lemon wedges and the reserved
   fennel fronds.

5. Slide a large serving spoon between the backbone and
   the top fillet to loosen the fillet. Serve each portion with
   a spoonful of the stuffing and a piece of the crisp skin.
   After the top fillet is removed, simply pull the frame of
   bones away to expose the bottom fillet. Warn your
   guests to be on the lookout for pinbones—it is impossible
   to serve a whole fish without getting a few.

:: **Note:** If stripers are out of season, you can substitute
cod, salmon, bluefish, black sea bass, or red snapper. Since
most fish is sold in fillets, you may need to place a special
order at your market; make sure to ask that the fish be
gutted and scaled.

## MCCORMICK & SCHMICK'S SEAFOOD RESTAURANTS—BOSTON

Boston Park Plaza Hotel
34 Columbus Avenue
Boston (Downtown)
(617) 482-3999

Faneuil Hall Marketplace
North Market Building
(617) 720-5522
www.mccormickandschmicks.com

**Regional senior chef | Chris Westcott**

One of the occupational hazards of a chef is gaining weight—all those tasting portions add up. Chris Westcott was destined to become a statistic until he underwent quadruple bypass surgery and lost a hundred pounds. He has since become a champion of healthy recipes at the Boston locations of McCormick & Schmick's Seafood Restaurants. For "Heart Health Month" each February, he runs low-fat specials accompanied by a nutritional analysis from Brigham and Women's Hospital in Boston. His goal, he says, is to create flavorful food while still being "mindful" of dietary concerns. This fish recipe fits the bill, he explains, with "some heat from the chipotle peppers along with offsetting sweetness from the orange marmalade." With a mere 5 grams of fat and no cholesterol, its nutritional profile looks good, too.

Fresh seafood comes first in all sixty locations of the Oregon-based McCormick & Schmick's, but regional chefs are given a lot of latitude to add their own items to the corporate menu. The gleaming green and white tile floor and crushed-ice-lined raw bar at the Park Plaza location look like a fish market. Tables and booths give you a quieter place to order crab cakes, stuffed shrimp, and almost any kind of fresh fish available in that day's market.

## TILAPIA WITH CHIPOTLE ORANGE GLAZE

### [SERVES 2]

**CHIPOTLE ORANGE GLAZE:**

MAKES APPROXIMATELY 1 CUP

3 ounces canned chipotle chile peppers in adobo sauce
    (see sidebar, page 59)
1 tablespoon rice wine vinegar
8 ounces orange marmalade
1 teaspoon freshly squeezed orange juice
1 teaspoon chopped fresh cilantro
1 tablespoon finely diced red onion

In a blender, blend the chipotle peppers and vinegar. In a nonreactive mixing bowl, combine the pepper-vinegar mixture with all the remaining ingredients. Set aside until you're ready to use it. Leftovers can be covered, refrigerated, and used as a sauce for other seafood dishes or as a condiment on sandwiches.

**TILAPIA:**

2 tilapia fillets (6 ounces each; see note)
3–4 tablespoons olive oil
Flour, for dusting
2 cups cooked white rice
2 cups mixed vegetables, steamed (your choice—such as
    zucchini, summer squash, carrots, or pea pods)
¼ cup Chipotle Orange Glaze (from recipe above)
2 tablespoons julienned bell peppers, preferably red,
    yellow, and green, for garnish
2 parsley sprigs, for garnish
2 lemon wedges, for garnish

1. Coat the fish with a little of the olive oil and dust with flour until coated on all sides. Heat a sauté pan and add the remaining olive oil. Sear the fish for 3 to 4 minutes per side.

2. Divide the rice and steamed vegetables between 2 plates. Place a fillet on each plate next to the vegetables. Ladle the chipotle glaze across the fish. Garnish with the bell peppers and parsley. Place a lemon wedge on the side of the plate.

:: **Note:** Other fish that could be used in this recipe are tuna, swordfish, marlin, and catfish.

# FANEUIL HALL MARKETPLACE

Faneuil Hall Marketplace proves the adage that everything old can be new again. Built in 1742, Faneuil Hall attracted early American patriots including Samuel Adams and George Washington to its speaker's platform. Close to the wharves on the Boston Harbor, its ground floor became a market for seafood, meat, and fresh produce. It prospered so much that another building, Quincy Market, was added in 1826. For nearly a hundred years, wagons, pushcarts, vendors, and shoppers crowded the area. Yet after World War II, much of Boston's commerce was no longer centered on the waterfront, and many residents had moved to the suburbs. The once thriving market was all but abandoned. Its crumbling buildings were scheduled for the wrecking ball until a preservation group, led by developer Jim Rouse and architect Ben Thompson (see Harvest, page 164), pushed to restore them.

The revitalized market—the first urban renovation project of its kind in the United States—opened in 1976. Its buildings now house a mix of retail shops, pushcart vendors, and eateries that range from quick snacks to sit-down steak dinners. Though locals sometimes grumble that tourists and national retail chains have taken over, it has remained one of the most consistently lively destinations in Boston. Civic and political groups still hold meetings in Faneuil Hall, topped with a metal grasshopper weather vane. The main corridor of Quincy Market has established itself as a take-out paradise of chowder, pretzels, sandwiches, ice cream, and cookies. (Massachusetts senator John Kerry co-founded the Kilvert & Forbes Bakeshop with some of his mother's recipes—the brownies are legendary—but has since sold the business.) Anything you order can be eaten at wooden tables in the two-story rotunda. The most historic restaurant in the marketplace is Durgin-Park, built in 1827, legendary for its corn bread, prime rib plates, coffee Jell-O, and tart-tongued waitresses. Cheers (see page 21) caters to the television generation. Celebrity-chef-watchers can sample Todd English's fare at Kingfish Hall (see page 92). Several national restaurant chains have also set up shop here, including Dick's Last Resort, Plaza III–The Kansas City Steakhouse, and McCormick & Schmick's seafood (see page 104).

Faneuil Hall Marketplace proved to be such a successful model for urban renovation that it inspired many other projects around the country, including Harborplace in Baltimore, and South Street Seaport in New York.

## OLEANA

134 Hampshire Street
Cambridge (Inman Square)
(617) 661–0505, www.oleanarestaurant.com

**Chef-owner | Ana Sortun**

Oleana is probably the only place in Boston where you can find Armenian bean-and-walnut pâté, almond soup with fried dates, and Turkish cheese pancakes on one menu. That's because Ana Sortun, who has staked out Mediterranean flavors as her territory, makes a wide sweep from Sicily through Greece, Turkey, North Africa, and Spain. Copper-edged tables topped with mosaic tiles, and a terra-cotta wine rack, enhance the Mediterranean theme. Sortun's husband, Chris Kurth, is commissioned to grow most of the vegetables for the restaurant at their farm near Boston.

Sortun puts her own spin on caponata, a traditional Sicilian sweet-and-sour vegetable side dish, by replacing eggplants with apples. The vinegary caponata, intensified by a hint of cocoa powder, complements mild-flavored swordfish. The easiest way to prepare the swordfish is to grill it.

Without a whole lot of extra effort, you can make involtini, an Italian-style sliced fish (or meat) rolled around a filling. "I love the involtini because they remind me of little fish dumplings," says Sortun. "It's not as hard as it sounds, and it makes a great summer dish." The recipe would also work with another firm-fleshed fish, such as salmon or monkfish. The caponata can also be used as a spread on crackers or toasted Italian bread, or even as a condiment with poultry.

# SWORDFISH WITH APPLE CAPONATA

[SERVES 4]

**APPLE CAPONATA:**

¼ cup golden raisins

4 apples, peeled and diced

2 onions, peeled and diced

½ cup finely chopped celery

½ cup extra-virgin olive oil

1½ teaspoons cocoa powder

1 cup peeled, seeded, and chopped tomatoes

1½ teaspoons tomato paste

2 teaspoons small capers

⅓ cup pitted green olives, roughly chopped

¼ cup balsamic vinegar

Place all the ingredients except the vinegar in a large, round sauté pan with plenty of surface area. Sauté until the apple and onion begin to soften, about 5 minutes, and add the vinegar. Simmer for 20 to 25 minutes, stirring occasionally, until the vegetables are soft and the flavors have blended. Set aside and let cool to room temperature.

**SWORDFISH:**

4 swordfish steaks (5 ounces each) for grilling, or
    1 (20-ounce) piece boneless swordfish for making involtini

2 tablespoons olive oil, divided

½ onion, minced

¼ cup minced celery

4 plum tomatoes

2 cups plain bread crumbs, preferably from baguettes

Pinch of fennel seeds

½ teaspoon dried oregano

Pinch of paprika or dried red pepper flakes

¼ cup grated Parmesan cheese

1 egg yolk

Salt and pepper, to taste

3 tablespoons water

1. If you'll be grilling the swordfish, sprinkle each side with olive oil, salt, and pepper. Grill until cooked through, about 4 minutes per side, depending on the thickness of the fish. At this point you could serve the swordfish with caponata on the side.

2. To make involtini, lay the swordfish against a cutting board. (Depending on the shape of the fish, you may need to slice it horizontally, laying your hand flat on top of the fish.) Use a sharp knife to cut it into 12 thin slices, each about ⅛ inch thick. Place 1 slice between 2 sheets of plastic wrap. Using a rolling pin, lightly pound the fish to flatten it to almost paper-thin width. Repeat until all pieces have been flattened. Set aside.

3. In a small sauté pan, heat 1 tablespoon of the olive oil over medium heat. Sauté the onion and celery until soft, about 4 to 5 minutes.

4. Split each tomato in half and use your fingers or a spoon to scoop out most of the seeds. Place a grater with large holes over a mixing bowl and grate each tomato until you have just the skin left in your hand. Discard the skin, keeping the juice and pulp in the bowl. Add the sautéed onion and celery, along with the bread crumbs, fennel, oregano, paprika, Parmesan, and egg yolk. Mix together with your hands. The mixture should hold its shape when squeezed together in one hand. If it's too dry, add a bit of olive oil.

5. Place a handful (about 3 tablespoons) of bread crumb stuffing at one end of each swordfish piece. Roll the fish around the filling as tightly as possible, forming a cigar shape.

6. In a sauté pan over medium heat, heat the remaining tablespoon of olive oil. Place each roll, seam-side down, in the pan. Sprinkle lightly with salt and pepper. (Go easy on the seasoning, as the thin swordfish has a delicate flavor.) When the swordfish has lightly browned, about 3 minutes, flip each roll to cook on the other side. After 1 minute, add the water. Lower the heat and cover the pan. Cook for another 2 minutes, until the swordfish is cooked through and the stuffing is warm.

7. Cut each involtini in half and place 6 halves on each serving plate. Spoon the juices from the sauté pan over the top, and then spoon some Apple Caponata on top or on the side. Arugula salad makes a good accompaniment.

## SEL DE LA TERRE

255 State Street
Boston
(617) 720-1300, www.seldelaterre.com

**Chef and co-owner | Geoff Gardner**

In the midst of jackhammers and scaffolding from the Big Dig, Sel de la Terre has provided a welcome distraction with its soothing beige color scheme and bright interpretations of the flavors of the south of France. Open since 2000, the restaurant gives owners Frank McClelland and Geoff Gardner a chance to expand beyond the ultrafine French dining at sister restaurant L'Espalier (see page 156). Gardner, who is also the chef at Sel de la Terre, notes that New England ingredients—and inspirations—"inevitably" make their way onto his menus. Green beans from a local farmer might be marinated and served with an herb-roasted chicken breast and a salad of pea greens. Macoun apples from a New Hampshire orchard could be paired with sautéed mussels and linguica. "We do different dishes that evolve from season to season, using the south of France as a starting point," says Gardner.

This swordfish recipe illustrates Gardner's interest in blending different traditions. Harissa, a North African hot pepper paste, is often used in France, as Tunisia and Morocco were once French colonies. Look for it at gourmet grocers or in specialty Middle Eastern markets. In Gardner's marinade the harissa gives mild-flavored swordfish a spicy kick. Succotash is thought to have originated with the Narragansett tribe of Native Americans in Rhode Island. Most versions—which have also become popular in the South—mix cooked corn and lima beans. This recipe adds chicory and cherry tomatoes for color as well as texture.

Now that Big Dig construction is complete, the type of traffic that predominates here is pedestrians, who come in for a loaf of fig anise or other fresh bread, a take-out sandwich, or a sit-down meal.

# HARISSA-MARINATED SWORDFISH WITH SUCCOTASH

[SERVES 6]

**SWORDFISH:**

5 ounces (150 g tube) harissa paste
Zest of 4 oranges
3 cloves garlic, peeled and chopped
1 shallot, peeled and chopped
1 teaspoon whole-grain mustard
1 teaspoon black pepper
1 cup canola oil
6 swordfish steaks (7 ounces each)
Salt and pepper, to taste

1. Make a marinade by placing the harissa paste, orange zest, garlic, shallot, mustard, and black pepper in a blender or food processor. Turn on the motor and slowly drizzle in the oil. Blend until smooth. Cover and refrigerate until ready to use. (In the refrigerator the marinade will keep for up to 2 weeks in a tightly closed container.)

2. Place the swordfish in a glass or ceramic container or a resealable plastic bag. Add the marinade and make sure each steak is coated. Cover (or reseal the bag) and let marinate in the refrigerator for at least 2 hours, but no more than 12.

3. When you're ready to cook, preheat the grill or broiler. Remove the fish from the marinade and season each side with salt and pepper. Grill over medium-hot coals or broil until it's cooked through, turning once so the fish cooks on both sides. (Cooking time will depend on the thickness of the fish.) Serve immediately with succotash (below) on the side.

**SUCCOTASH:**

½ cup uncooked pancetta or bacon, cut into bite-size pieces
2 cups fresh corn kernels (from 3–4 ears), cooked and cut off the cob, or 2 cups frozen corn kernels, cooked and drained (see sidebar, page 112)
1⅓ cups lima beans, preferably fresh, or frozen, cooked and drained
2 cups washed and chopped fresh escarole
20 cherry tomatoes, each cut in half lengthwise (through stem end)
2 teaspoons chopped fresh garlic
1⅓ cups heavy cream
½–¾ cup vegetable stock
½ cup grated Parmesan cheese
Salt and pepper, to taste

1. Place the pancetta or bacon in a 10-inch sauté pan over medium heat and sauté until the fat is rendered (turns to liquid). Remove from the heat. Strain; discard the fat, leaving only the pancetta in the pan.

2. To the pan, add the corn, lima beans, escarole, tomatoes, garlic, cream, ½ cup of the vegetable stock, and cheese.

3. Return to the stove and gently simmer for 4 to 5 minutes, stirring frequently, until the escarole is wilted and the tomatoes are soft but still hold their shape. If the sauce seems too thick, add a little more vegetable stock. Season to taste with salt and pepper. Serve immediately with the swordfish.

# HOW TO COOK CORN

Sweet corn has sustained New Englanders ever since the Pilgrims temporarily disembarked from the *Mayflower* and dug up a stash buried by Native Americans. The spot in Truro on Cape Cod is now named Corn Hill Beach. These days chefs still rely on corn, especially on their August and September menus, when the local harvest finally arrives. In the past freshly picked corn had to be cooked as soon as possible before its sugars turned to starch. Nowadays, thanks to supersweet hybrids, supermarket corn no longer invariably tastes like cattle feed. Still, the sweetest and freshest taste usually comes from locally grown corn. For maximum control over the preparation, many chefs cook the corn themselves and cut the kernels off the cob. The standard method of cooking—shucking each ear and immersing it in boiling water—may not bring out the best flavor. For tastier results, try the following.

Geoff Gardner of Sel de la Terre leaves the corn in its husk (the outer green part), which retains the natural moisture and flavor. Trim both ends of the husk, and pull off the toughest outer leaves. Place the corn on a baking sheet and bake at 400 degrees for about half an hour, until the kernels are soft. Let cool slightly before peeling the husk.

Corn can also be microwaved right in its husk. Follow the procedure above, but place 2 ears of corn at a time on a microwave-safe plate. Cook at full power for 5 to 10 minutes (depending on the strength of your oven), turning the corn and rotating the plate once or twice so the ears cook evenly. Let cool slightly before peeling.

To grill corn, remove the husk and silk completely. Preheat a grill to medium. Brush each ear of corn with melted butter on all sides. Grill the corn, turning and basting with additional butter, until the kernels are brown but not charred on all sides, about 5 minutes.

To cut cooked corn kernels from the cob, hold the cob at one end and place the other on a cutting board or in a shallow bowl. Use a sharp knife to scrape down the cob, a few rows of corn at a time. The kernels should pop right off. Rotate the cob until all the kernels have been removed.

## 33 RESTAURANT AND LOUNGE

33 Stanhope Street
Boston (Back Bay)
(617) 572–3311, www.33restaurant.com

**Chef | Anthony Dawodu**

While many chefs like to use ingredients from around the globe, Anthony Dawodu has sampled many of them on the spot. He grew up in Nigeria, his father's native country, then moved to London for culinary training and jobs in the kitchens of the Marriott and Hilton hotels. He arrived in Boston in 1996 to work at the Four Seasons. At 33, where the lights beneath the bar change colors every few minutes, he brings an exotic touch to familiar ingredients: pairing baked halibut with saffron okra curry gumbo, for instance, or lobster with a Japanese-inspired edamame pancake. His international sensibilities fit well with owners Greg Den Herder and Igor Blatnik, who were high school classmates in Switzerland.

Dawodu's technique for searing scallops is simple, but the accompaniments show his ingenuity. For surprising flavor and crunch, he mixes cooked parsnip puree with sea urchin paste, a bright orange Japanese delicacy made from the roe of sea urchins, available at Asian specialty markets. If you don't want to be that adventurous, you can substitute grilled corn kernels, or simply omit this step. The finishing touch is a French-style lemon butter sauce with Dijon mustard. Cultural confusion? Wait until you taste this before passing judgment.

# MAINE LOBSTER WITH SWEET CORN CUSTARD, ASPARAGUS TIPS, AND LOBSTER BISQUE SAUCE

[SERVES 4]

**LOBSTERS AND BISQUE:**

4 lobsters (2 pounds each)
¼ cup (½ stick) butter
2 stalks celery, roughly chopped
2 carrots, roughly chopped
2 onions, roughly chopped
2 plum tomatoes
2 bay leaves
2 sprigs fresh tarragon
½ cup red wine
1 cup water
3 cups heavy cream

1.  In a large pot of boiling salted water, add the lobsters and cook for 7 minutes. Remove from the water and place in a large bowl of ice water to cool. Remove the meat from the tail and claws of each lobster and refrigerate until ready to use. Discard the shells, rinse the bodies, and reserve.

2.  In a large pot, add the butter, celery, carrots, onions, tomatoes, bay leaves, tarragon, and lobster bodies. Cook and stir over high heat until all items turn golden in color. Add the red wine and simmer until the wine is reduced by half. Add the water and cream and let simmer until the sauce thickens.

3.  Strain the bisque through a fine strainer and reserve. Discard the solids.

**CORN CUSTARD:**

Kernels from 6 ears corn (for directions on removing kernels, see sidebar page 112)
2 eggs
1 cup heavy cream
1 tablespoon chopped fresh parsley
Salt and black pepper, to taste

Combine all ingredients in a bowl. Generously coat 4 ramekins or soufflé cups with nonstick spray and fill with the corn mixture. Place the cups in a water bath in a flat pan and bake at 350 degrees for 20 minutes or until fully cooked through.

**FINAL PREPARATION AND SERVING:**

¼ cup (½ stick) butter
Salt and pepper, to taste
2 bunches cooked asparagus, tips only (to yield about 2 cups asparagus tips)
Chervil or parsley, for garnish

1.  In a sauté pan over medium heat, melt the butter. Sauté the reserved lobster meat and season with salt and pepper. Add the lobster bisque sauce and asparagus tips.

2.  Unmold the custard from each ramekin: Run a knife around the inside edge of each ramekin, place a shallow soup bowl on top, and flip so the ramekin is upside down in the center of the bowl. Gently tap the bottom of each ramekin with the heel of your hand. The nonstick spray should help the custard release.

3.  Place the lobster meat, asparagus, and bisque sauce around the custard and serve. Garnish with a sprig of chervil or parsley.

## DELUXE TOWN DINER

627 Mount Auburn Street
Watertown
(617) 926–8400, www.deluxetowndiner.com

**Owners | Don and Daryl Levy**

*Retro chic* is perhaps the best way to describe the Deluxe Town Diner, a restored dining car from the 1930s. Here, old-fashioned eggs with corned beef hash and a bottomless cup of joe are offered alongside sweet potato waffles and warm spinach salad with goat cheese. The then-and-now menu seems to be one of the charms of the chrome-accented room with vinyl seats and coat hooks at the end of each booth. The diner is the kind of place where you can come in a business suit or sweatpants and still feel comfortable. You can take home the Deluxe's own pancake mix, as well as whimsical cupcakes (including sea urchins with spikes of frosting) from the Cosmo Cupcakes division of the business.

This turkey burger is a distant cousin to a plain hamburger. Toasted whole mustard seeds, curry powder, and chutney give it an Indian flair. It's not what Aunt Bea would have ordered in the 1950s, but it's just right for the customer who wants more pizzazz than a turkey dinner with mashed potatoes and cranberry sauce. The bulkie roll—a soft, fluffy sandwich roll similar in shape to a Kaiser roll—is a Boston-area peculiarity. Its name may derive from the Polish word for "roll."

# Poultry

# APPLE-CURRY TURKEY BURGER

[SERVES 4]

1 tablespoon mustard seeds
3 tablespoons applesauce
1 tablespoon plain yogurt
2 tablespoons mango chutney
2 teaspoons curry powder
¾ teaspoon salt
¼ teaspoon cayenne pepper
1 pound lean ground turkey breast
¼ cup chopped scallions (1–2 scallions, white and
   green parts)
¼ cup chopped fresh mint
2–3 tablespoons peeled and freshly grated apple
   (preferably Granny Smith)
Nonstick vegetable oil spray
Lettuce and sliced tomatoes, for serving
4 bulkie rolls or other bread, for serving

1.  Place the mustard seeds in medium skillet over low heat.
    Shake the skillet until the seeds begin to pop, about
    2 minutes.

2.  Transfer the seeds to a mixing bowl. Add the applesauce,
    yogurt, chutney, curry powder, salt, and cayenne pepper.
    Stir to combine. Add the turkey, scallions, mint, and
    apple. Mix together, but do not overmix. The consistency
    should be soft but manageable to shape into 4 patties,
    each ³⁄₄ inch thick.

3.  To cook the patties on a stove, spray a frying pan with
    nonstick vegetable oil or lightly brush the surface with oil.
    Place the patties inside and cook over medium heat. If
    using a grill, adjust the coals or gas to medium and spray
    each patty on both sides with the nonstick spray, or
    lightly brush with oil. By either method, cook thoroughly,
    about 5 minutes on each side.

4.  Serve with lettuce and sliced tomatoes on a bulkie roll
    or bread of your choice.

## OM RESTAURANT & LOUNGE

92 Winthrop Street
Cambridge (Harvard Square)
(617) 576–2800, www.omrestaurant.com

### Chef | Rachel F. Klein

Is Boston ready for a place that mixes Tibetan art, aromatherapy martinis, and wildly inventive combinations like foie gras with cardamom and rosewater-scented Moroccan funnel cake? OM, which opened in December 2005, has taken up the challenge. It is certainly a showpiece of design, with a carved wood front door that opens onto a textured black wall with water flowing down it. In the lounge one wall is completely covered by a giant Thangka religious Tibetan painting by co-owner Bik Yonjan's father. Upstairs in the main dining room hang more of these paintings, some on the ceiling. With its hardwood floors, beige walls, and statues of Buddha displayed in niches, the room looks as much gallery as dining room. Chef Rachel Klein feels at home in this atmosphere: She earned a degree from the Art Institute of New York before becoming a chef. Not surprisingly, she designs each plate with both color and flavor in mind, using many different elements. She enjoys putting together improbable combinations like tuna tartare with ginger gelée and a hibiscus spritzer, or parsnip soup with curry and caramelized pears.

A cookbook gave Klein the idea of using bay leaves in a starring role. "I had always thought of bay leaves as something to put into a stock or sauce to bump up the flavor, not as the base of a sauce," she says. With its concentrated, earthy flavors, the cream became "the winner on the plate." As more of an accent than something to pour over food, Bay Cream works well with chicken and mushrooms. Klein also found other successful combinations—scallops, mild-flavored cod, or haddock for protein; sautéed greens, potatoes, or rutabagas for vegetables. "What I like about the Bay Cream is that it is not just reserved for one thing. It's a base that you can build from."

# ROAST CHICKEN WITH BAY CREAM AND MUSHROOMS

[SERVES 4]

**BAY CREAM:**

1½ teaspoons unsalted butter
¾ cup finely diced shallots
¾ cup finely diced celery
½ cup finely diced fresh fennel root
1 cup white wine
1 quart chicken stock
8 bay leaves
2 cups heavy cream
¼ cup roasted garlic (see note)
Sugar, to taste
Salt and white pepper, to taste

1. In a large pot, melt the butter over medium-low heat. Add the shallots, celery, and fennel. Sauté until they start to soften, about 5 minutes. Do not let them brown.

2. Add the white wine to deglaze the pan. Bring to a boil over high heat, reduce the heat to low, and let simmer until the wine has almost evaporated, about 20 minutes.

3. Add the chicken stock and bay leaves. Bring to a boil, reduce the heat to low, and let simmer until the liquid is reduced by half, 25 to 30 minutes.

4. Add the cream, bring to a boil, reduce the heat to low, and let simmer until the sauce thickens enough to coat the back of a spoon.

5. Stir in the garlic. Strain through a fine sieve, discard the solids, and season to taste with sugar, salt, and pepper. This sauce should be very light—not brown.

:: **Note:** To make ¼ cup roasted garlic, peel 4 large or 6 small garlic cloves. Place on a sheet of aluminum foil, fold up the ends, and place directly on the rack in a 375-degree oven for 1 hour, or until the cloves are brown and completely soft. You can scrape the garlic right off the foil into the sauce.

**ROAST CHICKEN:**

4 split chicken breast pieces, bone in (approximately 12 ounces each)
1 tablespoon olive oil
Salt, pepper, and paprika, to taste

Preheat the oven to 375 degrees. Place the chicken pieces skin-side up in a roasting pan. Drizzle olive oil over each. Sprinkle with salt, pepper, and paprika. Roast for 45 minutes, or until the chicken is no longer pink inside (insert a knife into its thickest part to test) and its juices run clear.

**PAN-ROASTED MUSHROOMS:**

1 tablespoon canola oil
½ pound king oyster mushrooms, sliced (see note)
½ pound hen-of-the-woods mushrooms, sliced
1 tablespoon unsalted butter
Salt and pepper, to taste

In a nonstick sauté pan, heat the canola oil on high heat until it's smoking. Place the mushrooms in the pan. Add the butter and season with salt and pepper. Sauté the mushrooms until they're golden brown and the cooking liquid has almost evaporated.

:: **Note:** Use any fresh, seasonal mushrooms if you can't find king oyster or hen-of-the-woods mushrooms. (For more information about mushrooms, see the sidebar on page 122.)

**FINAL PREPARATION AND SERVING:**

Place a portion of chicken on each plate, with the mushrooms next to it. Spoon the cream onto the plate next to the mushrooms.

# ABOUT MUSHROOMS

Until about fifteen years ago, most people thought of gourmet mushrooms as baked stuffed cocktail party fare. But in the 1990s portobello mushrooms—a meaty variety that can grow as big as hockey pucks—became all the rage. Since then, dishes that highlight the variety of shapes, textures, and flavors of mushrooms have become a welcome addition to restaurant menus. Many Boston chefs order their supplies from Benjamin Maleson, an elfin man with a gray beard nicknamed "the Mushroom Man," who forages for fresh, exotic varieties. He sometimes sells his picks at local farmers' markets. Daniel Bruce of Meritage at the Boston Harbor Hotel (see page 10), and Frank McClelland of L'Espalier (see page 156), are among the chefs who have gone foraging with Maleson, then prepared special mushroom dinners in their restaurants.

If you're buying mushrooms, the cultivated, pale white button variety, with a subtle flavor, can be found almost anywhere. The most reliable place to find the more exotic mushrooms is at a gourmet grocery store with a well-stocked produce section. Never pick your own unless you are accompanied by an expert, as varieties that look edible sometimes turn out to be poisonous.

Here are a few of the most commonly available types:

**Cremini:** A brown version of the button mushroom, with slightly more flavor.

**Portobello:** This is the full-grown version of the cremini, with a thick, meaty texture and flavor (for a recipe, see page 147).

**Shiitake:** Dark brown, with a cap resembling a wide-brimmed hat and a dense, woodsy flavor. The stems are usually too tough to eat.

**Oyster:** Tan, with wide, overlapping stems that resemble a fan, and a delicate flavor.

**Hen-of-the-woods:** Found at the base of oak trees, this mushroom looks a bit like the feathers on a hen's body, with small, overlapping ruffles and a firm texture.

Do not wash mushrooms under running water, as they will become soggy. Brush or wipe them with a damp cloth or paper towel to remove any dirt that clings to them.

Dried mushrooms can be found at a gourmet grocery store or through mail order. Delicate morels and porcinis are often sold this way. Reconstitute them by placing them in a bowl, adding lukewarm water to cover, and soaking for 15 to 30 minutes.

## CORIANDER BISTRO

5 Post Office Square
Sharon
(781) 784-5450, www.corianderbistro.com

**Chef-owner | Kevin Crawley**

Leave it to a chef to find a way to dress up those boring but handy boneless, skinless chicken breasts. Kevin Crawley turns to two French techniques for a colorful topping. In the first step, called a brunoise, several different vegetables are diced into pieces about the size of a pea and sautéed. The next step purees chicken with egg white and cream, so it can form a sort of dumpling called a quenelle. A red wine sauce adds color and contrasting flavor. "It's an approachable dish with a really pretty presentation," says Crawley.

Crawley's use of French techniques brings city sophistication to suburban Sharon, about 25 miles south of Boston along I–95. At his restaurant he also serves scallops with crepes, and puts wild mushrooms and goat cheese into a tart shell. To reach out to the community, he regularly teaches cooking classes in the restaurant kitchen.

## Squeeze Bottles

To a chef, a squeeze bottle is like a ratchet wrench to a mechanic—or, to take a higher-minded view, a paintbrush to an artist. Most chefs place the sauces and oils that they use for garnishes in plastic bottles fitted with a tip that has a small opening for the liquid to be squeezed through. This gives the chef control over how fast the liquid comes out, and the opportunity to squeeze out zigzags, squiggles, and other decorations. You can sometimes find them at kitchen, housewares, and art supply stores. Just make sure they are clean before using. You can cheat by placing the sauce in a re-sealable plastic sandwich bag, cutting a tiny hole in the corner, and squeezing. But once you start to see the design possibilities, you'll probably want the real thing.

# BONELESS CHICKEN BRUNOISE

[SERVES 4]

**BRUNOISE:**

2 tablespoons olive oil

¼ cup finely diced carrots (approximately
⅛ x ⅛-inch cubes)

¼ cup finely diced celery

¼ cup finely diced onions

¼ cup finely diced shallot

¼ cup finely diced zucchini

¼ cup finely diced red pepper

¼ cup finely diced leeks (white part only; see sidebar,
page 35)

Heat the olive oil in a sauté pan. Add the diced vegetables and lightly sauté over medium-low heat until the vegetables start to soften and the onions are translucent, but not brown. (The vegetables will continue to cook in the oven.) Cool and reserve.

**QUENELLE:**

1 boneless, skinless chicken breast half (6 ounces)

1 egg white

1 teaspoon chopped shallot

Pinch of ground nutmeg

Salt and white pepper, to taste

Approximately ½ cup heavy cream

Cut the chicken breast into chunks. Place in the bowl of a food processor along with the egg white, shallot, nutmeg, salt, and pepper. Pulse once or twice to mix the ingredients. With the motor running, slowly pour in the cream until the mixture develops a pastelike consistency (you may not need to use all the cream). Set aside.

**CHICKEN:**

4 boneless, skinless chicken breast halves (6 ounces each)

Olive oil, as needed to drizzle over chicken

¼ cup chicken stock

¼ cup white wine

1. Preheat the oven to 350 degrees. Place each of the 4 chicken breasts between 2 sheets of plastic wrap. Using a rolling pin or a meat mallet, lightly pound the meat to an even thickness. Place each chicken breast in a 9x13-inch baking pan.

2. Put 2 to 3 tablespoons of the quenelle mixture (from the recipe above) on each breast, spreading over the meat but leaving a small border (about ⅛ inch) all around. Place about 2 tablespoons of the brunoise mixture (from the recipe above) on top.

3. Drizzle the chicken with olive oil. Pour the chicken broth and white wine into the pan.

4. Bake for 12 to 15 minutes, or until the topping is cooked, the chicken is no longer pink inside (insert a knife into its thickest part to test), and its juices run clear.

**SAUCE:**

1 cup red table wine

1 sprig thyme

1 bay leaf

1 cup veal demi-glace (available at specialty markets)

Salt and pepper, to taste

In a saucepan, bring the red wine, thyme sprig, and bay leaf to a boil. Reduce the heat and simmer until the liquid is reduced by half. Add the demi-glace and continue simmering over medium heat until the mixture thickens enough to coat the back of a spoon. Season with salt and pepper.

**FINAL PREPARATION AND SERVING:**

Place 2 to 3 tablespoons of the red wine sauce on a serving plate. With a slotted spoon that allows the cooking liquid to drain, transfer the chicken to the plate, serving it on top of the red wine sauce. Alternatively, drizzle the sauce around the chicken on the plate. A squeeze bottle works well for this (see previous page).

## LES ZYGOMATES

129 South Street
Boston (Downtown)
(617) 542-5108, www.winebar.com

**Chef-owner | Ian Just**

As a French-style bistro, Les Zygomates is hardly a poseur. It is modeled after a bistro with the same name (the French word for the muscles in your face that make you smile) on rue de Capri in Paris. Ian Just worked at the Paris location for nearly three years after he became fluent in French and graduated from a cooking school in France. Though it was tempting to become a permanent expatriate, Just was eventually drawn back to his New England roots. (He grew up in Vermont.)

Just opened Les Zygomates in 1994, serving hearty bistro classics like foie gras, escargots, and steak frites. For variety, he offers crab cakes with chile-pepper-spiked aioli, or grilled swordfish with purple sticky rice, spicy squid, and mango. Equally important has been the wine list. Weekly tastings, organized around a theme like California Cabernets, have become so popular that they now include two seatings. A jazz cafe adds entertainment to the package.

This duck recipe comes from the traditional bistro part of the menu. With two opportunities to flambé the sauce as it cooks, you are sure to impress whoever is watching you prepare it. (Just be careful not to set the kitchen on fire.) The sauce is a complex combination of sweetness from the cherries and port, and savory stock and foie gras. Look for duck breasts, foie gras, and dried cherries at a specialty food or meat market.

## ROAST DUCK BREAST WITH FOIE GRAS

[SERVES 4]

2 tablespoons canola oil, divided
2 boneless duck breasts (approximately 1 pound each)
2 whole shallots
2 tablespoons dried cherries
¼ cup brandy
½ cup port wine
2 cups duck or chicken stock
Salt and pepper, to taste
2 ounces foie gras, diced

1. Preheat the oven to 450 degrees. In a large, ovenproof sauté pan, heat 1 tablespoon of the canola oil over high heat. Add the duck breasts and sear until golden brown on one side, approximately 2 to 3 minutes. Flip over and sear on the other side for another 2 to 3 minutes.

2. Place the pan in the oven to finish cooking the duck. Let roast for about 5 minutes, then flip over and continue cooking until medium rare, approximately 5 minutes more. Remove the pan from the oven, place the duck on a plate, and set aside.

3. Pour out and discard the fat from the pan. Place the pan over medium heat on the stove. Add the remaining tablespoon of canola oil and sauté the shallots until translucent. Add the cherries to the pan, then the brandy. Flambé the brandy by lighting a match (turn away from the stove as you do this), then carefully touching the flame to the top of the liquid in the pan until it catches fire. Let the flame burn until the alcohol burns off. Simmer until the liquid is reduced by half.

4. Add the port and flambé again. Let the port simmer until the liquid is reduced by half. Add the stock and continue simmering until, once again, the liquid is reduced by half.

5. Season with salt and pepper and add the foie gras. Place each duck breast on a serving plate and ladle a portion of sauce on top. Serve with au gratin potatoes or crusty bread.

## GARGOYLES ON THE SQUARE

219 Elm Street
Somerville (Davis Square)
(617) 776-5300, http://gargoylesonthesquare.com

**Chef | Jason Santos**

You have to expect plenty of culinary risk taking from a chef who regularly dyes his hair blue. ("Kids point to me and ask about it so often, I've lost track of how many times," he says, chortling.) Jason Santos delivers, seeking out mini coconuts the size of grapes, white yams, and other exotic produce. Even the color scheme of Gargoyles—sage green and orange—is unpredictable, but it somehow works for the neighborhood customers who stream in for a dose of spring rolls with cactus leaf salsa, or tuna grilled in oolong tea. Chef Santos owns over 300 cookbooks and spends days off scouring ethnic markets and other restaurants for new inspirations. At any given time a dozen different ideas might be ricocheting around his kitchen—and he seems to thrive on the commotion.

Using his characteristic method of tossing and tasting different ingredients, Santos transformed a basic dressing for steak tartare into what he calls "a funky, chunky version of a mayonnaise-based dressing." It even looks pretty, with a nice contrast of red jam and green watercress on top of the meat. So what if you think tomato dressing doesn't really go with steak? Santos has the gumption to try it and make it work.

# Meat

# GRILLED SKIRT STEAK WITH TOMATO JAM

[SERVES 4]

**TOMATO JAM:**

1 tablespoon olive oil

1 tablespoon chopped garlic

1 tablespoon diced onion

1 tablespoon chopped fresh parsley

2 tablespoons red wine

1 cup diced canned tomatoes

2 tablespoons mayonnaise

1 tablespoon Dijon mustard

1½ teaspoons minced cornichons

1½ teaspoons minced capers

1. In a small saucepan, heat the olive oil. Add the garlic and sauté until brown. Add the onion and cook until translucent. Add the parsley and sauté for 1 or 2 minutes, until it wilts.

2. Add the red wine to deglaze the pan. Simmer until the liquid has almost evaporated. Add the tomatoes and continue to simmer over low heat, stirring occasionally, for 30 to 40 minutes, until the tomatoes have become quite soft and most of the liquid has evaporated.

3. Place the tomato mixture in a food processor and pulse to mix thoroughly—but still leave a slightly chunky texture. With a spoon, fold in the mayonnaise, mustard, cornichons, and capers.

**STEAK:**

2 pounds skirt or rib eye steak, approximately
    1 steak per person (8 ounces each)

Salt and pepper, to taste

1 bunch watercress, rinsed and dried

Season the steak on both sides with salt and pepper. Grill until cooked to medium rare (or to your liking), about 5 minutes per side. Serve with a few sprigs of watercress and a spoonful of Tomato Jam on top.

## TEMPLE BAR

1688 Massachusetts Avenue, Cambridge (between Harvard and Porter Squares)
(617) 547–5055, www.templebarcambridge.com

### Chef | Tom Berry

As a chef who has built a career in New England, Tom Berry understands all too well the fleeting nature of the local growing season. This steak works best in spring and summer, when fresh herbs are in season and you can stand at the grill without shivering. The herbs of faraway Provence are what originally inspired Berry: tarragon, lavender, basil, and oregano. The Herb Salad with the contrasting color and crunch of sliced radishes is a refreshing change from a tossed salad, and goes well with the meat. "It's meant to be a little contrast, not a big side salad," he says. In summer and fall fresh herbs can be picked up at a local farmers' market (see the sidebar on page 158). Look for dried lavender at a specialty tea shop or a natural foods store with a wide selection of bulk herbs and spices.

The steak, served with french fries, fits right into the casual, neighborhood atmosphere at Temple Bar. Inspired by the Temple Bar in Dublin, a major retail, restaurant, and tourist district, this Cambridge spot is a loose, eclectic interpretation. Running the length of the room is a polished copper bartop, with a mirror behind it to reflect cylindrical light fixtures that appear to be woven from thin strips of wood. Berry, who arrived in 2005, has also added Asian accents to the menu, an affinity he learned as Ming Tsai's sous chef (see Blue Ginger, page 180). Menu best sellers are a salmon seviche with a sushi rice cake and passion fruit vinaigrette and a Japanese seafood cioppino with udon noodles. Less adventurous eaters can find cheese fondue, braised short ribs, and other comfort foods. "The food here can be eaten once or twice a week, not just when it's a special occasion," Berry says.

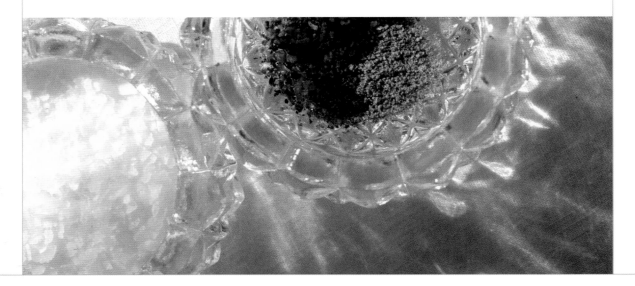

# GRILLED STEAK DE PROVENCE
## WITH LAVENDER AIOLI AND HERB SALAD

[SERVES 4]

**STEAK:**

¼ cup whole fennel seeds
4 cloves garlic
1 cup fresh basil leaves
1 cup fresh tarragon leaves
½ cup fresh oregano leaves
2 tablespoons dried savory
1 tablespoons Dijon mustard
1 cup pure olive oil
4 flatiron or flank steaks (10 ounces each)
Kosher salt and freshly ground black pepper, to taste

1. Heat a small skillet over high heat. Add the fennel seeds and shake the skillet or toss the seeds with a spoon until toasted and fragrant, 3 to 4 minutes.

2. In a food processor or a blender, puree the toasted fennel seeds, garlic, basil, tarragon, oregano, savory, mustard, and olive oil until smooth.

3. Thoroughly coat the steaks with the marinade and let them marinate in the refrigerator for 24 hours.

4. Preheat a grill until very hot. Season the steaks on both sides with salt and pepper. Grill for 3 to 4 minutes per side for medium rare. Let the steaks rest for 4 minutes before slicing against the grain. Serve the slices of steak with Herb Salad on top and Lavender Aioli on the side.

**HERB SALAD:**

2 tablespoons Banyuls or sherry vinegar (see note)
2 tablespoons olive oil
¼ cup fresh tarragon leaves
¼ cup fresh flat parsley leaves
¼ cup fresh chervil leaves (or substitute an additional ¼ cup parsley leaves)
¼ cup chives, cut into 1-inch pieces
½ cup thin red radish slices
Kosher salt and freshly ground black pepper, to taste

Mix the vinegar and oil together. Just before serving toss all the herbs and radish together with the vinaigrette. Season with salt and pepper.

:: **Note:** Banyuls vinegar is made from sweet wine from the southwestern French region of Banyuls-sur-Mer. Its flavor is more mellow than other vinegars.

**LAVENDER AIOLI:**

1 tablespoon dried lavender
2 tablespoons hot tap water
1 tablespoon Dijon mustard
1 teaspoon minced garlic
1 teaspoon minced shallot
Pinch of sugar
1 teaspoon fresh lemon juice
1 cup good-quality commercial mayonnaise
Kosher salt and freshly ground black pepper, to taste

Place the dried lavender in a small bowl. Add the hot water and let the lavender steep for 5 minutes. Drain and add the lavender to a large mixing bowl, along with the mustard, garlic, shallot, sugar, lemon juice, and mayonnaise. Stir to combine. Season well with salt and pepper. If possible, re-frigerate for 2 to 3 hours before serving, so the flavors have time to blend.

## DAVIO'S

75 Arlington Street
Boston (Back Bay)
(617) 357–4810, www.davios.com

**Co-chefs | Stephen Brown and Eric Swartz**

When Davio's opened in the 1980s, it was one of the first restaurants to bring Italian food to fashionable Newbury Street. Its menu ventured beyond the pasta with red sauce that was once the mainstay of traditional Italian American restaurants. In 2002 Davio's moved into more spacious quarters that overlook busy Park Square. Large white columns rise from each end of the bar to the dramatically high ceiling. Over the years the menu has evolved into a Northern Italian steak house, with Eric Swartz and Stephen Brown also turning out hearty veal tenderloin, cioppino, and crispy chicken livers. A take-out counter serving salads, Italian sandwiches, and pastries faces into a sunny atrium furnished with tables and couches.

This recipe takes a tough cut of beef and braises it until the meat is fork-tender and slightly sweet from the brown sugar. Introduced during one of Boston's famously long winters, the short ribs are now listed in the "classics" section of the menu. "We tried to take them off the menu in the summer, but people went crazy asking for them. They wouldn't let us," says owner Steve DiFillippo. Leftovers make great sandwiches—if you get that far.

# BRAISED SHORT RIBS

[SERVES 4-6]

2 quarts veal and/or beef stock
8 pounds beef short ribs (with bone)
Salt and black pepper, to taste
3 cups flour
Canola oil, as needed
1 large carrot, finely diced
1 large Spanish onion, finely diced
2 stalks celery, finely diced
1½ cups red wine, any variety except sweet
2 cups balsamic vinegar
1 cup brown sugar
2 tablespoons finely chopped fresh rosemary leaves,
    plus additional sprigs for garnish
1 whole hot chile pepper (fresh or dried)

1.  Preheat the oven to 400 degrees.

2.  In a saucepan, heat the stock to a slow boil.

3.  Pat dry the ribs with paper towels and season with salt and pepper.

4.  Place the flour in a large bowl. Add the ribs and toss until the ribs are lightly coated in flour.

5.  In a large skillet, pour in canola oil until it reaches a depth of ½ inch; heat over a medium-high flame. Carefully add a few ribs at a time to the hot oil and turn to brown on all sides. Transfer the browned ribs to a large roasting pan. Continue until all the ribs are done.

6.  Discard the excess oil from the skillet. Return the skillet to the stove over medium-low heat and add the carrot, onion, and celery. Sauté the vegetables until they're lightly brown and transfer them to the roasting pan with the ribs.

7.  Add the red wine to the skillet. Simmer until the liquid is reduced by half, stirring to deglaze the pan. Add the vinegar and brown sugar to the red wine. Stir until the sugar completely dissolves. Stir in the rosemary and hot pepper. Pour the mixture into the roasting pan with the ribs.

8.  Pour the hot stock into the roasting pan, submerging the ribs.

9.  Cover the roasting pan with foil and bake for 2½ hours, or until the meat is tender and easily falls away from the bone.

10. To serve, gently remove the ribs from the braising liquid and place on a serving plate (use a shallow bowl or plate with a raised rim). Ladle some of the braising sauce over the ribs and garnish with a fresh rosemary sprig. Serve with mashed potatoes and a sautéed green vegetable.

## EVOO

118 Beacon Street
Somerville
(617) 661–3866, www.evoorestaurant.com

**Chef-owner | Peter McCarthy**

Playfulness is part of the concept at EVOO, whose name is short for "extra-virgin olive oil." A popular entree is Duck, Duck, Goose (duck prepared two ways, with sliced goose breast). Another is beef and shrimp packed with vegetables and rice into a Chinese take-out box, then inverted onto a dinner plate. The casual decor—wire mesh lamp shades that that look like giant window screens, and close-up photos of spoons and forks—fits right in.

Behind it all is Peter McCarthy's serious devotion to New England ingredients. He owns a share in a Boston-area farm, and runs daily specials to highlight seasonal picks. "A third of the menu stays the same, and a third changes all the time," he says. Restaurant-made pickles and jams are served year-round. McCarthy came up with this lamb dish by doing what he likes to do best—brainstorming with pots and pans. "I started thinking about what to do with coffee . . . ," he says, smiling mischievously as his voice trails off. At first bite, the coffee is more of an undertone than a flavor that dominates the meat, but the aftertaste feels like you've just taken a sip. The espresso vinaigrette would overwhelm a salad but goes well with meats, poultry, and richer-flavored fish. It can even be spooned over a baked potato. A sweet potato tamale accompanies the lamb at EVOO, but McCarthy simplified his recipe for home cooks. What's next? "Chile peppers go well with cheesecake," he deadpans.

# COFFEE-MARINATED ROAST RACK OF LAMB
## WITH CORN RELISH AND ESPRESSO VINAIGRETTE

[SERVES 4]

**LAMB AND COFFEE MARINADE:**

¼ cup finely ground dark-roast coffee beans

2 tablespoons chopped garlic

1½ tablespoons Dijon mustard

2 tablespoons chopped fresh cilantro

½ teaspoon ground cinnamon

½ cup lemon juice

¼ cup vegetable oil

¼ cup hot coffee

1 tablespoon dark brown sugar

2 Frenched racks of lamb (1¾–2¼ pounds each; see note)

1. In a mixing bowl, combine all the ingredients except the lamb. Place the lamb in a large, nonreactive bowl. Pour the marinade over the top, making sure to coat all sides. Cover and let marinate in the refrigerator overnight.

2. Lift each rack of lamb from the marinade and place it in a roasting pan, with the bones facing up. Roast at 450 degrees until the internal temperature reaches 115 degrees for medium rare. (This temperature may sound low, but it will go up another 20 degrees as it continues to cook outside the oven.) Remove the lamb from the oven and let it rest for at least 10 minutes at room temperature before cutting. Letting the meat rest is very important and should not be skipped. If the meat does not rest, it will be very rare in the center and the juices will run out.

**:: Note:** To French a rack of lamb means to cut away part of the meat from the end of the ribs, leaving part of the bone exposed. (Each individual rib with the meat attached would be a lamb chop.) Gourmet markets sometimes sell lamb already prepared this way; if your market does not, ask the butcher to do it for you.

**CORN RELISH:**

2 cups corn kernels, cut from the cob (see sidebar, page 112)

¼ cup diced, peeled, seeded tomatoes

¼ cup diced red onion

¼ cup chopped fresh cilantro

¼ cup diced red peppers

¼ cup diced green peppers

1½ tablespoons lime juice

2 tablespoons extra-virgin olive oil

1½ teaspoons kosher salt

¼ teaspoon freshly ground black pepper

Combine all the ingredients.

**ESPRESSO VINAIGRETTE:**

6 ounces (¾ cup) espresso or strong black coffee

1½ teaspoons Dijon mustard

2 tablespoons chopped garlic

2 tablespoons chopped fresh cilantro

½ thinly sliced scallion (white and green parts)

2 tablespoons lime juice

6 tablespoons extra-virgin olive oil

1½ tablespoons honey

½ teaspoon ground cinnamon

1½ teaspoons kosher salt

¼ teaspoon freshly ground black pepper

Whisk together all the ingredients until well combined.

**FINAL PREPARATION AND SERVING:**

Cilantro sprigs, for garnish

Slice the rack of lamb into individual lamb chops. Place 2 to 3 lamb chops, meat-side down, in the center of a serving plate. To serve, spoon some of the Corn Relish into the center of a plate. Arrange 2 or 3 chops, bone-side up, on the relish. Spoon the Espresso Vinaigrette over the meat and garnish with cilantro sprigs. Repeat to make 4 servings.

## BAKER'S BEST

27 Lincoln Street
Newton Highlands
(617) 332-4588, www.bakersbestcatering.com

**Owner | Michael Baker**

It's always party time at Baker's Best, where platters of everything from quesadillas to grilled chicken wings are rushed out each day from the busy catering department. Equally successful is a cafe, where the take-out counter fronts a bustling, open kitchen. Prepared foods, including orange ginger beef tenderloin salad, and spinach mushroom lasagna, can be brought home or eaten on the spot at a table in the side room. The business has expanded several times since owner Michael Baker opened it in 1984.

A popular entree is this rack of lamb, which is often cut into baby lamb chops and passed as an appetizer at parties. "The great thing about this glaze is that you get sweet, savory, and spicy all at the same time," says former chef Geoff Skillman. It finishes with a zing.

# HONEY PEPPERCORN LAMB RACK

[SERVES 4]

**LAMB RACK:**

2 racks domestic lamb (1¾–2 pounds each)
1 teaspoon fresh thyme leaves
1 teaspoon fresh rosemary leaves
1 teaspoon chopped fresh garlic (about 2 cloves)
1 teaspoon diced shallot
3 ounces (6 tablespoons) extra-virgin olive oil

1. Split each lamb rack in half, to yield 4 portions with 4 bones per rack.

2. Coarsely chop the fresh rosemary and thyme with a sharp knife. Be careful not to chop the herbs too much, or they will turn black.

3. In a bowl, mix together the fresh herbs, garlic, shallot, and oil.

4. Rub the herb oil all over the lamb. Put the lamb into a plastic or glass container, cover, and marinate in the refrigerator for at least for 2 hours, preferably overnight.

**HONEY PEPPERCORN GLAZE:**

1 tablespoon chopped fresh parsley
½ teaspoon chopped fresh thyme leaves
½ cup brown sugar
¼ cup grainy mustard, such as Pommery
2 tablespoons Dijon mustard
1 teaspoon diced shallot
1 teaspoon chopped fresh garlic (about 2 cloves)
Dash of Tabasco sauce
Dash of Worcestershire sauce
1 teaspoon freshly ground pepper, preferably from
    mixed peppercorns (white, pink, and black)
¼ cup honey

Thoroughly combine all the ingredients in a small mixing bowl. Set aside.

**FINAL PREPARATION AND SERVING:**

2 tablespoons vegetable oil

1. Preheat the oven to 350 degrees.

2. In a large sauté pan, heat the oil. Sear each rack of lamb in the hot oil for about 2 minutes per side—or you can use a gas grill on the high setting to grill each rack for about 2 minutes per side. (This step will ensure that the meat stays moist throughout the cooking process.)

3. Rub the Honey Peppercorn Glaze over the seared or grilled meat.

4. Place each rack of lamb on the top of a broiler pan. Bake until the internal temperature (measured on a meat thermometer) reaches 110 degrees for rare, or 120 for medium rare, about 10 to 12 minutes. (Check once during the cooking time to make sure you don't overcook the lamb.) Let rest 10 minutes before serving. Good accompaniments are mashed potatoes accented with roasted garlic or parsnips; rosemary-roasted baby red potatoes; or wild rice.

## ICARUS

3 Appleton Street
Boston (South End)
(617) 426-1790, www.icarusrestaurant.com

**Chef-owner | Chris Douglass**

Back when most chefs ordered their produce from giant distributors, Chris Douglass was foraging for wild mushrooms and finding local farmers to deliver specialties like heirloom cranberries. An emphasis on seasonal ingredients has helped Icarus stay in business since 1977—an eternity in the volatile restaurant world. So have dishes like polenta with braised exotic mushrooms, and grilled shrimp with mango and jalapeño sorbet. Icarus was an early anchor in upscale dining in the South End, a category that has steadily expanded to include more than a dozen restaurants within about a square mile.

This simple pork chop recipe is surprisingly flavorful. Take the time to soak the meat in the brine, which tenderizes it and makes it juicier. The Maple Mustard Sauce can also be used as a condiment on sandwiches. It works especially well with turkey or chicken.

## GRILLED PORK CHOPS WITH MAPLE MUSTARD SAUCE

[SERVES 4]

1 quart water
¼ cup salt
2 tablespoons sugar
4 double-cut pork chops
Vegetable oil, as needed
2 onions, sliced (optional)
2 zucchini, sliced lengthwise (optional)
2 red or green bell peppers, sliced lengthwise (optional)
½ cup whole-grain mustard
¼ cup maple syrup

1. Make a brine by combining the water, salt, and sugar in a nonreactive pot or bowl. Add the pork chops and make sure they are covered with the liquid. Cover the bowl and let the meat soak for 6 to 8 hours in the refrigerator.

2. Drain and pat the pork chops dry on paper towels. Rub oil on the cooking grate of a grill, so the meat won't stick, and preheat the grill to medium. Rub oil on the outside of the vegetables, if using. Grill the chops until no pink remains but the meat is still tender, approximately 5 minutes on each side. Grill the vegetables at the same time until they're soft, approximately 5 minutes on each side.

3. Meanwhile, in a small bowl, stir together the mustard and maple syrup to use as a dipping sauce. You can also brush a little of this mixture over the pork chops at the final stage of cooking to give them a slight glaze.

4. Serve the pork chops with the grilled vegetables. Pass the Maple Mustard Sauce on the side.

## PAOLO'S TRATTORIA

251 Main Street
Charlestown
(617) 242-7229, www.paolosboston.com

**Founder and former chef | Paul Delios**

Paolo's feels like the sort of neighborhood place you would find in Italy, with a brick pizza oven glowing in back, cozy tables tucked next to exposed brick walls, and indomitable portions of pasta. Founding chef Paul Delios was well trained by growing up in a predominately Italian neighborhood in Saugus. His grandfather owned a bakery in Greece. After the family emigrated to Boston, they owned Tony's Spa in Chelsea, Mrs. Foster's in Lynn, and Kane's Donut House in Saugus (which is still in the family). After years as the chef-owner at Paolo's and a partner at the now-closed Greek restaurant, Meze, Delios can be found at Kane's, where he plans to add a line of savory dishes.

To create a knockout sauce for pork tenderloin, Chef Delios looked no farther than his pantry. "I took two traditional ingredients from Southern Italy and put them together," he cheerfully explains, making it sound easy. Astringent juniper berries (also used as the base for gin) contrast with sweet Marsala. Pine nuts and raisins add a delightfully nubby texture. This dish is almost too good for an ordinary weeknight—it deserves an adoring audience.

# PORK WITH MARSALA AND JUNIPER BERRIES

[SERVES 4]

¼ cup plus 3 tablespoons extra-virgin olive oil, divided

2 tablespoons fresh thyme

2 cloves garlic, minced

Salt, to taste

2 pork tenderloins (1½–2 pounds each)

2 tablespoons (¼ stick) unsalted butter, divided

1 small shallot, finely minced

¼ cup pine nuts

1–2 tablespoons dried juniper berries (available in the spice section of most supermarkets)

1 cup Marsala wine

1 cup beef stock

1 tablespoon cornstarch dissolved in ¼ cup cold water

¼ cup raisins

¼ cup sun-dried tomatoes (not packed in oil)

Black pepper, to taste

1. Preheat the oven to 450 degrees.

2. In a small bowl, mix together ¼ cup of the olive oil with the thyme, garlic, and salt. Rub this mixture over the pork, making sure to coat all sides. Place in a roasting pan and roast in the oven until the center is pink (130 degrees on a meat thermometer), about 15 to 20 minutes.

3. Meanwhile, in a medium-size sauté pan over medium heat, heat 1 tablespoon of the butter, the remaining 3 tablespoons of olive oil, and the shallot, pine nuts, and juniper berries. Sauté until the shallot is translucent and the nuts brown slightly, about 3 to 4 minutes. Add the Marsala, raise the heat, and bring the mixture to a boil. Cook, stirring constantly, until the liquid is reduced by a third, about 5 to 6 minutes. Remove the pan from the stove and set aside.

4. In a small saucepan, heat the beef stock to just under a boil. Stir in the dissolved cornstarch and continue stirring until the mixture thickens, about 2 minutes. Return the pine nut mixture to the stove over medium heat. Add the thickened beef stock to the pine nut mixture, plus the raisins and sun-dried tomatoes. Bring to a boil and let simmer until the liquid is reduced by a third, stirring constantly, about 5 to 6 minutes. Remove from the heat. Stir in the remaining tablespoon of butter and salt and pepper to taste. Keep warm.

5. Slice the tenderloin into medallions. Spoon sauce over the top and pass more sauce on the side. Serve with oven-roasted potatoes with rosemary, or rice.

## DARWIN'S LTD.

148 Mount Auburn Street
Cambridge (Harvard Square)
(617) 354-5233

1629 Cambridge Street
Cambridge
(617) 491-2999, www.darwinsltd.com

**Former head chef | Justin Turner Bennett**

Tucked behind a blue-and-white Busch beer sign on Mount Auburn Street, Darwin's looks more like a convenience store than a place to find a top-quality take-out counter and espresso bar. Neighbors know better, and the late Julia Child, who lived within walking distance, was among the regulars. She raved about the egg salad, saying, "It was the best I've ever had," reports former head cook Justin Bennett. Egg salad is still a lunchtime staple, and it's typically served on seven-grain bread with avocado, lettuce, and tomato. Perhaps the secret to its success is Worcestershire sauce, which tints the mixture light brown and puts a bite behind the salt and pepper.

A second location of Darwin's opened in 2005 to offer a similar mix of sandwiches (all named after streets in Cambridge—the egg salad is "The Chapman"), baked goods, take-out dinners, and coffee drinks. Just in case you did expect a convenience store, you can pick up a loaf of bread, a piece of fruit, a soda, and other basics at either location.

# Vegetarian

## AWESOME EGG SALAD

### [SERVES 4 AS A SANDWICH FILLING]

12 hard-boiled eggs, cooled and peeled
2 stalks celery, finely chopped
1 tablespoon Worcestershire sauce
1–2 teaspoons kosher salt
1 teaspoon black pepper
¼ cup mayonnaise

Over a mixing bowl, gently use your hands to break the hard-boiled eggs into bite-size pieces. Add the remaining ingredients and mix gently to combine. (Do not overmix or the salad will become gooey.) Serve on a sandwich or on a bed of lettuce.

# JULIA CHILD

One of the most beloved chefs in Boston never owned a restaurant or worked in one. Yet Julia Child, the original television celebrity chef, transcended the usual categories, becoming as famous for her cheery, warbling voice as for her cooking demonstrations on public television's *The French Chef.* By the time she died in 2004 at age ninety-one, Child had also established herself as the grande dame of Boston's culinary community. She often invited local chefs to join her in the kitchen of her Cambridge home (since reconstructed and on display at the Smithsonian Institution), and patronized their restaurants. Among her protégés were Lydia Shire (see page 184) and Jasper White (see page 102). Mark Sapienza (see page 90), Michael Schlow (see page 160), and John Merrill (see page 116) fondly remember the honor of being asked to cook a birthday meal for her.

Jody Adams, now chef at Rialto (see page 84), credits Child with helping her find her first job in Boston in the 1980s. More than a dozen years later, Child invited Adams to appear on *In Julia's Kitchen with Master Chefs,* one of her late-career shows. "She had such a generosity of spirit," says Adams. "She was always in the moment, always appreciative of the work every person was doing. Everyone felt connected to her. She was right within reach." When Child dined at Rialto, she was unfailingly gracious to the fans who interrupted her meal by asking for her autograph.

Child is also fondly remembered at Savenor's Market, the gourmet grocery at 92 Kirkland Street, Cambridge (between Harvard and Central Squares), where she used to shop. (A second location at 160 Charles Street, Boston [Beacon Hill], kept the business going when the Cambridge location burned and was closed for many years.) Jack Savenor, whose son, Ron, now runs the business, was a frequent guest on *The French Chef* television show. A giant black-and-white portrait of Child interviewing Savenor on the set is posted near the entrance of the Cambridge store. EVERY WOMAN SHOULD KISS HER BUTCHER, the caption reads.

At WGBH-TV, the Boston PBS station, Child taped her cooking shows for some thirty years. She was merely trying to publicize the cookbook she co-authored, *Mastering the Art of French Cooking,* when she agreed to be a talk-show guest at the station in 1961. When her on-camera demonstration of how to whisk egg whites received unprecedented accolades, she developed a pilot for *The French Chef.* The first shows aired in 1962.

Born Julia McWilliams in Pasadena, California, in 1912, Child didn't become interested in cooking until she was in her forties. After graduating from Smith College with a degree in history in 1934, she worked for the U.S. Office of Strategic Services (which later became the CIA) in Sri Lanka and China. Only when her husband, Paul Child, took a job in Paris in the late 1940s did she begin studying at the Cordon Bleu cooking school and writing her book with two French colleagues. The couple bought their home in Cambridge, Massachusetts, in 1959.

The collection of Child's personal papers at the Schlesinger Library at the Radcliffe Institute for Advanced Study at Harvard University chronicles the development of her Emmy Award–winning program. These papers are open to the public, but must be read inside the library. Child also donated her personal collection of cookbooks to the library. Among the thirty-five cartons of correspondence, scripts, audiotapes, and recipes are fan letters responding to the earliest episodes of the show. In August 1962, for instance, a woman from Auburndale called the coq au vin demonstration "really and truly one of the most surprisingly entertaining half-hours I have spent in front of the TV in many a moon. . . . I love the way she projected over the camera directly to me, the watcher. Her to-do about the brandy firing was without parallel for that rare, tongue-in-cheek sort of humor the viewer longs for in this day of over-rehearsed ad-lib." Child responded two weeks later: "Thanks so much for your good letter about 'The French Chef.' If more people would write with such pleasant enthusiasm, perhaps we shall have a sponsor and be able to continue the programs."

The French Chef did indeed continue. Though Child may have seemed off-the-cuff on camera, her files from 1963 reveal that she carefully prepared for each episode. She diagrammed the set down to the location of tasting spoons on the countertop and the contents in each drawer beneath her counter (a butter dish and butter knife on the right, folded paper towels on the left). Though she had a typewritten script, she often wrote changes in the margins, adding in one case, "boeuf bourguignon is one of the best stews devised by man . . . a king couldn't ask for a better dinner." A handwritten list of equipment to "always take to TV shows" included three clean aprons, three clean blouses, powder, lipstick, masking tape, a stopwatch, "cooking" glasses (for reading, with a reminder, EXTRA GLASSES, written in bold letters), cigarettes, and gum.

As Child became more experienced, the script added estimated times for each section and more cryptic notes. The fan mail changed, too, from praise for Child's showmanship to more personal notes. In April 1966 a high school student from East Providence (Rhode Island) Senior High sent a report—written in French—that named Child as one of the grand masters of French cooking. Another viewer sent in a poem about bouillabaisse. Still more enclosed their favorite recipes along with their holiday greeting cards. By 1975 fans were suggesting new cookbook topics (Child published six major cookbooks in her career, including two based on The French Chef). They also asked for her advice about attending culinary school, and requested autographed photos. Child personally answered many of these letters, signing them "Mrs. Paul Child."

Child was frequently asked to appear on commercial television, but she steadfastly remained at WGBH. The other nonprofit organization she always supported was the American Institute of Wine and Food, which she helped start in 1981. The national group is still going strong, following its original mission to promote education and understanding of food and wine. Though Child could be sharp tongued when it came to the "ninnies" who wanted to wring the butter and fat out of every classic recipe, she generally celebrated the pleasures of food. "Dining with one's friends and beloved family is certainly one of life's primal and most innocent delights, one that is both soul-satisfying and eternal," she wrote in the introduction to her seventh book, The Way to Cook. "In spite of food fads, fitness programs, and health concerns, we must never lose sight of a beautifully conceived meal." Chefs in Boston still use her as an inspiration, even if they were not lucky enough to meet her around town.

## REDBONES

55 Chester Street
Somerville (Davis Square)
(617) 628–2200, www.redbones.com

**Chef | José Perez**

Redbones—best known for its barbecue—is a get-your-fingers-dirty kind of place, with stacks of paper napkins on each table to keep pace with the giant platters of smoked brisket and ribs. A southern theme extends from the collage of country and blues band posters on the wall to the iced tea served in wide mouthed canning jars. But behind the aw-shucks veneer are surprises like valet parking for bikes, a large selection of craft-brewed beers, and a chef who was born in El Salvador and raised in California.

Another surprise at Redbones is the menu's appeal to vegetarians, who regularly make a meal of sides like corn pudding and fried okra. Because barbecue is hard to make at home without special equipment, chef José Perez gave us a popular alternative entrée—a portobello mushroom sandwich. The Portobello is a fully grown version of the familiar button mushroom; it ranges in diameter from a soda can to a martini glass. Here the mushrooms are grilled and served in a hamburger bun. The accompanying house-made Onion Jam is versatile enough to go with meat dishes, too.

# GRILLED PORTOBELLO MUSHROOM SANDWICH
## WITH ONION JAM

[SERVES 4]

**ONION JAM:**

¼ cup olive oil

½ pound onions, sliced

2 tablespoons brown sugar

½ cup orange juice

½ cup red wine vinegar

Salt and pepper, to taste

1. In a sauté pan over medium heat, heat the oil and add the onions. Sauté for about 2 minutes.

2. Add the brown sugar and orange juice and sauté for another 2 minutes. Add the red wine vinegar and stir, scraping up the browned bits from the bottom of the pan.

3. Add salt and lots of pepper. Continue cooking until most of the liquid has evaporated and the onions are golden brown.

**PORTOBELLO MUSHROOM SANDWICH:**

2 teaspoons chopped fresh garlic

½ cup olive oil

¼ cup red wine vinegar

Pinch of dried thyme

Salt and pepper, to taste

4 large or 8 medium portobello mushrooms

4 hamburger buns

1. In a small bowl, mix the garlic, oil, vinegar, thyme, salt, and pepper.

2. Place the mushrooms in a large bowl. Pour the garlic mixture over them and marinate for an hour at room temperature.

3. Place the mushrooms in an ovenproof dish and bake at 350 degrees for 20 minutes, until they become soft. Finish cooking on the grill, or under the broiler, for about a minute, until the tops of the mushrooms turn brown and firm up a bit.

4. Place 1 large or 2 medium mushrooms in each bun and serve with Onion Jam on the side. Redbones serves the sandwich with a small salad or choice of vegetables.

## OLIVES

10 City Square
Charlestown
(617) 242–1999, www.toddenglish.com

### Chef-owner | Todd English

Olives started in 1989 in a fifty-seat space on Main Street in Charlestown, with exposed-brick walls, a brick oven, and an American chef who had recently apprenticed in Italy. The rest is the stuff of legend. Todd English cooked, and customers rushed in for the pasta, the pizza, and the rustic Olives tart topped with olives and anchovies. Before long Olives moved to a larger space around the corner, and English opened Figs in its place. The accolades for the food at Olives, which by this point had become a layered, complex interpretation of Mediterranean ingredients, led to magazine and television stories. English became one of the nation's first celebrity chefs. His far-flung empire now includes restaurants in New York, Las Vegas, and Mohegan Sun. In the Boston area he still owns Olives and Figs, as well as Kingfish Hall (see page 92) and Bonfire.

This lasagna typifies how English can start with a basic Italian dish and take it in a surprising direction. It is more sweet than savory, as the noodles are layered with crushed amaretti (crisp, almond-flavored Italian cookies) and mascarpone cheese. Baking the dish inside a hollowed-out pumpkin makes a dramatic presentation. Make sure you get a sugar pumpkin, bred to be eaten, not the stringy jack-o'-lantern variety. Otherwise, layer the noodles in a baking dish, cover with foil, and bake. What the latter lacks in showmanship, it makes up for in simpler preparation. For something simpler yet, serve the Butternut Squash Sauce on top of cooked pasta, and sprinkle with crushed amaretti, almonds, and Parmesan cheese. The toasted pumpkin seeds and watercress can garnish any of these presentations.

# OLIVES PUMPKIN LASAGNA

[ S E R V E S   8 ]

**BUTTERNUT SQUASH SAUCE:**

1 butternut squash (approximately 2 pounds)
1 bunch fresh rosemary, leaves removed and chopped
1 cup half-and-half, or more as needed
1 cup heavy cream, or more as needed
¼ cup (½ stick) butter
¼ cup maple syrup
Salt and pepper, to taste

1. Peel the squash and dice it into large pieces. Place the squash in a saucepan. Add the rosemary, plus enough half-and-half and cream to immerse the squash pieces. Bring to a simmer and continue simmering until the squash becomes soft.

2. Drain off the liquid and reserve. Place the squash into a blender. Add just enough of the cooking liquid to cover and blend until smooth. Add the butter and maple syrup. Blend again. Season to taste with salt and pepper. Add more of the cooking liquid if necessary. The consistency should be liquid but not runny.

**LASAGNA:**

1 sugar pumpkin (3–4 pounds)
7 fresh lasagna sheets, cut into 5x5-inch pieces, or
     7 (5x5-inch) no-boil lasagna sheets
Butternut Squash Sauce (from recipe above)
½ cup mascarpone cheese
¼ cup ground amaretti cookies
¼ cup ground almonds
½ cup grated Parmesan cheese, plus more for
     sprinkling on top
Watercress sprigs, for garnish

1. Preheat the oven to 400 degrees. Slice off the top of the pumpkin. Scoop out the seeds and stringy parts. Clean the pumpkin seeds and spread them in a single layer on a baking sheet. Toast in the oven until lightly brown, about 10 minutes, stirring once or twice so they brown evenly. Place the pumpkin on a baking sheet and roast for 40 minutes, or until the inside meat is cooked.

2. Lower the oven temperature to 350 degrees. If you're using fresh pasta, immerse 1 sheet in the Butternut Squash Sauce so the sauce clings to each side. Lay 1 sheet of pasta in the bottom of the pumpkin (it might not fit exactly, but you can let the edges come up the sides of the pumpkin, if necessary). Spread 1 to 2 tablespoons of mascarpone cheese on top, then sprinkle with cookie crumbs, ground almonds, and Parmesan cheese. If you're using no-boil lasagna sheets, break the edges to fit into the pumpkin if necessary. Spread a little Butternut Squash Sauce under each sheet, and then more on top. Continue layering until the pumpkin is filled. Top with Parmesan cheese and bake for 30 minutes. Slice the pumpkin open and serve each piece on a wedge of cooked pumpkin. Garnish with watercress and toasted pumpkin seeds.

## PETIT ROBERT BISTRO

468 Commonwealth Avenue
Boston (Kenmore Square)
(617) 375-0699

480 Columbus Avenue
Boston (South End)
(617) 867-0600
www.petitrobertbistro.com

**Chef and co-owner | Jacky Robert**

In a city where most of the chefs who expertly make European food are Americans, Jacky Robert is a rarity—a chef born and trained in France. His last name is well known in Boston, as his uncle, Lucien Robert, owned the fine-dining Maison Robert (now closed) for more than thirty years. Jacky worked there early in his career, then returned in the 1990s to be the executive chef. In between, he owned a restaurant in San Francisco.

Petit Robert gives the chef a chance to re-create a French bistro with home-style food. Some of the dishes are exactly what you would find in France—house-made pâté, duck confit, roast rabbit. Robert also leaves room on his menu for lighthearted additions like the Burgerdog—ground beef shaped like a hot dog, grilled, and served on a split baguette—a favorite among Red Sox fans who file past en route to nearby Fenway Park. One of the desserts leans a miniature chocolate Eiffel tower against a slice of cake. The setting in a row of old brownstones is more American than French, but the ambience recaptures the French *joie de vivre* around a table.

This recipe shows Robert's flair for re-imagining classics. Ratatouille, a vegetable stew from Provence, is transformed when it is placed between the sheets of crisp dough that characterize a napoleon. Phyllo dough (sometimes spelled *fillo*) is a tissue-thin pastry that originated in Greece. It usually comes packaged in frozen sheets, available at a well-stocked supermarket. For a simpler variation, serve the ratatouille as a crepe filling, or as a garnish for fish or meat.

## RATATOUILLE NAPOLEON

[SERVES 4]

1 small eggplant, peeled and cut into ¼-inch cubes
Salt, to taste
3 tablespoons olive oil, divided
2 tablespoons finely chopped onion
1 green bell pepper, seeded and cut into ¼-inch cubes
2 tomatoes, peeled, seeded, and finely chopped
2 tablespoons finely chopped garlic
Bouquet garni made from 2–3 sprigs each of fresh thyme and
    parsley, plus 1 bay leaf, wrapped in cheesecloth and tied
    with a string
Cayenne pepper, to taste
1 small zucchini, cut into ¼-inch cubes
About 2 tablespoons (¼ stick) butter
4 sheets frozen phyllo dough, thawed
Parmesan cheese, for sprinkling
Fresh basil, cut into julienne, for garnish

1. Place the eggplant in a colander and sprinkle with salt. Place in a sink and let sit for 30 to 60 minutes to purge the bitterness.

2. In a large saucepan, heat 1 tablespoon of the olive oil. Sauté the onion and pepper for 5 minutes.

3. Add the tomatoes and garlic and simmer for 15 minutes. Add the bouquet garni. Season with salt and cayenne pepper.

4. Wash the salted eggplant pieces with running water and drain on paper towels. In a sauté pan, heat another tablespoon of the olive oil. Add the eggplant and sear until brown on all sides. Add to the tomato-onion mixture and cook for 10 minutes.

5. In a clean sauté pan, heat the remaining tablespoon of olive oil. Quickly sauté the zucchini pieces until they begin to brown. Add to the tomato-onion mixture and cook for another 10 minutes. Remove and discard the bouquet garni.

6. Preheat the oven to 350 degrees. Line two baking sheets with parchment paper. Melt the butter. Unroll one sheet of phyllo dough on a cutting board or work surface. Brush the top with butter. Unroll another sheet of phyllo dough and place on top of the first sheet. Using a sharp knife, cut the dough into 8 rectangles (3x4 inches each), each made from a double layer of dough. Carefully place the rectangles on a baking sheet. Brush the tops with butter and sprinkle with Parmesan cheese. Repeat the procedure to make 8 more rectangles on a second baking sheet.

7. Bake for 5 to 7 minutes, or until crisp and brown. Remove from the oven and let cool slightly.

8. Assemble each napoleon by placing a tablespoon or so of ratatouille on each of 4 serving plates. Place a double-layer rectangle of phyllo dough on top, then about 2 tablespoons of ratatouille. Continue until you have made 3 layers of phyllo and ratatouille. Place a double-layer rectangle of phyllo dough on top, sprinkle the top with basil, and serve. Repeat to make 4 servings.

## SWEET BASIL

942 Great Plain Avenue
Needham
(781) 444-9600, www.sweetbasilneedham.com

**Chef-owner | Dave Becker**

Before you even reach the front door of Sweet Basil, out wafts the aroma of garlic to guide your way. Along with basil, garlic is one of Becker's favorite ingredients. "I can't even taste it if there's less than a tablespoon of garlic in anything," he jokes. Both contribute to his real specialty: bold flavors. The menu's mainstays are robust Italian dishes such as rosemary chicken with pancetta and asparagus, and handmade four-cheese ravioli in basil marinara sauce. He improvises dishes like Gouda cheese baked in phyllo dough according to his mood and what's in the pantry.

From the kitchen at the back of the dining room, Becker often calls out greetings to customers. They stream in all day to eat, pick up menus, and just chat, giving the place the feel of a friend's house. Becker, who has been working in restaurants since he was growing up on Boston's North Shore, seems well adapted to the nonstop pace.

Becker put together this mushroom dish on the fly. The Italian word *ragu* means "sauce" as well as "appetite stimulant." "It's not supposed to be too saucy—it has a real vegetable flavor," he notes. The herbs, and plenty of ground black pepper, provide the accents. The sauce can be served plain, or over polenta or pasta.

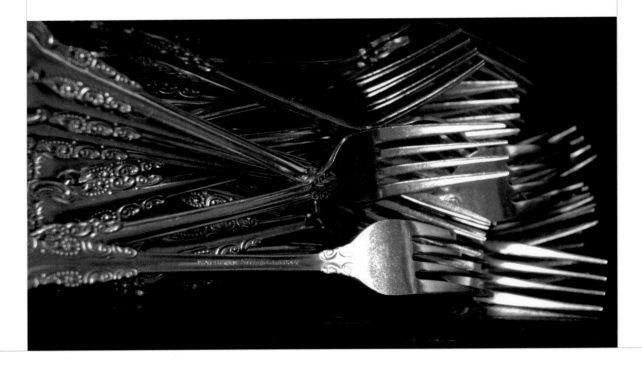

# POLENTA WITH MUSHROOM RAGU

[SERVES 4]

**POLENTA:**

2 cups water

2 cups heavy cream

1 teaspoon salt

1 cup yellow cornmeal

In a large saucepan, stir together the water, cream, and salt. Bring to a boil. Slowly stir in the cornmeal. Cook over low heat, stirring frequently, until the polenta is thick and pulls away from the side of the pan when it is stirred, 20 to 25 minutes. Turn out the polenta onto a plate or shallow bowl. Smooth the top with a wooden spoon. Let it cool slightly, then cut into wedges for serving.

**MUSHROOM RAGU:**

3 tablespoons olive oil

1 large Spanish onion, chopped

2 cups chopped carrots

½ stalk celery, chopped

2 tablespoons minced fresh garlic

Pinch each of rosemary, sage, and chile pepper flakes

4 portobello mushrooms, stems removed, each sliced into ½-inch-wide pieces

12 shiitake mushroom caps, sliced in half if large

12 button mushrooms, sliced thin

1 cup port wine (an inexpensive brand is fine)

1 cup chicken stock or water, as needed

1 cup diced tomatoes

Salt and pepper, to taste

2 tablespoons (¼ stick) butter

Parmesan cheese, for garnish

Chopped fresh parsley or basil, for garnish

1. In a large sauté pan, heat the olive oil. Add the onion, carrots, and celery. Sauté until the onion is brown. Add the garlic, herbs, and mushrooms. Continue to sauté until the mushrooms soften and begin to give off their liquid.

2. Deglaze the pan with the port. Simmer until the liquid is reduced by about half. Add enough stock or water to cover the mushrooms with liquid. Continue to simmer until the liquid is reduced and the sauce is thick. Add the tomatoes and simmer until they're incorporated. Season with salt and pepper. Add the butter, stirring until it melts.

3. Serve over wedges of Polenta (from recipe above) or pasta. Garnish with Parmesan, parsley, or basil.

# SIDE DISHES

Certain side dishes have become an almost essential part of the entrees they accompany—baked potatoes with steak; slaw with barbecue; sweet peppers and onions with sausages. As a result, many chefs find that their selection of side dishes simply falls into place. Instead of trying to reinvent mashed potatoes or creamed spinach, their challenge becomes how to liven up starchy rice, cornmeal, and potatoes. In this chapter vegetables from the Copley Square Farmers' Market reinvigorate risotto at L'Espalier. Chef Michael Schlow of Radius tosses lobster meat and ginger into fried rice. At Flora sweet potatoes are baked in a casserole with cornmeal and maple syrup.

No cookbook about Boston would be complete without a recipe for baked beans. The recipe from the venerable Union Oyster House, which has served meals continuously since 1826, upholds the tradition started by Puritans. Forbidden from cooking on the Sabbath, they found a solution by baking navy beans with salt pork and molasses a day ahead and eating them on Sunday. This widespread practice gave Boston its nickname *Beantown;* some nineteenth-century restaurateurs called the beans "Boston strawberries." A more modern interpretation of a bean side dish comes from Harvest, where cranberry beans are mashed and mixed with crème fraîche. A bean supper fed many a family in the past, though now beans have become more of a side dish, because meat is so much more readily available.

Whatever form they take, side dishes by definition do not become stars. Still, they are prized for their role as supporting players that enhance an entree.

## L'ESPALIER

30 Gloucester Street
Boston (Back Bay)
(617) 262–3023, www.lespalier.com

**Chef-owner | Frank McClelland**

When growers unload their vegetables at the Copley Square Farmers' Market (see the sidebar on page 158), Frank McClelland isn't far behind. He searches for glistening, just-harvested freshness, as well as ingredients for the night's menu. "That's why I'm in this business. It's very inspirational to make what's in season," says McClelland, who grew up on a farm in New Hampshire and purchased L'Espalier in 1988. This risotto recipe is a direct result of one of McClelland's shopping excursions. "I saw the beets and kale, and thought, *What can I do with these?*" The recipe works best in fall, when these vegetables are in season and goes well with roast chicken. For a gourmet touch, boil apple cider until the liquid is reduced and the flavors are concentrated, and drizzle a little around the plate of risotto.

L'Espalier's name is French for "carefully pruned tree," and McClelland does use some French techniques, but New England ingredients come first. The restaurant occupies a Back Bay mansion built in 1886; this is McClelland's laboratory for stunning combinations of the familiar and the luxurious—lobster gratin with white asparagus and fried quail egg; Valrhona dark chocolate fondant with chicory lime sauce. The attention to detail in each dish, and the Victorian setting, put this among the most romantic restaurants in Boston. One of the three dining rooms is informally called the "seduction room," because so many marriage proposals have been made at its tables. Particularly appealing is the built-in seat under a bay window containing five panes of stained glass. Potted orchids top the mantels everywhere. Because each room contains only about ten tables, dinner here feels like eating in a private home—not the home of an ordinary friend, but of a finely bred, gracious millionaire with impeccable taste.

## BEET AND KALE RISOTTO

[SERVES 4]

1 cup small-diced beets
3 cups vegetable stock or chicken stock
1 tablespoon olive oil
1 tablespoon butter
½ cup diced onion
½ cup Arborio rice
2 teaspoons garlic
½ cup white wine
⅓ cup heavy cream
½ cup grated Parmesan cheese
1 tablespoon kosher salt
¼ teaspoon ground white pepper
2 teaspoons lemon juice
2 teaspoons white truffle oil
½ cup kale leaves, washed, dried, and coarsely chopped

1. Place the beets in a saucepan. Add the stock, making sure the beets are covered with liquid. Simmer until tender. Drain and reserve the cooking liquid.

2. In a heavy-bottomed saucepan over medium-high heat, heat the olive oil and butter. Add the onion and sauté until it is translucent.

3. Lower the heat and add the Arborio rice. Sauté, stirring, for 3 to 4 minutes. Add the garlic and cook for 15 seconds.

4. Raise the heat to medium high. Add the white wine and stir constantly until it has been absorbed. Add the reserved cooking liquid from the beets, a little at a time, and repeat the same process. (The process of stirring and letting all the liquid absorb takes about 18 to 20 minutes altogether.) When all the liquid has been absorbed, add the beets, heavy cream, cheese, salt, pepper, lemon juice, and truffle oil.

5. Simmer until tender. Fold in the kale and let it warm through. Serve immediately.

# FARMERS' MARKETS

The first farmers' markets in the Boston area were decidedly unglamorous—farmers in flannel shirts selling muddy vegetables from the backs of their trucks. In the past fifteen years, however, their popularity has grown as city dwellers have rediscovered the quality and flavor of truly farm-fresh produce. Now these outdoor markets are held in parks, parking lots, and public squares all around Massachusetts (an estimated 125 were open in 2006, according to the Massachusetts Department of Agriculture). In Boston some of the most visible are at City Hall Plaza and Copley Square, Harvard Square in Cambridge, Coolidge Corner in Brookline, and Davis Square in Somerville. Farmers and other food producers display their offerings under tents, with amenities like produce scales and shopping bags.

The stock-in-trade is whatever produce is in season, though some vendors also sell farm-made cheese, flavored oils and vinegars, jams, and even fruit pies.

The Massachusetts Department of Agricultural Resources lists farmers' markets throughout the state at www.mass.gov/agr/massgrown. A year-round indoor market in the city is also being planned through the nonprofit Boston Public Market Association (www.bostonpublic market.org).

## RADIUS

8 High Street
Boston (Financial District)
(617) 426–1234, www.radiusrestaurant.com

**Chef-owner | Michael Schlow**

Almost always ahead of the curve in food trends is Radius, where you'll find locally grown string beans fried as tempura, salmon with caviar sauce, and french fries dusted with Parmesan cheese and truffles. It's all in good fun for Michael Schlow, who once threw a 92-mile-per-hour fastball but turned down a baseball scholarship to attend culinary school. He then worked at some of New York's top restaurants.

After moving to Boston, Schlow and his business partners opened Radius in 1999. The space complements the restaurant's name, with a sleek curved bar and a circular ceiling molding anchored by two white columns. Following the success of Radius, Schlow's team went on to open the

Italian-themed Via Matta in Park Plaza and Great Bay seafood restaurant in Kenmore Square.

This recipe gives Schlow, who calls himself an "alchemist" as well as chef, a chance to meld a fundamental New England ingredient and an Asian-style side dish. Ginger, rice wine vinegar, and soy sauce complement the naturally briny flavor of lobster. "I liked the way everything went together," Schlow reports. Have everything lined up: Once the pan is hot, you'll sprint through the cooking in less than 15 minutes. A nonstick pan helps keep everything from burning. Turn this into a main course by serving it with a salad. Make sure to squeeze lime juice on the final dish—it really boosts the flavors.

## SPICY LOBSTER AND SHIITAKE MUSHROOM FRIED RICE

[SERVES 4]

2 tablespoons canola oil
1 small carrot, finely diced
1 teaspoon chopped fresh gingerroot
2 cups cooked rice
1 cup sliced shiitake mushrooms
2 tablespoons lobster stock or vegetable stock
1 tablespoon soy sauce
¼ teaspoon hot sauce, such as Sriracha or Tabasco
1 tablespoon rice wine vinegar
1 tablespoon mirin (sweet Japanese rice wine)
1 small scallion, sliced
1 tablespoon chopped fresh cilantro
Salt and pepper, to taste
6 ounces cooked lobster meat, chopped into small pieces
4 lime wedges, for garnish

1. Place a large sauté pan over high heat. Add the oil and heat for 1 minute.

2. Add the carrot and ginger and cook for 30 seconds.

3. Add the rice and sauté for 1 to 2 minutes.

4. Add the shiitake mushrooms and cook for 1 to 2 minutes.

5. Add the lobster (or vegetable) stock, soy sauce, hot sauce, vinegar, and mirin. Cook for 30 seconds.

6. Add the scallions, cilantro, salt, pepper, and lobster meat. Heat for 30 seconds to 1 minute. Taste and adjust the seasoning if necessary.

7. Divide the rice among 4 plates. Garnish each serving with a lime wedge.

## UNION OYSTER HOUSE

41 Union Street
Boston (Downtown)
(617) 227–2750, www.unionoysterhouse.com

**Chef | Bill Coyne**

You can't get more historic than Ye Olde Union Oyster House, which has served meals continuously since 1826. The front door of the modest, three-story brick building still welcomes LADIES & GENTS. In 2003 it was designated a National Historic Landmark. A more modern touch for tourists on the Freedom Trail (a walking tour, marked by a red line painted on the sidewalk, past more than a dozen of Boston's historic sites) is the red neon sign for the restaurant mounted on the roof. Newcomers to Boston sometimes get their first up-close look at live lobsters in the tank near the front door. The semicircular oyster bar, where Daniel Webster once ordered a tumbler of brandy with half a dozen oysters, still draws a crowd for chowder and oysters on the half shell. The low ceiling (people were shorter back then) and the ship's model in the window add charm to the historic dining room. Specialties include the Lazy Man's Lobster (with the meat already removed from the shell and baked with bread crumbs), fried seafood platters, and broiled scrod (which is not a type of fish, but a special cut of cod or haddock).

For those who want a taste of Ye Olde Beantown, this recipe for baked beans has been in constant use over the years. No one is sure exactly when it was written down, but Bill Coyne is the latest chef to make it for customers.

### BOSTON BAKED BEANS

[SERVES 8]

1 pound dry white beans (navy or
    white Michigan)
3 ounces salt pork, rind removed
½ medium onion
2 cups tomato juice
1 cup light molasses
1 tablespoon brown sugar
1 tablespoon dry mustard
1 tablespoon garlic powder
Salt and pepper, to taste

1. Pick through the beans to remove pebbles and foreign objects. Place in a large bowl. Add cold water to cover. Set aside and let soak for 12 hours.

2. Dice the salt pork into ¼-inch cubes. In a 3-quart saucepan, sauté until the fat is rendered and the pork is browned. Add the onion and sauté until soft. Add the tomato juice, molasses, sugar, mustard, garlic powder, salt, and pepper. Mix well.

3. Add the beans and simmer over low heat for 2 hours, until the beans are tender and the sauce is brown and about the thickness of plain yogurt.

## HARVEST

44 Brattle Street
Cambridge (Harvard Square)
(617) 868-2255, www.harvestcambridge.com

**Executive Chef | Keith Pooler**

Harvest, one of the first restaurants in Boston to promote seasonal New England food, opened in 1976 with the celebrity appeal of its owner, architect Ben Thompson. He's the local hero who also helped revitalize Faneuil Hall Marketplace (see the sidebar on page 106). Trendsetting chefs soon followed, and the kitchen helped launch Lydia Shire (see page 184), Chris Schlesinger (see page 94), and Frank McClelland (see page 156).

Completely redecorated from its days of mod 1970s chic, Harvest is now owned and managed by the team responsible for Grill 23 & Bar (see page 30) and Excelsior (see page 44). The outdoor garden terrace—with heat lamps to extend the season—is a linden-and-umbrella-shaded urban oasis. Keith Pooler has remained true to Harvest's original mission to bring out the best in New

England food. His poached halibut comes with baby fennel confit and black trumpet mushrooms. Corn bread croutons top a Bibb lettuce salad.

One year the fall harvest of cranberry beans (also called shell or borlotti beans) caught chef Pooler's attention. The cream-colored beans, also grown in Italy, have distinctive red streaks and a slightly nutty flavor. He came up with a side dish akin to a New England version of refried beans. The beans are simmered with seasonings and then mashed (not pureed). "The fresh beans have a velvety texture, and the crème fraîche adds a little tang to them," he says. Their assertive, almost smoky flavor stands up well to hearty pork, duck, and beef entrees. Serve them as an alternative to mashed potatoes.

## CRANBERRY BEAN MASH

[SERVES 6 AS A SIDE DISH]

1 tablespoon butter
1 large onion, diced
2 stalks celery, finely chopped
3–4 cloves garlic, minced
½ pound prosciutto trimmings (optional)
4–5 sprigs thyme
5 cups fresh shelled cranberry, or dried borlotti or white, beans (if using dried beans, soak 2 cups overnight, then proceed)
6–7 cups chicken stock
Kosher salt and pepper, to taste
Approximately ½ cup crème fraîche

1. In a sauté pan, melt the butter. Sauté the onion, celery, and garlic until the onion is translucent. Add the prosciutto and thyme. Wrap this mixture in cheesecloth and tie with a string (dental floss works well) to make a bouquet garni.

2. In a heavy-bottomed pot, place the sachet and the beans. Add enough chicken stock to cover the beans by 1 to 1½ inches. Bring to a boil and then reduce the heat and simmer for 1 hour, occasionally stirring gently for even cooking. The beans should then be tender.

3. Add salt and pepper to the beans immediately when they are done cooking. This is important because as the beans cool, they will soak up the flavorful liquid and take on the seasoning as well. Let the beans cool; then strain them, reserving the liquid. Discard the bouquet garni. Stir the crème fraîche into the beans. If necessary, adjust the consistency by adding a little of the cooking liquid or additional crème fraîche.

4. In a saucepan, gently reheat the beans, mashing with a fork as they warm, leaving some whole or in large pieces to give the mash texture. Do not use a food processor.

## LINEAGE

242 Harvard Street
Brookline
(617) 232-0065, www.lineagerestaurant.com

**Chef-owner | Jeremy Sewall**

When Jeremy Sewall finally found a spot for his soon-to-open restaurant, he noticed a street sign nearby for Sewall Avenue. He already knew that one of his ancestors, Judge Samuel Sewall, had presided at the Salem witch trials. What he soon learned was that Samuel's son inherited an estate in Brookline and was the first town clerk. "I wish we still owned the estate," he jokes. Still, the family connections gave him the idea for the restaurant's name—Lineage—and the sense that "this was meant to be."

With its yellow walls and wood-burning oven in the center, the dining room creates a comfortable backdrop for thoughtfully composed dishes. Sewall and his wife, Lisa, print a new menu each day so they can take advantage of whatever is fresh. Seafood is a specialty—roasted halibut, spicy seviche tacos, house-smoked salmon. When possible, Sewall shops at the farmers' market for accompaniments that in spring might include fava beans, wild ramps, and spring onions.

The extended Sewall family also figures prominently into this recipe for New England fall vegetables. "I made this dish for a Thanksgiving dinner one year. There are some vegetarians in the family, and I wanted to make something they could enjoy," he recounts. His mix of parsnips, potatoes, and squash, seasoned with browned butter and fresh lemon juice, was such a hit that he added the dish to the Lineage menu. "It's attractive on the table. The colors are beautiful!"

# FALL VEGETABLE HASH

[SERVES 6-8]

1 pound fingerling potatoes, washed well
2 tablespoons olive oil
1½ teaspoons chopped fresh rosemary
1½ tablespoons unsalted butter
1 small butternut squash, peeled and diced
    into ¼-inch pieces
2 parsnips, peeled and diced into ¼-inch pieces
1½ shallots, peeled and sliced thin
1 clove garlic, minced
½ cup dried cranberries (optional)
1 cup baby spinach leaves
Juice and zest of ½ lemon
Salt and pepper, to taste

1. Preheat the oven to 350 degrees. Slice the fingerling
   potatoes into quarters and place in a roasting pan. Toss
   with the olive oil and rosemary. Bake for 20 to 30 minutes, or until lightly brown. Cool at room temperature.

2. In a large, nonstick pan, melt the butter and continue
   heating until it begins to brown. Add the squash and
   parsnips. Cook until they brown and begin to soften.
   Add the shallots and garlic. Sauté for 2 minutes. If the
   garlic and shallots begin to brown, lower the heat.

3. Add the reserved potatoes, cranberries, and spinach.
   Gently stir until the spinach is wilted. Season with lemon
   juice, lemon zest, salt, and pepper. Serve at once.

### FLORA

190 Massachusetts Avenue
Arlington
(781) 641-1664, www.florarestaurant.com

**Chef-owner | Bob Sargent**

Flora makes the most of New England ingredients by sending its staff to shop at the Arlington Farmers' Market and taking deliveries from small-scale farmers as long as the growing season holds out. Seafood, cheeses, and meats from local providers—credited by name—figure prominently on the menu. Bob Sargent's ingenuity for combining these ingredients shows up in crisp cod cakes with spicy tomato caper sauce and in maple panna cotta with poached pears. Open since 1996, the main dining room was originally a bank built in the 1920s. It retains some of the original

architectural flourishes, including two-story windows, a vaulted ceiling, and a mahogany vestibule. Despite the formal silk curtains, this is a lively place for couples and groups of friends to pass plates around while watching the action in the open kitchen.

This side dish is a fun twist on southern spoon bread, using maple syrup as the sweetener. The cornmeal adds a slight crunch to its otherwise light texture. It goes well with meat or poultry, making a nice change from the standard accompaniments of bread or white potatoes. Leftovers make a good breakfast. Hard-core maple syrup fans can even drizzle a bit on top for a flavor boost.

## SWEET POTATO SPOON BREAD

[SERVES 4-6]

2 sweet potatoes (approximately 1 pound each)
1 cup milk
6 tablespoons cornmeal
2 eggs
3–4 tablespoons maple syrup
1 teaspoon baking powder
½ teaspoon salt

1. Grease an 8x8-inch baking dish with butter and set aside. Preheat the oven to 400 degrees. Scrub the potatoes and prick them with a fork. Place the potatoes on a baking sheet or directly on the oven rack. Bake until soft, approximately 1 hour. Remove and let cool. Peel the potatoes, mash them lightly with a fork, and measure out $1^{1}/_{2}$ cups of cooked sweet potato. Set aside.

2. Lower the oven temperature to 350 degrees.

3. In a large saucepan, bring the milk to a boil. Turn off the heat and whisk in the cornmeal, a little at a time, as if you were making polenta. Let it cool a bit. Stir in the $1^{1}/_{2}$ cups cooked sweet potatoes until fairly smooth (no need to fret over small lumps).

4. Meanwhile, separate the eggs. Using an electric mixer, whip the egg whites with the maple syrup until soft peaks form.

5. Mix the egg yolks, baking powder, and salt into the cornmeal-potato mixture. Fold in the egg whites.

6. Pour into the prepared baking dish and bake at 350 degrees for about 40 minutes, or just until a toothpick inserted in the center comes out dry.

# DESSERTS

In seventeenth-century Massachusetts there was no such thing as dessert. Anything sweet—pie, custard, or pudding—was served along with the rest of the meal. The public has made up for it since then. In the past twenty-five years, the state legislature has designated several official sweets, in many cases at the request of schoolchildren: the chocolate chip cookie (created in 1930 at the Toll House Restaurant in Whitman), the corn muffin, the Boston cream pie (which bested the Toll House cookie and Indian pudding for the title of the state's official dessert), and the Boston cream doughnut.

All these official desserts have given pastry chefs a strong base from which to launch their own creations. In this chapter, continuing a classic is the Omni Parker House, where the Boston cream pie originated. Also sticking close to New England tradition is Prose's maple custard with three ingredients—eggs, maple syrup, and cream. Gabriel Bremer of Salts stakes out less familiar territory by adding thyme and sage to his honey-glazed poached pear. Chefs get crazier with cranberries. Ming Tsai of Blue Ginger mixes them with lychees for a sweet salsa to go with shortcakes.

Chocolate represents a newer wave of New England desserts. Finale, Boston's own dessert-focused restaurant, packs plenty of high-quality bittersweet and semisweet chocolate into its recipe for moist, chewy cookies. In a final blow to the Puritan ethic of self-denial, the Chocolate Bar at the Langham Hotel sets out a buffet each week with more than seventy selections of cakes, pies, and truffles—with gluttony encouraged.

## PROSE

352A Massachusetts Avenue
Arlington
(781) 648-2800, www.prosefood.com

**Chef-owner | Deborah Shore**

Walking into Prose feels a bit like walking into a friend's quirky, eclectically furnished home. Deborah Shore puts her personal touch on the tableware, a mismatched assortment of Melmac, Fiesta ware, Depression glass, and other flea market finds. One salt-and-pepper pair might be a replica of King Kong and the Empire State Building; another might be ceramic apple slices. There is a folk CD on the stereo, and photos of New York City street scenes adorn the mustard-yellow-painted wall.

Shore changes her menu nearly every day to reflect both the season and her mood. Her flourishes shine through in pomegranate glaze on chicken potpie, and saffron mustard caraway cream on beet fettuccine. This maple custard has been a mainstay of the dessert menu since Prose opened in 1996. "It's a take on classic custard, using maple syrup instead of sugar. It's sort of retro," she reports as she scurries between the dining room and kitchen, her curls peeking out from beneath a scarf. As if to prove it, she adds with a chuckle, "I bake it in my mother's Pyrex dish from the 1970s." An unadorned, beige slice looks humble on the plate, but one bite packs a wallop of maple flavor. Forget comparing it to plain syrup or crumbly maple sugar candy. This dense, smooth custard is an irresistible vehicle for delivering that essential New England taste of maple.

## MAPLE CUSTARD

[SERVES 10-12]

5 egg yolks
4 whole eggs
1⅓ cups pure maple syrup, preferably Grade B
    (see sidebar)
1 quart heavy cream

1. Leave the ingredients at room temperature for 1 hour before you begin baking.

2. Preheat the oven to 400 degrees.

3. In a large bowl, whisk together the egg yolks, whole eggs, and maple syrup. Whisk in the cream.

4. Pour the batter into an ungreased, 9x11-inch Pyrex baking dish. Place the Pyrex dish in a water bath.

5. Carefully place both pans (you don't want the water to slosh out) into the oven. Bake for 45 minutes to 1 hour, rotating the pans every 15 minutes so the custard cooks evenly. The custard is done when it is slightly jiggly, the top is golden brown, and a knife inserted in the center comes out clean.

6. Remove both pans from the oven and let the custard cool to room temperature in the water bath. Then cover the custard with plastic wrap and refrigerate. Slice into individual rectangles and serve.

# Maple Syrup

Maple syrup is nothing more than tree sap that has been boiled—and boiled and boiled. Native Americans were the first to slash the trunks of sugar maples in early spring, to let the sweet sap drip out. In the 1700s settlers were doing the same and boiling the sap to thicken it and concentrate its sweetness. Most of it was made into sugar and used as an alternative to the expensive white sugar produced in the Caribbean. Vermont is now the country's leading maple syrup producer. Massachusetts ranks sixth nationwide, with its farmers producing about 50,000 gallons of syrup annually, according to the Massachusetts Maple Producers Association (www.massmaple.org).

Maple syrup is graded by color and flavor, based on a federally regulated scale. Grade A Light Amber is the lightest and has the most delicate flavor. Grade A Medium and Grade A Dark Amber have successively darker color and stronger flavor. The darkest of all, Grade B, has the most intense maple flavor—verging on caramel—which makes it a good choice for baking.

## SALTS

798 Main Street
Cambridge (Central Square)
(617) 876–8444, www.saltsrestaurant.com

**Chef-owner | Gabriel Bremer**

Red velvet drapes, fresh flowers, and candles in glass chandeliers make Salts feel like an elegant country inn. From a kitchen that only fits three people at one time come thoughtfully composed dishes like boneless chicken tied in a bundle and served with apricot white bean puree, fried sage leaf, and cocoa citrus brown butter. The soft-spoken Bremer, who often pauses to gather his thoughts before speaking, sums up his philosophy this way: "We like to keep familiar flavors, but use new techniques and modern elements." His father grows many of the vegetables; the kitchen staff sometimes take a field trip to harvest them.

At Salts this poached pear is served in a trilogy of desserts meant to "frame and highlight each other," explains Bremer, who wears his hair in a ponytail. He and pastry chef Francisco Samaron came up with pear sorbet and bay-leaf-spiced flan to accompany the pear, which literally shines with its honey glaze. At home you can garnish each serving of pear with vanilla ice cream or sweetened fresh ricotta—or just serve it plain.

### ROASTED SECKEL PEAR WITH HONEY AND CLOVE

[SERVES 6]

¼ cup honey, preferably wild mountain
  (available at specialty markets; see notes)
½ teaspoon whole cloves
6 ripe Seckel pears, peeled and cored (see notes)
2 tablespoons (¼ stick) unsalted butter
3 sprigs fresh thyme
1 fresh bay leaf (optional)
Pinch of salt

1. Preheat the oven to 350 degrees. In a large ovenproof sauté pan over low heat, simmer the honey and cloves until the mixture begins to reduce and caramelize, about 4 to 5 minutes.

2. Add the pears, butter, thyme, and bay leaf and simmer over low heat until the pears begin to turn light golden, about 10 minutes. Transfer to the oven and roast the pears until tender, 10 to 20 minutes, basting with the pan juices every 5 minutes.

3. Drizzle the honey mixture from the pan juices over the pears and serve hot or warm.

:: **Notes:** Wild mountain honey comes from bees that gather nectar from wildflowers; its flavor is stronger than the more commonly found clover honey.

The Seckel pear is a small, firm variety that stands up well to poaching. You can substitute Bosc or another firm-fleshed pear in this recipe.

## VERRILL FARM

11 Wheeler Road
Concord
(978) 369-4494, www.verrillfarm.com

**Owner and baker | Jennifer Verrill Faddoul**

As one of the owners of Verrill Farm in Concord (see page 36), Jennifer Verrill Faddoul has unlimited access to rhubarb and fresh berries from the fields. Her fruit pies, which she sells at the farm stand, are a local legend. At the height of the growing season, the farm might sell 125 in one day. Varying the mix of fruits according to what's in season, Faddoul seems to capture the essence of summer. She has managed to find the right proportions of butter and sugar, so whatever fruit combination she chooses for the filling is not overwhelmed by sweetness or a heavy crust. Ice cream or whipped cream only enhances each slice of this classic combination of two early-season crops: tart rhubarb and sweet strawberries.

# STRAWBERRY RHUBARB PIE

[MAKES 1 (9-INCH) PIE]

**PIECRUST:**

2¼ cups flour
¼ cup sugar
½ teaspoon salt
1 cup (2 sticks) cold butter, cut into approximately
    ¼-inch pieces
¼ cup cold water

1. In the bowl of a food processor, add the flour, sugar, salt, and butter. Process until the butter is the size of coarse crumbs. Add the water and pulse until the dough begins to come together. Alternatively, place the flour, sugar, and salt in a mixing bowl. Add the butter and use a pastry knife or your fingers to mix in the butter.

2. Shape the dough into a ball and cover with plastic wrap; refrigerate for at least 1 hour before rolling out. This recipe makes 3 (9-inch) pie shells. Leftover dough may be wrapped in plastic and kept in the freezer for several months.

3. To make one pie, cut off a third of the chilled dough. Sprinkle flour on a clean, flat work surface. Using a rolling pin, roll the dough out until it is about 11 inches in diameter. Place the dough on top of a 9-inch pie plate and gently press it down so it rests against the sides. Trim any crust that hangs over the rim. Use your thumb to press the remaining crust on top of the rim, forming a decorative edge. Set aside until ready to fill.

**FILLING FOR ONE PIE:**

4½ cups sliced rhubarb (½- to ¾-inch pieces)
1½ cups hulled and sliced strawberries
¾–1 cup sugar, to taste
3 tablespoons cornstarch
Pinch of orange zest

Gently mix all the ingredients together in a bowl.

**CRUMB TOPPING:**

1 cup flour
¼ cup granulated sugar
¼ cup brown sugar
½ cup (1 stick) cold butter, cut into approximately
    ¼-inch pieces

Place all the ingredients into the bowl of a food processor. Process just until coarse crumbs form. Do not overprocess. Alternatively, place the flour and sugars in a bowl. Add the butter and use a pastry cutter or your fingers to mix it in.

**FINAL PREPARATION AND SERVING:**

1. Preheat the oven to 375 degrees.

2. Spoon the filling into the pie shell, smoothing it with the back of the spoon so it is evenly distributed.

3. Sprinkle with about 2 cups of the crumb topping, completely covering the fruit so none is visible. (Extra topping can be refrigerated for future use.)

4. Bake for about 55 minutes, until the juices are thick and bubbly and the crumb topping is crisp. If the juices are too watery, return the pan to the oven for about 5 minutes and check again.

5. Let cool and serve with whipped cream or vanilla ice cream (both optional).

## LUMIÈRE

1293 Washington Street
West Newton
(617) 244–9199, www.lumiererestaurant.com

**Chef-owner | Michael Leviton**

Michael Leviton grew up right near the restaurant he now owns, but he took a roundabout route to get there. After earning a degree in psychology, he moved to San Francisco and decided to become a chef—in large part, he admits, "because I couldn't sit still, and cooking kept me physically occupied while I was also learning a lot." He worked in some of the city's top restaurants, including Square One with chef Joyce Goldstein. A visit to France sparked his interest in cooking at French restaurants in California and New York. By the time he moved back home and opened Lumière in 1999, he could confidently re-create French bistro dishes, but also let in New England touches. His highly personal style is reflected in artichoke soup with lemon crème fraîche, mint, and croutons; and Cape Cod haddock with green beans, chanterelle mushrooms, almonds, and lemon brown butter.

Gauzy curtains and booths backed with fabric in swirls of burgundy add sophisticated touches to the airy dining room. "Strawberry shortcake with a twist" is how Leviton describes this recipe. He made the biscuits when he stumbled across Bakewell Cream, a type of baking powder made only in Maine, by going to a general store in a tiny town where he was vacationing. Pairing the biscuits with strawberries naturally followed—especially the berries grown nearby. "They have a ton more flavor than what comes from California, and we're keeping the recipe local," he says. Orange juice adds a surprise element to the berries and cream.

# BISCUITS WITH NATIVE STRAWBERRIES
# AND ORANGE WHIPPED CREAM

[ S E R V E S   6 ]

## BISCUITS:

2 cups flour
½ teaspoon salt
2 teaspoons baking powder (see note)
2 tablespoons butter, chilled
2 tablespoons shortening, chilled
¾ cup milk
1 egg
1 tablespoon milk
Coarse sugar, for sprinkling

1. Preheat the oven to 450 degrees.

2. In a mixing bowl, sift together the flour, salt, and baking powder.

3. Cut the butter and shortening into pea-size pieces. Add the butter and shortening to the flour mixture. Using your fingers, quickly pinch together the shortening and butter so the pieces break up and incorporate into the dry ingredients. Add the ¾ cup milk, mixing gently with your free hand. Turn the dough out onto a clean counter or other flat work surface and finish gathering it together into a ball.

4. Press the dough into a ½-inch-thick disk. Using a biscuit cutter or an overturned glass, cut out biscuits about 2½ to 3 inches in diameter.

5. In a small bowl, beat together the egg and with 1 tablespoon milk to make an egg wash. Brush the tops of the biscuits with the egg wash. Sprinkle lightly with sugar. Bake for 10 minutes. Turn the oven off, but allow the biscuits to cook for 5 more minutes before removing them from the oven.

:: **Note:** If you have Bakewell Cream, use 2 teaspoons of it and 1 teaspoon of baking soda in place of the baking powder.

## STRAWBERRIES:

3 cups strawberries, rinsed and quartered
Juice of ½ orange
3 tablespoons sugar

Combine the ingredients and let sit for 30 minutes.

## ORANGE WHIPPED CREAM:

1 cup heavy cream, very cold
2¼ teaspoons granulated sugar
½ tablespoon orange zest
½ tablespoon orange juice

Combine all the ingredients in a mixing bowl and beat vigorously with an electric mixer until soft peaks form. Place the cream in the refrigerator until needed.

## FINAL PREPARATION AND SERVING:

1. Preheat the oven to 475 degrees.

2. Cut 4 biscuits crosswise. Place the biscuit halves, cut-side up, on a sheet pan and place in the oven for 3 to 5 minutes, until hot and slightly crispy on the edges.

3. Place one of the bottom biscuit halves, cut-side up, in the center of each plate. Top with the berries. Use the liquid from the berries as your sauce and spoon a little around the plate. Top with the whipped cream and then the top biscuit half.

## BLUE GINGER

583 Washington Street
Wellesley
(781) 283–5790, www.ming.com

**Chef-owner | Ming Tsai**

In the WGBH-TV studio where Julia Child once taped her shows, Ming Tsai is a standout in the new generation of showbiz chefs. His relaxed, personable style helps demystify Asian ingredients for the viewers of *Simply Ming*. Blue Ginger, open since 1998, is where you can taste the "East meets West" dishes that define his style. Unexpected combinations like lobster with lemongrass fried rice, or chicken with tamarind hoisin sauce, keep the dining room buzzing. The well-dressed crowd comes to be wowed, and the stainless-steel kitchen, which runs lengthwise down the main dining room, obliges. It sizzles with meats being pan-seared, and bustles with cooks angling for the precise placement of garnishes like Thai basil.

Asian accents in the dining room are subtle—a rice-paper panel dividing one room from another, a scroll in a corner. Tsai was well prepared to reinterpret East and West by growing up in Dayton, Ohio, where his family owned a Chinese restaurant. He earned degrees from Yale and Cornell before becoming a chef.

You can't get more New England than the cranberry, or more Asian than the lychee, a white fruit approximately the size of a golf ball that is a delicacy in China (canned lychees are most easily found in the United States). Tsai coarsely chops both for a shortcake topping. "Salsa isn't just for savory applications," he says. "I enjoy making a sweet salsa and using it in a variety of ways." Don't omit the whipped cream, which ties together the different components. With the enthusiasm that makes his show so much fun to watch, he says, "I love the contrast in this dish of the sweet-tart salsa with the mild whipped cream and buttery biscuit." You might like the combination so much, you'll eat up eating it for breakfast.

# LYCHEE CRANBERRY SHORTCAKE

[SERVES 4]

**LYCHEE CRANBERRY SALSA:**

MAKES 1 QUART

2 cans lychees, drained (20 ounces each; available
    at Asian specialty markets)
1 bag cranberries (12 ounces)
½ cup sugar
Zest of 1 orange
Juice of 1 orange
2 teaspoons vanilla extract

Combine all the ingredients in a food processor and blend
until medium coarse in texture. Transfer to a container,
cover, and refrigerate for up to 2 weeks. In addition to using
this recipe in desserts, it's great as an accompaniment to
pork or poultry.

**SWEET BISCUITS:**

MAKES 24 BISCUITS (2½–3 INCHES EACH)

¾ cup (1½ sticks) butter, very cold
5 cups all-purpose flour
2 teaspoons salt
1 tablespoon baking powder
⅔ cup sugar
Zest of 1 lemon, grated
2 eggs
2 cups heavy cream, plus more as needed
2 teaspoons vanilla extract
Turbinado or coarse sugar, for sprinkling

1.  Cube the butter into walnut-size pieces and place in the
    refrigerator.

2.  In a large mixing bowl, whisk together the flour, salt, bak-
    ing powder, sugar, and lemon zest. Using an electric mixer,
    mix the butter into the dry ingredients until the butter is
    broken down in size a bit, but not fully incorporated.

3.  In a medium bowl, whisk together the eggs, cream, and
    vanilla extract. Add the egg mixture slowly to the flour
    mixture until well incorporated, but not overmixed.

4.  Remove the dough from the bowl and place it on a
    lightly floured surface. Form it into a loose ball and
    cover tightly in plastic wrap. Place in the refrigerator
    for 30 minutes.

5.  Preheat the oven to 350 degrees.

6.  Remove the dough from the refrigerator and place it on
    a floured work surface. Roll to ½ inch thick, fold it in half,
    and roll it back out to ½ inch thick. Cut it into 2½- to
    3-inch squares.

7.  Line 2 baking sheets with parchment paper or lightly
    grease them with butter. Put the shortcakes on the bak-
    ing sheets. Brush the top of each with heavy cream and
    sprinkle with sugar. Bake for 20 to 30 minutes, or until
    golden brown. Remove from the oven and let cool.

**FINAL PREPARATION AND SERVING:**

4 Sweet Biscuits (from recipe above), or best-quality
    store-bought biscuits
2 cups Lychee Cranberry Salsa (from recipe above)
2 cups sweetened whipped cream
Mint sprigs, for garnish (optional)

Split each biscuit in half horizontally and spoon a generous
amount of Lychee Cranberry Salsa onto the bottom half.
Replace the top biscuit half and cover with more salsa and
whipped cream. Garnish with a mint sprig.

## CASABLANCA

40 Brattle Street
Cambridge (Harvard Square)
(617) 876–0999, www.casablanca-restaurant.com

**Former chef | Ruth-Anne Adams**

For its first thirty-five years, Casablanca paid tribute to the classic movie in name and decor only. It was mostly a bar with giant murals depicting scenes from the movie. When Sari Abul-Jubein and other investors bought it in 1991, they added the menu that had been missing all those years—North African and Mediterranean fare.

A mural with Bogart at one end and Bacall at the other still dominates the dining room, with ceiling fans and an atrium adding an appropriately airy touch. Wicker chairs enhance the tropical feel. Former chef Ruth-Anne Adams, who is equally well versed in Mediterranean and New England fare, paid tribute to a Massachusetts favorite with this Cranberry Pecan Praline Tart. Adams outlines the steps that led her to this recipe: "I wanted a nut dessert, and I always loved pecans and chocolate together. The cranberries were to add some high tones to the sweet dessert, and the color was nice as well. The coconut was the influence of the pastry cook, and I thought it would make a nice addition to the texture of the crust." All the ingredients come together in a thoughtful reinterpretation of pecan pie. To work ahead, mix the crust one day and bake the tart the next.

# CRANBERRY PECAN PRALINE TART

[MAKES 1 TART (SERVES 8)]

**CHOCOLATE COCONUT CRUST:**

¾ cup plus 1 tablespoon (1½ sticks plus
    1 tablespoon) butter
½ cup sugar
1 egg
1 egg yolk
½ teaspoon vanilla extract
2½ cups (12 ounces) pastry flour
⅓ cup cocoa, sifted
Pinch of salt
2 tablespoons shredded coconut, toasted

1.  In the bowl of an electric mixer, cream the butter and
    sugar. Add the egg and the yolk, mixing well after each
    addition. Add the vanilla and mix in.

2.  Add the flour, sifted cocoa, and salt. Mix until just com-
    bined. Mix in the coconut. Form into a large disk, cover,
    and refrigerate for at least 2 hours.

**CRANBERRY TOPPING:**

2 cups fresh cranberries, rinsed and drained
¼ cup sugar

In a saucepan, sauté the cranberries with the sugar over
medium heat just until the sugar dissolves, but the cranberries are still whole. Set aside.

**NUT FILLING:**

2 eggs
½ cup sugar
¼ cup (½ stick) butter, melted
1½ teaspoons all-purpose flour
Pinch of salt
½ teaspoon vanilla extract
½ cup corn syrup
1½ cups pecans, toasted and roughly chopped
    to the size of peas
½ cup shredded coconut, toasted (see note)

In a mixing bowl, mix the eggs with a whisk. Add the sugar,
melted butter, flour, salt, vanilla, and corn syrup. Stir in the
pecans and coconut.

**:: Note:** Coconut can be toasted in a dry skillet. Heat the
skillet over high heat, add the coconut, and toss with a
spoon until it's fragrant and lightly brown, 5 minutes or less.
Watch carefully: Coconut burns easily.

**FINAL PREPARATION AND SERVING:**

Whipped cream or crème fraîche, for garnish

1.  Use a 9½ x 1-inch tart shell with a removable bottom.
    Spray the shell with nonstick spray. Roll the chocolate
    dough with a little flour to ¼ inch thick. Press the shell
    into the pan and refrigerate for 30 minutes. (You may
    have crust left over, which you can roll out, cut, and bake
    as cookies.)

2.  Prebake the tart shell in a 350-degree oven for 7 minutes.
    Remove from the oven and pour in the nut filling. It
    should fill to just below the top of the shell. Sprinkle the
    cranberries evenly on the top.

3.  Bake at 350 degrees for 15 minutes. The tart should look
    underbaked in the middle and set around the edges.
    Garnish each slice with whipped cream or a spoonful of
    crème fraîche sweetened with a little sugar.

## LOCKE-OBER

3 Winter Place
Boston
(617) 542–1340, www.locke-ober.com

**Chef-partner | Lydia Shire**

The Locke-Ober is a Boston legend, but gone is the upper-crust atmosphere that once welcomed celebrities including poet Ogden Nash and President John F. Kennedy, but excluded women from its dining rooms until 1970. Now directing the kitchen is a woman with bright red hair and even more dazzling culinary ideas. She's Lydia Shire, who shook up the city's beans and brown bread stalwarts in the 1990s by serving offal as well as lobster pizza at BIBA, her first (and now closed) restaurant.

Shire purchased Locke-Ober with a business partner in 2001. She kept traditional steak au poivre and JFK's lobster stew on the menu while overseeing more creative dishes like mini lobster melts with fried clams, and halibut with grilled oysters and lemongrass lime sauce. "It's half old, half new recipes," she says.

Shire frequently makes this Baked Lemon Pudding with ginger cookies for family and friends at her suburban home. Nearly every surface in the kitchen here is decorated with the knick-knacks that she collects, from art glass to miniature tableware. Her design sense is as playful as her food. So what if the light fixtures and knobs on the cabinets don't match? She happily justifies it by stating, "There's a great beauty in things not being symmetrical."

# BAKED LEMON PUDDING

[SERVES 8]

**PUDDING:**

1 cup (2 sticks) butter
1 cup sugar
6 egg yolks
¼ cup flour
1 teaspoon salt
¾ cup freshly squeezed lemon juice (from 3–4 lemons)
1 cup milk
1 cup buttermilk
½ cup heavy cream
6 egg whites

1. Preheat the oven to 350 degrees. Using an electric mixer, mix the butter and sugar until light and creamy. Add the egg yolks 1 at a time, mixing well after each addition. Add the flour and salt and mix until well incorporated.

2. In a separate bowl, combine the lemon juice, milk, buttermilk, and heavy cream.

3. With the beater running, pour the butter mixture into the lemon-milk mixture and continue beating for 1 to 2 minutes. The mixture will not stick together, appearing broken. (This is because the lemon juice, an acid, reacts with the milk and cream, curdling it. In this case, curdling is just a chemical reaction and does not mean the batter is spoiled!)

4. Pour this mixture into a large bowl and set aside.

5. Clean and thoroughly dry the mixing bowl. Add the egg whites and beat until soft peaks form. Fold into the butter-lemon mixture.

6. Pour the batter into a greased 9x13-inch baking pan. Place this pan into a water bath. Bake until golden brown and set, 45 to 60 minutes.

7. Serve warm with softly whipped cream and ginger cookies (recipe follows).

**GINGER COOKIES:**

MAKES ABOUT 5 DOZEN

¾ cup (1½ sticks) butter
1 cup packed brown sugar
1 egg
1½ cups flour
1 teaspoon salt
½ teaspoon baking soda
2 teaspoons chopped crystallized ginger

1. Preheat the oven to 350 degrees. Using an electric mixer, beat the butter and brown sugar until light and creamy, stopping once or twice to scrape down the sides of the bowl.

2. Add the egg and continue beating to combine.

3. In a separate bowl, sift together the flour, salt, and baking soda.

4. Place the crystallized ginger in the bowl of a food processor, add a pinch of flour, and process into small pieces. (Do not overprocess, or the ginger will clump up and turn sticky.) Stir into the flour mixture.

5. Add the flour mixture to the butter mixture and beat just until combined. Do not overmix.

6. Line a cookie sheet with parchment paper. Scoop out the batter by the heaping teaspoon, leaving at least ½ inch in between each cookie. Bake for 10 to 12 minutes, or until golden brown. (Bake less for softer, chewier cookies; more for crisp ones.) Cool on a wire rack before serving.

## BRICCO

241 Hanover Street
Boston (North End)
(617) 248–6800, www.bricco.com

**Former chef | Marisa Iocco**

Bricco represents the wave of more modern Italian restaurants in the North End (for a neighborhood overview, see the sidebar on page 190). It offers a similar mix of cutting-edge and traditional food as sister restaurant Umbria (see page 6). Bricco's menu takes risks with traditional dishes—wrapping cod with eggplant slices; pairing Maine lobster with angel-hair pasta, sausage, and chestnuts. For more conventional appetites a wood-burning oven turns out a late-night pizza menu. With mahogany-trimmed windows and seats facing the sidewalk, the dining room attracts a chic crowd from the hordes strolling Hanover Street. Still, everyone seems to go for this homey bread pudding, developed by former executive chef Marisa Iocco. Though many bread pudding recipes call for mixing in raisins, nuts, or cinnamon, Iocco prefers to keep things simple, reaffirming the adage: "Less is more."

### SIGNATURE BREAD PUDDING

[SERVES 6-8]

1 loaf (1 pound) crusty, day-old Italian bread
1 vanilla bean, split in half lengthwise, or
    1 teaspoon pure vanilla extract
2 cups heavy cream
2 cups whole milk
1 cup sugar
3 eggs
Caramel sauce, for serving (available in jars at
    grocery stores)

1.  Preheat the oven to 375 degrees. Remove the crusts from the bread and discard. Cut the bread into 1-inch cubes.

2.  If you're using the vanilla bean, combine the cream, milk, sugar, and vanilla bean in a heavy-bottomed pot. Bring to a slow boil. Remove from the heat and let the mixture cool and steep for 1 hour. If you're using vanilla extract, simply whisk together the cream, milk, sugar, and extract.

3.  In a large mixing bowl, whisk the eggs briefly. Pour in the vanilla-cream mixture and stir to combine. Add the bread cubes, pressing down with the back of the spoon. Let sit until they absorb most of the liquid.

4.  Pour the mixture into a 9x13-inch baking pan and cover tightly with foil. Place this pan into a water bath.

5.  Bake for 50 minutes to 1 hour, until the custard is firm. Remove from the oven and let cool slightly to settle. Cut into squares and serve with warm caramel sauce.

## MARIA'S PASTRY SHOP

46 Cross Street
Boston (North End)
(617) 523-1196

**Owner and baker | Maria Merola**

When you push open the glass door at Maria's, you leave traffic-choked Cross Street and enter a warm room redolent of sugar and baking dough. Bags of Italian candy hang behind the counter, and waffle-like pizzelle cookies line a glass display case. Other cookies come in all shapes and textures, from chewy macaroons to crunchy almond biscotti. The hard, sesame-covered zuccherati are nicknamed *passa tempo* ("time passers") because they take so long to finish. People come from all over Boston for the sfogliatelle, flaky pastries shaped like clamshells and filled with cheese and citron fruit. Pastries are sold the old-fashioned way, in cardboard boxes tied with string, though many people don't even make a pretense of saving them for later, devouring them on the spot at one of the round tables in the pastry shop.

With traditional Italian recipes and a deft touch, Maria Merola has built her bakery into a local legend. "I've been coming through that door since 1968," says the vivacious Merola, laughing. She started as a salesclerk and ended up buying the business in 1982. Most days she can be found patting out dough in the kitchen out back, speaking Italian with her mother and sister, who work with her. "If I don't like it, I don't make it," she declares. She warns that even if you follow her recipe, your ricotta tart won't be exactly the same as hers. "It all depends on how you roll and how you mix everything." But this will come close, especially if you use the best-quality ricotta cheese you can find. And whatever you do, don't add vanilla. "Fresh ricotta has no flavoring. If I wanted to taste vanilla, I'd buy a vanilla biscuit," she insists.

Michele Topor of North End Market Tours (see the sidebar on page 190) adapted this recipe for the home cook.

## TORTA DI RICOTTA (ITALIAN CHEESECAKE)

[MAKES 1 (9-INCH) CAKE]

**PASTA FROLLA CRUST:**

½ cup sugar
½ cup (1 stick) unsalted butter, room temperature
1 large egg
¼ cup milk or water
½ teaspoon baking powder
¼ teaspoon salt
2½ cups flour

In a large bowl, combine the sugar, butter, egg, milk or water, baking powder, and salt. Mix well. Fold in the flour but do not overmix; make sure that the mixture remains cool and does not become pasty. Shape the dough into a disk, wrap in plastic, and refrigerate for 30 to 60 minutes, or until firm.

**RICOTTA FILLING:**

1½ pounds ricotta cheese
½ cup sugar
4 large eggs

Place the ricotta in a large bowl. Stir in the sugar, then the eggs 1 at a time. Do not overmix.

**FINAL PREPARATION AND SERVING:**

1 large egg
Pinch of salt
Few drops of water

1. Preheat the oven to 350 degrees.

2. Cut off half of the *pasta frolla* dough and reserve. Roll half the dough into a 14-inch disk. Carefully fit it into the bottom and sides of a 9-inch cake pan. Allow the dough to hang over the edge of the pan.

3. Roll out the reserved dough into a 10-inch circle. Set aside.

4. Pour the ricotta filling into the crust base. Lay the reserved 10-inch circle of dough on the top of the filling. Trim the excess to an overlap of about $1/2$ to $3/4$ inch. Roll the overlapping dough back onto itself so it no longer hangs over the edge of the pan.

5. Make an egg wash by beating the egg with the salt and water. Brush the top of the *torta* with this mixture. Place the *torta* in the lower third of the oven and bake for about 45 minutes, until the filling is set (it should no longer jiggle in the center when the pan is gently shaken) and the crust is golden brown. Remove from the oven and let cool in the pan. Serve warm, or at room temperature.

# NORTH END

Boston's version of Little Italy, called the North End because of its location along the northern coastline of the city, has been a colorful place since Paul Revere lived there from the 1730s through the Revolutionary War (when he made his famous ride to Lexington and Concord to warn colonists that British troops were coming). Later the neighborhood's proximity to the waterfront made it home to groups of new immigrants. Italians settled in the late 1800s; by 1930 the neighborhood had become 99 percent Italian, according to neighborhood advocacy site NorthEndBoston.com.

In the past twenty years, high real estate prices and demographic changes have brought many non-Italians into the North End, but the population is still 41 percent Italian American. Crammed into less than a square mile bordered by Haymarket and the waterfront are about eighty-five restaurants—almost all of them Italian. You can still hear Italian spoken on the streets, and find Italian-language newspapers in some of the cafes. The streets are also home to specialty grocers that stock Italian imports and to bakeries selling biscotti and freshly stuffed cannoli—like

Maria's. Many of the small meat and produce markets look like they have been transplanted from Italy.

"The biggest business here is food," says Michele Topor, a longtime resident who has been leading North End Market Tours since 1994. "When [Italian] people got here, the food they were used to eating was not available. So they started bakeries, butchers, and shops to take care of themselves."

Calling out greetings in English and Italian, Topor takes visitors through the maze of narrow streets to about a dozen stores. These include Giuffre's Fish Market (the owner goes to the docks every day); Polcari Coffee (which also sells spices, flour, tea, nuts, and licorice); Salumeria Italiana (imported pantry items, cheeses, and cooking accessories); and Dairy Fresh Candies (confections and baking ingredients). The tour also stops in liquor stores specializing in Italian wines and liqueurs like limoncello and sambuca.

The food served at North End restaurants ranges from the traditional red-sauce-and-pasta menus (see Cantina Italiana, page 76) to more modern interpretations (see Bricco, page 187). "You are seeing more emphasis on better-quality ingredients," Topor says. "More people are traveling to Italy and coming back, wanting those ingredients. It's the food as well as the implication of the life that goes along with it—the romance and the abundance."

By now Italian restaurants in Boston have established themselves well beyond the North End. Still, they cannot possibly re-create the context of Old World neighborhoods where, in warm weather, people set up folding chairs on the sidewalk to play cards, and saints are celebrated at street festivals. The North End remains Boston's most colorful place for a plate of pasta, a tiny cup of espresso, and a stroll through the streets.

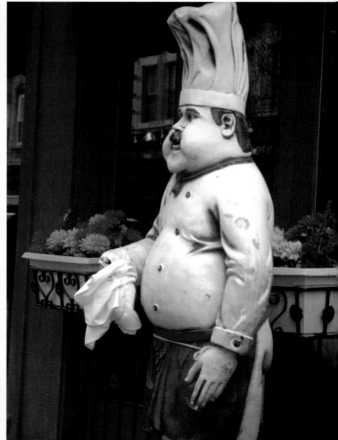

## TOP OF THE HUB

Prudential Tower
Fifty-second floor
800 Boylston Street, Boston
(617) 536-1775, www.topofthehub.net

**Executive pastry chef | Tak Chuen (Tommy) Choi**

The major attraction at the Top of the Hub is not on top of the tables. It's the view of planes angling up from Logan Airport, traffic bunching on Route 93, and boats leaving white streaks in Boston Harbor. Still, there are good reasons to turn your attention to the plates in front of you. Chef Mark Porcaro has fun taking off from basic ingredients in dishes like a coconut milk lobster soup, and sole with shiitake mushroom ravioli.

Since 1995, pastry chef Tommy Choi has built elaborate desserts at Top of the Hub from caramelized pineapple, toasted coconut, white Godiva chocolate sauce, and other rich components. A Hong Kong native, he grew up with a style of cheesecake that didn't weigh down the fork. His goal in this recipe was to combine this lightweight cheesecake with an American favorite: apple pie. "I wanted the flavor of the pie with the soufflé-like cake," he says. He certainly succeeds in re-imagining both desserts. It's nearly impossible to re-create his presentation—an individual cheesecake with a miniature candied apple on the side—but the inventive combination still shines in this home adaptation. This recipe has many steps, though none is complicated. Start by making the apple chips the day before. For an easy shortcut, use packaged apple chips and commercially made, chunky applesauce instead of the apple filling. The apple coulis—a thick sauce spooned onto the plate underneath each slice—accents the cake.

## TOP OF THE HUB'S APPLE CHEESECAKE

[MAKES 1 (9-INCH) CHEESECAKE]

**DRIED APPLE SLICES:**

1 Granny Smith apple, skin on, core removed,
   but apple left whole
¾ cup confectioner's sugar

1. Preheat the oven to 200 degrees. Cover a baking sheet with parchment paper.

2. With a sharp knife, or a mandoline, going horizontally through the apple, cut slices as thinly as possible.

3. Place the sugar in a shallow bowl and dip each apple slice to coat both sides. Arrange the slices on the baking sheet. Bake for 1½ hours.

4. Turn off the oven and keep the apples inside for several hours, or until totally dry—it's best if you can leave them overnight. Apple slices should keep their white color.

**CRUST:**

6 ounces graham crackers, crushed
2½ tablespoons granulated sugar
½ cup (1 stick) unsalted butter, melted

Combine all the ingredients and pat down evenly with the back of a spoon into the bottom of a 9-inch pan with removable sides. Set aside.

**APPLE FILLING:**

5 Granny Smith apples, peeled, cored, and cut in ¼-inch cubes
1½ tablespoons fresh lemon juice
1 cup granulated sugar
1 teaspoon ground cinnamon
2 tablespoons (¼ stick) unsalted butter

In a medium saucepan, combine all the ingredients. Cook over medium-low heat, uncovered, until the apples are soft but still hold their shape. Let cool.

**CHEESE FILLING:**

8 ounces cream cheese, left at room temperature to soften
4 egg yolks
½ cup heavy cream
1½ tablespoons flour
¼ teaspoon ground cinnamon
5 egg whites
½ cup sugar
¼ teaspoon cider vinegar
Approximately 1 cup apple filling (from recipe above)
    or chunky applesauce
Confectioners' sugar, as needed

1. Preheat the oven to 350 degrees.

2. In a large mixing bowl, using an electric mixer, beat together the cream cheese, egg yolks, and heavy cream until well combined.

3. Add the flour and cinnamon. Beat until combined, about 30 seconds.

4. In a separate mixing bowl, using an electric beater, beat the egg whites on low speed until they begin to foam. With the mixer still running, slowly add the sugar and then the vinegar, continuing to beat, increasing the speed to high, until stiff peaks form. Gently fold the beaten eggs into the cream cheese mixture.

5. Pour a quarter of the cheesecake batter evenly into the prepared crust. Spoon in the apple filling or applesauce to cover the top. Pour in the remaining cheese filling (it should come about three-quarters of the way to the top of the pan).

6. Bake for 40 to 45 minutes, or until the top is light golden brown. Turn the oven off. Partially open the oven door, keeping the cake inside for 20 additional minutes. The cake will fall as it cools. Remove from the oven.

7. After the cake is completely cool, sprinkle the top with confectioners' sugar.

**APPLE COULIS:**

½ cup sugar
1 cup water
2 tablespoons light corn syrup
¾ cup applesauce
1½ teaspoons cider vinegar

1. Place the sugar, water, and corn syrup in a saucepan. Bring to a boil and reduce the heat. Let simmer until the liquid reduces slightly, 4 to 5 minutes.

2. Stir in the applesauce and let cook for another 2 to 3 minutes.

3. Turn off the heat and stir in the vinegar. Let cool until you're ready to serve.

**FINAL PREPARATION AND SERVING:**

Spoon about 2 tablespoons of Apple Coulis (from the recipe above) on the bottom of a dessert plate. Place a slice of cheesecake on top. Garnish with dried apple slices and whipped cream (optional).

## OMNI PARKER HOUSE

60 School Street
Boston (Downtown)
(617) 227–8600, www.omniparkerhouse.com

**Executive chef | Gerry Tice**

The official dessert of Massachusetts, the Boston cream pie, started off as a basic chocolate pie at the Parker House Hotel (now the Omni Parker House), which opened in 1855. When it became popular, the word *Boston* was added to identify it to out-of-town visitors. The hotel developed two other famous American recipes as well—Parker House rolls and scrod (a special cut of cod or haddock). The hotel's claim to fame also includes famous employees: Malcolm X (who in the 1940s lived with his half sister in Roxbury) once worked here as a busboy; several years earlier the bakery employed a young Ho Chi Minh, the future leader of North Vietnam.

Today the concept of Boston cream pie has sometimes been stretched quite far from the original two-layer sponge cake with pastry cream filling and swirled chocolate-and-white frosting. You can find doughnut filling, cake mix, yogurt, and cheesecake all named Boston cream pie. Many Boston restaurants also serve variations, shrinking it into individual servings, adding fruits like banana to the filling, or drizzling the top with caramel sauce. This recipe comes straight from the source, but it has been adapted for the home cook.

# BOSTON CREAM PIE

[MAKES 1 (10-INCH) ROUND PIE]

**SPONGE CAKE:**

7 eggs

1 cup sugar, divided

1 cup flour

2 tablespoons melted butter

1. Butter the bottom and sides of a 10-inch round cake pan. Preheat the oven to 350 degrees.

2. Separate the eggs, placing the yolks and whites in separate mixing bowls.

3. Add $1/2$ cup of the sugar to each bowl. Using an electric mixer on high speed, beat the yolks until light and fluffy. Beat the whites until stiff peaks form.

4. With a rubber spatula, fold the beaten egg whites into the yolk mixture. Gradually add the flour, a little at a time, mixing it in with a wooden spatula. Mix in the butter.

5. Bake for about 20 minutes, or until spongy and golden. Remove from the oven and allow to cool fully.

**PASTRY CREAM:**

1 tablespoon butter

2 cups milk

2 cups light cream

$1/2$ cup sugar

$3 1/2$ tablespoons cornstarch

6 eggs

1 teaspoon dark rum

1. In a saucepan, bring the butter, milk, and light cream to a boil.

2. While this mixture is heating, combine the sugar, cornstarch, and eggs in a bowl. Using an electric mixer, whip until ribbons form.

3. When the cream mixture reaches the boiling point, whisk in the egg mixture. Return to a boil and let boil for 1 minute.

4. Pour into a clean bowl and cover the surface with plastic wrap. Let cool to room temperature, then chill in the refrigerator for several hours, or overnight if possible. When chilled, whisk to smooth out the consistency. Then whisk in the rum.

**CHOCOLATE ICING:**

4 ounces ($1/2$ cup) semisweet chocolate

$1/2$ cup heavy cream

Melt the chocolate in the top of a double boiler set over gently boiling water. Place the cream in a mixing bowl. When the chocolate is melted, add it to the cream and beat with a whisk for 15 to 30 seconds, just until it lightens slightly in color. Do not overwhisk.

**WHITE ICING:**

1 cup confectioners' sugar

2 tablespoons ($1/4$ stick) butter

3 tablespoons heavy cream, heated

In a mixing bowl, beat together the sugar, butter, and cream. Thin with water, if necessary. Place into a pastry bag fitted with a $1/8$-inch tip, or into a squeeze bottle (see the sidebar on page 124).

**FINAL PREPARATION AND SERVING:**

4 ounces slivered, toasted almonds

1. Using a slicing knife, level off the top of the sponge cake. Carefully slice the cake into 2 layers. Spread the pastry cream over 1 layer, reserving a small amount to spread on the sides. Top with the second cake layer.

2. Spread a thin layer of chocolate icing on the top of the sponge cake. Using the white icing in the pastry bag or squeeze bottle, immediately squeeze out a spiral line, starting from the center of the cake. Score the white lines with the point of a paring knife, starting at the center and pulling outward to the edge.

3. Spread the sides of the cake with a thin coating of the reserved pastry cream. Press on the toasted almonds and serve.

## RENDEZVOUS CENTRAL SQUARE

502 Massachusetts Avenue
Cambridge (Central Square)
(617) 576-1900, www.rendezvouscentralsquare.com

**Chef-owner | Steve Johnson**

With its orange walls, square lamps, and the 1950s lettering in its logo, Rendezvous has the comfortable, understated vibe of a rec room. Its menu also feels more personal than institutional, reflecting Steve Johnson's long relationships with local seafood providers (he's an avid fisherman himself), farmers, and other New England purveyors. Building on a base of comfort foods like roast chicken with chestnuts, cremini mushrooms, and sherry, his menu also makes room for Mediterranean-influenced dishes like grilled Portuguese sardines or tuna with Italian tonnato sauce. Though Johnson put in many years toiling in the kitchen while guests dined, he decided at Rendezvous to cook during the day so he could greet customers at night. His warm, friendly manner (he has mentored many kitchen workers) helps welcome people and keep service running smoothly.

This Warm Chocolate Cake shows how Johnson puts his own signature on a classic American dessert. It came together, as many recipes do, through two seemingly unrelated activities: He was baking Julia Child's Queen of Sheba cake, and talking to friends who were researching coffee in Mexico. Soon after, he decided to add a bit of ground coffee to a chocolate cake batter. "This cake has been following me around over the last twenty years," jokes Johnson, who throughout his career has remained in close touch with his high school friend Chris Schlesinger of the East Coast Grill (see page 94). The cake was the most popular dessert when Rendezvous opened in fall 2005. When it's served warm, with hints of cinnamon as well as espresso, you can taste why.

# WARM CHOCOLATE CAKE

[MAKES 1 (9-INCH) CAKE]

12 ounces semisweet chocolate, cut into pieces
1½ cups (3 sticks) unsalted butter
1 cup sugar
1 teaspoon ground espresso beans
6 egg yolks
½ cup all-purpose flour
½ teaspoon ground cinnamon
½ teaspoon salt
6 egg whites

1.  Preheat the oven to 350 degrees. Rub a little butter on the bottom and sides of a 9-inch cake pan with removable sides. Sprinkle with flour, tilting the pan to coat the bottom and sides, tapping out the excess. Set aside.

2.  In the top of a large, metal mixing bowl set over barely simmering water, gently melt the chocolate. Be careful to only heat the chocolate enough to melt it completely, then turn off the heat and allow it to stand at room temperature while you prepare the rest of the ingredients.

3.  In a large mixing bowl, using a stand mixer with the paddle attachment, or using an electric hand mixer, mix the butter and the sugar together, adding the sugar in three separate steps, until the batter becomes creamy, fluffy, and white in color. Add the ground coffee and beat it in. Add the egg yolks 1 at a time, beating after each addition.

4.  In a small bowl, stir together the flour, cinnamon, and salt. Add them to the butter-sugar-egg mixture and mix very briefly, just to combine. Pour the batter into the mixing bowl of melted chocolate. Using a rubber spatula or a wooden spoon, fold the melted chocolate into the batter very quickly, being careful not to overmix. Streaks of batter and chocolate may remain.

5.  In a separate bowl, beat the egg whites just until soft peaks form. Do not overbeat! Fold them into the cake batter quickly but in 3 separate steps. When the batter is smooth, turn it into the prepared cake pan and bake for 45 minutes, or until the top starts to crack and a toothpick inserted in the center comes out clean.

6.  Allow the cake to set for 20 minutes before removing the sides of the pan. This cake tastes best when served warm because of the cinnamon and espresso in the batter. If you prepare the cake well ahead of time, reheat it gently for a few minutes prior to serving.

SABAYON MOUSSE MARTINI

# CHOCOLATE HEAVEN

The Chocolate Bar at the Langham Hotel will make you feel like a kid in a candy store—but with far classier choices. Here the buffet tables are laden with sweets that define deluxe: chocolate coconut almond mousse pie, white chocolate lime panna cotta, chocolate sabayon in martini glasses, and s'mores for grown-ups to eat with a spoon. Playing the role of Willy Wonka is Alejandro Luna, who each week devises at least seventy creations, including sushi (white chocolate "rice" rolled around a fruit-and-candy filling) and pizza (chocolate crust topped with raspberries and coconut). The showstopper is a four-tiered fountain of liquid chocolate with an assortment of fresh fruit, waffle chunks, and pretzel rods for dipping. The room is festive, with chairs and drapery in floral fabric and the aroma of chocolate crepes being made to order. Servers in red shirts dart through, bringing coffee and water to counteract the sugar overload.

The Chocolate Bar, the first buffet of its kind when it opened in 1988, is a well-known splurge for families and groups celebrating weddings and other special events. (For savory menus, go to the hotel's Café Fleuri restaurant; see page 90.) Intrepid, calories-be-damned members of a senior citizens' club in New Hampshire even charter a bus for a weekly excursion. People walk in happy and leave even happier. "You should come here to experience what chocolate is all about," says Luna, who grew up in Miami and worked at the Wynn Las Vegas hotel before arriving in Boston in 2005. His philosophy—and that of the entire Chocolate Bar—shows how far Boston has come from its restrained Puritan beginnings. "At the end of the day, it's all fun," enthuses Luna.

## CHOCOLATE BAR

Langham Hotel
250 Franklin Street
Boston (Financial District)
(617) 451-1900, www.langhamhotels.com

**Pastry chef | Alejandro (Alex) Luna**

Chef Alex Luna of the Chocolate Bar finds passion fruit a particularly refreshing flavor. "I always keep a little container in my freezer at home because I love to eat it," he says. Using passion fruit curd as a base, it didn't take him long to build a tart with a layer of chocolate ganache and a meringue topping. The bite-size version has become a staple at the Chocolate Bar. This recipe makes a large tart that is likely to be a conversation piece at a dinner party because of its unusual mix of flavors. Though each step in making the tart is fairly easy, you need to plan at least 2 days in advance because the passion fruit curd needs to sit overnight in the refrigerator, and the finished tart needs be frozen before serving. Frozen passion fruit can often be found at the supermarket. For a substitute, use the same quantity of freshly squeezed lemon juice or pureed raspberries. Frozen orange juice concentrate also works, as long as you omit the ½ cup sugar in the curd recipe. Similarly, milk chocolate, dark chocolate, or white chocolate can be used in the ganache. In fact, the components of the tart are so versatile that almost any combination of pureed fruit and chocolate would go together—which is how Luna likes to work. No idea, it seems, is too outlandish to fit into his philosophy: "The only boundary to what you can do with chocolate is your mind."

## CHOCOLATE PASSION FRUIT TART

[MAKES 1 (9-INCH) TART]

**PASSION CURD:**

1 cup pureed passion fruit
3 eggs
½ cup sugar
¼ cup (½ stick) butter

One day before assembling the tart, place the pureed passion fruit, eggs, and sugar in the top of a double boiler. Fill the bottom of the double boiler with water and heat on medium high. When the water is barely simmering, place the passion fruit mixture on top and cook, stirring constantly, until it thickens enough to form ribbons (188 degrees on a candy thermometer). Remove from the stove and set aside until it's warm to the touch, but not hot

(104 degrees). Add the butter and stir until it's melted and well incorporated. Cover with plastic wrap, patting the wrap directly onto the surface of the curd to keep a skin from forming. Refrigerate overnight.

At this point, you could also make the dough for the tart shell and refrigerate it overnight.

## TART SHELL:

7 tablespoons (3½ ounces) butter
1 cup confectioners' sugar
1 egg
1½ cups plus 2 tablespoons pastry flour
¼ teaspoon baking powder

1. Again the day before assembling the tart, use an electric mixer to cream the butter with the sugar. Incorporate the egg.

2. In a separate bowl, whisk together the flour and baking powder. Stir the dry ingredients into the butter mixture. Gather the batter together into a ball of dough.

3. Wrap the dough in plastic wrap and refrigerate for 2 hours. When you're ready to bake, preheat the oven to 375 degrees. On a countertop or another flat surface, roll the dough into a circle to fit into a 9-inch tart pan with a removable bottom. Gently press the dough into the pan so it evenly covers the bottom and the sides.

4. Cover the crust with parchment paper and fill with dry beans or pie weights. (This step, called blind baking, prevents the crust from rising unevenly.) Bake the shell for 15 minutes. Carefully remove the paper and beans and continue baking for an additional 8 to 10 minutes, until lightly brown. Set aside until you're ready to use it.

## CHOCOLATE GANACHE:

1 cup heavy cream
8 ounces dark or milk chocolate, chopped

1. The day before assembling the tart, place the cream in a saucepan and bring to a boil. Add a third of the chopped chocolate, stirring until well incorporated. Add the remaining chocolate a third at a time, stirring well after each addition to achieve a nice emulsion and a smooth ganache. Remove the double boiler from the heat, but leave the ganache on top so it stays warm until ready to use.

2. Assemble the tart in the prepared shell. Spread the passion fruit curd over the bottom, filling the shell halfway. Carefully pour the warm ganache over the curd, enough to cover. Be careful not to fill too high, or the ganache will spill over. Cover with foil and place in the freezer overnight.

## MERINGUE:

3 egg whites
½ cup plus 2 tablespoons sugar

Just before serving the tart, mix the egg whites and sugar in a clean, stainless steel bowl. Place on top of a double boiler set over medium-low heat, stirring constantly until the grains of sugar have completely dissolved. Remove the bowl from the heat. Using an electric mixer, whip until stiff peaks form.

## FINAL PREPARATION AND SERVING:

Remove the tart from the freezer. Fill a pastry bag with the meringue and pipe it on top, or spread the meringue on top with a spoon. Brown the meringue by placing it directly under a very hot broiler. Serve immediately. Garnish with fresh raspberries, if desired.

## FINALE DESSERTERIE & BAKERY

1 Columbus Avenue
Boston
(617) 423-3184

30 Dunster Street
Cambridge (Harvard Square)
(617) 441-9797

1306 Beacon Street
Brookline (Coolidge Corner)
(617) 232-3233
www.finaledesserts.com

**Executive pastry chef | Nicole Coady**

Instead of making dessert an afterthought, Finale Desserterie & Bakery specializes in upscale sweets served anytime, for any occasion. The idea started as a Harvard Business School project for classmates Kim Moore and Paul Conforti. By the time they graduated, they were ready to take it into the marketplace and opened their first location in Park Square in 1998. Nicole Coady, executive pastry chef since the beginning, builds works of art from super-premium ingredients like Valrhona chocolate, Tahitian vanilla beans, and Morello cherries. Lined up in the pastry case for counter service or takeout might be an Ultimate Chocolate Cake with a fresh orchid on top, tiramisu with a checkered pattern on its sides, and a glossy Chocolate Decadence Cake with a dot of gold frosting in the center.

The candlelit dining room, where red velvet banquettes line one wall, specializes in plated desserts. The savory food—soups, sandwiches, pizza—is appropriately called a prelude, "a light bite before you indulge in something sweet."

These chocolate cookies, adapted here for home cooks, have been on the menu since Finale opened. Their intense flavor makes them anything but the ordinary bake-sale variety. The key, says Coady, is to use the best chocolate you can find (look for Valrhona or Callebaut; avoid the baking squares). It will seem like a lot of expensive chocolate, but "this is no mistake." Line up your ingredients: The batter comes together quickly after you melt the chocolate. Plan to eat the cookies within 24 hours of baking them—which shouldn't be a problem once you take the first buttery, intensely chocolate bite.

# DOUBLE CHOCOLATE COOKIES

[MAKES 3-4 DOZEN COOKIES]

6 ounces bittersweet chocolate
17 ounces semisweet chocolate
1 cup (2 sticks) unsalted butter
6 eggs
2½ cups granulated sugar
1 tablespoon vanilla extract
1 cup all-purpose flour
½ teaspoon baking powder
¾ teaspoon salt

1. Melt the chocolate and butter together in a double boiler, stirring frequently with a wooden spoon, until blended.

2. In a separate bowl, using an electric mixer, whip the eggs, sugar, and vanilla until thick and light.

3. In another bowl, sift the flour, baking powder, and salt together.

4. With the mixer on low speed, slowly add the chocolate mixture to the egg mixture. Slowly fold in the flour mixture. The cookie batter will be liquid. Let it sit for 3 hours in a cool place.

5. When you're ready to bake, preheat the oven to 350 degrees. Make a doubled cookie sheet by placing one sheet inside another. Spray the top sheet lightly with nonstick cooking spray. Scoop heaping tablespoons onto the cookie sheet at least 3 inches apart. Bake for 10 to 15 minutes, or until the center of the cookie is firm to the touch (cakelike firmness). The second and subsequent batches may need less baking time, as the doubled cookie sheet retains heat. Avoid overbaking—the cookies will become dry and powdery instead of moist and chewy. Cool on wire racks. Serve as close to baking time as possible.

## FLOUR BAKERY + CAFÉ

1595 Washington Street
Boston (South End)
(617) 267-4300

12 Farnsworth Street
Boston (Fort Point Channel)
(617) 338-4333
www.flourbakery.com

**Chef-owner | Joanne Chang**

As a child with an insatiable sweet tooth, Joanne Chang always wanted to try new desserts—
even before she had the slightest idea of how to cream butter and sugar. Once she learned how
to bake, she never stopped, even while she was earning a degree from Harvard. She now master-
minds the snickerdoodle cookies, ooey-gooey caramel nut tarts, lemon raspberry cakes, and
dozens of other desserts at Flour, her bustling bakery. Open since 2000, Flour has become a
neighborhood favorite: 80 to 85 percent of its customers are regulars who expect to order the

same thing every day from the menu posted on a chalkboard. Though pastries are the base of the business, Chang gives equal importance to the cafe menu of sandwiches, soups, and salads.

As is the case with many recipes, these Cornmeal Lime Cookies started as an experiment. "We had a big batch of quince jam and wondered what to do with it. So we decided to make thumbprint cookies from a cornmeal batter." When the jam ran out, the staff still liked the cookies, so they looked for another complementary ingredient. Since lemon, cinnamon, vanilla, and nuts were already in heavy rotation, they decided to try lime. The result—a crumbly, not-too-sweet cookie with a surprising jolt of citrus in the batter as well as the pale green frosting—was a keeper.

## CORNMEAL LIME COOKIES

[MAKES ABOUT 30 COOKIES]

**COOKIES:**

½ cup (1 stick) butter

⅓ cup plus 2 tablespoons sugar

1 egg

1 tablespoon lime zest (from about 3 medium limes)

½ teaspoon vanilla extract

1¼ cups all-purpose flour

⅓ cup plus 1 tablespoon cornmeal

1 teaspoon baking powder

¼ teaspoon salt

1. Cream the butter and sugar, mixing together they're until well blended and creamy. Mix in the egg, lime zest, and vanilla.

2. In a separate bowl, sift together the flour, cornmeal, baking powder, and salt. Fold the dry ingredients into the butter mixture.

3. Shape the dough into a round log approximately 1 inch in diameter, wrap it in plastic wrap, and refrigerate for at least 1 hour until the dough is well chilled, or as long as overnight.

4. When you're ready to bake, preheat the oven to 350 degrees. Slice the dough into cookies about ¼ inch thick and place on a lightly greased cookie sheet. Bake until the edges are golden brown, 12 to 15 minutes. Let cool and spread with Lime Glaze (recipe follows).

**LIME GLAZE:**

1½ cups confectioners' sugar

Approximately 2 tablespoons lime juice

1 tablespoon lime zest

Put the confectioners' sugar in a bowl. Mix in the lime juice and lime zest until the consistency is thin enough to spread. Glaze the cookies on the rack where they cooled to let the excess drip off. Wait several minutes before serving to let the glaze set. Sprinkle the top of each cookie with additional lime zest or strips of lime peel, if desired.

# BRUNCH

After the frenzy of a busy Friday or Saturday night, most chefs are relieved to change the pace at brunch. Tables turn over at a more comfortable pace, as customers need not rush out for movie or concert tickets. In Boston brunch is typically served on Saturdays as well as Sundays, with menus sticking closely to classic eggs Benedict, pancakes, waffles, and French toast. What varies more is atmosphere. At the casual extreme is the Pajama Brunch at Tremont 647, where the entire staff comes to work in bathrobes and slippers. The recipe for Gingerbread Pancakes with Lemon Curd typifies the adventurous American style of chef-owner Andy Husbands. The more formal brunch at the Four Seasons Hotel starts the day with a sumptuous spread that includes chocolate-stuffed French toast, sushi, a carving station, and a dessert buffet that sometimes features Lemon Poppy Seed Tea Bread. This chapter also introduces you to an urban hot spot (Union Bar and Grille), a deli with a fat lady on its logo (Zaftigs), and a bakery and cafe that doubles as a job-training program for the homeless (Haley House).

## ZAFTIGS DELICATESSEN

335 Harvard Street
Brookline (Coolidge Corner)
(617) 975–0075, www.zaftigs.com

**Chef | Lisa Hicks Clark**

A more-than-pear-shaped lady in a tight, red dress sets the tone for Zaftigs, whose name means "pleasantly plump" in Yiddish. A portrait of this mascot, nicknamed Louise, presides over a counter where you can pick up a coconut cupcake or a peanut butter and jelly bar to go. The dining room is the place to order chicken soup, brisket, and about two dozen hot or cold sandwiches. This deli is Jewish influenced but not kosher, hectic but friendly compared with brusque New York places. It's also a neighborhood hangout where you might see a uniformed policeman, a couple with a child in a high chair, and college students staring into their laptops. Whimsical work by local artist Danny O'Connor is often on display; a plaque announces his place in *The Guinness Book of World Records* for fitting 11,430 toy balls into a mosaic.

One of the mainstays of Zaftigs is breakfast, which can be ordered right up until closing time. To supplement the menu's challah French toast, potato pancakes, and eggs, Lisa Hicks Clark added her version of banana bread. "The recipe is actually an updated version of my father's," she says. "I loved banana bread when I was a kid, but I didn't like the large chunks of walnuts (I loved the walnuts, just not the skin, which would get stuck between my teeth)." Chopping the walnuts into tiny pieces eliminated this problem. Grilling adds another dimension, as it brings out the flavor in the nuts and turns the crust crispy. "That's where the flavor is," she confides with a grin. "The date butter melts into the warm toast, and it's like heaven." This spread also works well with cinnamon raisin toast.

# TOASTED BANANA NUT BREAD
# WITH DATE AND CINNAMON BUTTER

[MAKES 1 LOAF]

**BANANA BREAD:**

1¾ cups all-purpose flour

1¼ teaspoons baking powder

½ teaspoon baking soda

1 teaspoon salt

½ cup granulated sugar

⅔ cup packed light brown sugar

1 cup (2 sticks) unsalted butter, room temperature

2 eggs

2 tablespoons whole milk

5 overripe bananas (3 mashed, 2 cut into large chunks)

¼ cup chopped, toasted walnuts, divided

1. Preheat the oven to 325 degrees. Spray a 9x5x3-inch loaf pan with nonstick cooking spray, or lightly grease it with butter.

2. In a large mixing bowl, combine the flour, baking powder, baking soda, and salt.

3. Using an electric mixer, beat both sugars with the butter for 5 minutes, scraping the sides of the bowl often, until light and fluffy.

4. Beat in the eggs 1 at a time. Add the milk 1 tablespoon at a time. Beat at medium speed for 1 minute.

5. Add the butter mixture to the dry ingredients. Use a spoon to fold in the bananas and 2 tablespoons of the nuts until all is combined (stir gently so the banana chunks retain their shape).

6. Pour the batter into the prepared loaf pan. Top the batter with the remaining 2 tablespoons of walnuts. Bake for 50 to 60 minutes. Check for doneness with the toothpick test.

7. The bread can be sliced and served warm. To toast it, let it cool completely and cut into slices 1½ inches thick. Spray a nonstick sauté pan with cooking spray and heat over medium-high heat. Add the slices of banana bread to the pan and brown on both sides. Serve with Date and Cinnamon Butter (recipe follows).

**DATE AND CINNAMON BUTTER:**

½ cup (1 stick) unsalted butter, room temperature

½ teaspoon pure vanilla extract

1 teaspoon ground cinnamon

3 tablespoons chopped, pitted dates

With an electric mixer, cream the butter on low speed for 1 minute. Add the vanilla, then the cinnamon, and mix for another minute. Add the dates and mix until combined, pausing to scrape down the sides of the bowl often so the ingredients mix evenly.

## AUJOURD'HUI

Four Seasons Hotel Boston
200 Boylston Street
Boston
(617) 338–4400, www.fourseasons.com

**Executive pastry chef | Tim Fonseca**

During the week the Four Seasons Hotel is known as a power-breakfast spot where deals go down between the first and third cups of coffee. On Sunday the pace slows for the clientele—mostly families and couples of all ages—to sample the lavish buffet at Aujourd'hui (located upstairs, above the hotel's other restaurant, the Bristol Lounge, see page 38). The fresh freesias on each table, cloth napkins, and dark wood armchairs put children on their best behavior. So does the view of the Boston Public Garden, especially if the Swan Boats are cruising the lagoon. The youngest diners usually appreciate the French toast stuffed with chocolate, served from a silver chafing dish.

Anyone can appreciate the selection—poppy seed waffles, assorted fresh berries and tropical fruits, granola, and pancakes cooked to order. Farther around the horseshoe-shaped buffet is a station for dumplings and other Chinese dim sum treats. More lunch-friendly fare goes from a carving station to tossed salads. A separate seafood station turns lox and bagels into a work of art: Thinly sliced limes garnish the lox platter, while florets of cream cheese and butter are piped around the edge of each serving bowl. Oysters on the half shell, lobsters, and shrimp top giant bowls of crushed ice.

Pastry chef Tim Fonseca takes charge of the dessert buffet, an artistically arranged assortment of parfaits, miniature crème brûlée ramekins, wedges of chocolate cake—more than a dozen selections. There's even a dessert soup—white chocolate with Grand Marnier—with dried cherry chocolate biscotti for dipping. The selection changes almost every week, but you might find this poppy seed bread, enlivened by the zest of three lemons. Tim Fonseca says it can be served all day long. "Because of its bold lemon flavor, it holds up on its own. I have even caught myself eating slice after slice without needing to top it with butter or jam."

## LEMON POPPY SEED TEA BREAD

[MAKES 1 (9X5X3-INCH) LOAF]

1 cup (2 sticks) butter
1¾ cups sugar
6 eggs
Finely grated zest from 3 lemons
¼ teaspoon vanilla extract
2 cups all-purpose flour
1½ teaspoons baking soda
¾ teaspoon salt
1 cup sour cream
¼ cup poppy seeds

1. Preheat the oven to 350 degrees. Spray a 9x5x3-inch loaf pan with nonstick cooking spray or grease lightly with butter.

2. Using an electric mixer, cream the butter and sugar until light. Slowly add the eggs, 2 at a time, scraping the bowl after each addition. Add the lemon zest and vanilla extract. Mix just until incorporated.

3. In a separate bowl, combine the flour, baking soda, and salt. Add to the butter mixture.

4. Add the sour cream and poppy seeds. Mix for 1 minute, scrape the sides of the bowl, and mix for 30 seconds more. Make sure the sour cream is completely mixed in.

5. Pour the batter into the prepared pan. Bake for approximately 45 minutes or until a toothpick comes out clean.

# TEA

Boston's most famous tea is a variety that nobody ever sipped, much less poured into a china cup. On the night of December 16, 1773, in the turmoil leading up to the Revolutionary War, colonists staged the Boston Tea Party to protest the taxes that England levied on tea shipped to the American colonies. They boarded cargo boats and dumped 342 chests of tea into Boston Harbor.

After the Revolution, Bostonians found more pleasant reasons to take tea together. Tea is now a social event at hotels and restaurants around town. Once the province of elderly ladies in below-the-knee skirts sipping from Wedg-

wood china cups, tea has been updated to make room for everything from pink peppercorn–spiced cookies to tea-infused cocktails. Here are a few fun places to go.

At UpStairs on the Square (see page 62), tea is served in a room with hot-pink walls and gold-trimmed doors. "It's a progression of flavors, my inner old lady coming out," jokes co-owner Deborah Hughes. You can find finger sandwiches on the three-tiered display, but also chive biscuits shaped like stars, and profiteroles stuffed with chicken salad. Sweets might include date nut bread, a peppermint brownie, or a few slices of candied orange peel. The teapot's handle is covered with velvet so you don't burn yourself.

The mansion setting of L'Espalier (see page 156) contrasts with Frank McClelland's playful tea menu. Children feel welcome with the "Make Way for Ducklings" special that includes pink peppercorn madeleine cookies, orange blossom meringues, and chocolate-dipped strawberries. Red Riding Hood's basket comes stuffed with petits fours and canapés. Adults can order the caviar and champagne tasting menu, or the "Three Blind Mice" cheese tray.

For British-style afternoon tea (scones with cream and jam, finger sandwiches, pastries) in a dining room overlooking some of the best scenery in Boston, go to the Four Seasons (see page 210) or Intrigue cafe at the Boston Harbor Hotel (see page 10). The Langham Hotel (see pages 90 and 200) serves familiar fare, with menu selections named after London landmarks including Windsor Castle and Buckingham Palace. To connect to history, you can still visit a restored Boston Tea Party ship (closed for renovations until 2008) moored by the Congress Street bridge across Fort Point Channel, opposite the Children's Museum, and even buy a Boston Tea Party blend to brew at home.

## SWANS CAFÉ

Boston Park Plaza Hotel
64 Arlington Street
Boston
(617) 426–2000, www.bostonparkplaza.com

**Tea sommelier | Cynthia Gold**

Though the term *sommelier* is usually reserved for wine experts, Cynthia Gold treats tea tasting as seriously as anyone who swirls, sniffs, and sips wine. Not only does she select the blends served at the hotel's Swans Café (see page 78), but she also leads tea tastings, if arranged in advance. The usual progression goes from white tea—made from leaves that have been minimally processed—to green, then black. Without consulting notes, Gold can eloquently explain the origins and attributes of tea varieties including Gen-Mai-Cha (Japanese green tea with roasted rice floating in it), Rare-Aged Pu-Erh (an earthy-tasting Chinese black tea), and Dunsandle Estate (a slightly sweet black tea from India).

Gold has also developed tremendous expertise in recipes that use tea. "You're not trying to make things taste like tea—that would be out of balance," emphasizes Gold, who used to own a specialty tea shop in Cambridge. "Tea enriches or enlivens different flavors." One of her most successful experiments has been blending tea with liquor in cocktails that range from the delicate white port jasmine tea to the bright green apple mar-tea-ni. She and sous chef Darrel Lazier have also perfected crème brûlée infused with the hotel's own Swan's Grey blend. Tea also finds its way into their scallops, sorbets, and poached fruits.

Teatime edibles—almost an afterthought, given all the choices of tea—come on a two-tiered silver tray. The assortment of sandwich toppings on the bottom tier can be tailored for vegetarians, children, and seafood lovers. Petits fours, chocolate-covered strawberries, and other sweets line the tray's top tier. Scones, with accompaniments in ladylike cut-glass dishes, come with any menu. This version uses dried cranberries to perk up British-style raisin scones with New England flavor.

## CRANBERRY RAISIN SCONES

[MAKES 18 SCONES]

½ cup (1 stick) butter, softened
½ cup sugar
2 eggs
6 cups all-purpose flour
3 tablespoons baking powder
2 teaspoons baking soda
2 teaspoons salt
Zest of ½ orange
5 ounces dried cranberries
3 ounces raisins
1½ cups whole milk
1 teaspoon vanilla extract
Coarse sugar, for sprinkling

1. Line 2 baking sheets with parchment paper. Preheat the oven to 425 degrees.

2. In a mixing bowl, using an electric mixer on medium speed, cream the butter and sugar. Add the eggs 1 at a time, beating after each, until they're incorporated into the batter.

3. In a separate bowl, sift together the flour, baking powder, baking soda, and salt. Add to the butter mixture, beating just until combined.

4. Using a spoon, stir in the orange zest, cranberries, and raisins.

5. Add the milk and vanilla and stir just until mixed. There will still be signs of unmixed flour, but for a tender scone, be sure not to over mix.

6. Scoop out the batter into tennis-ball-size scones and place on the prepared baking sheets. Sprinkle the tops with coarse sugar.

7. Bake for 15 minutes, or until golden brown. Let cool on a wire rack. Serve with butter and jam.

## SEAPORT HOTEL & SEAPORT WORLD TRADE CENTER

1 Seaport Lane
Boston
(617) 385–4000, www.seaportboston.com

**Executive chef | Richard Rayment**

Boston's Seaport District is gradually being transformed from acres of old warehouses into the headquarters for the Boston Convention Center and new hotels, offices, and condominiums. The Seaport Hotel, which opened in 1988, was one of the first to arrive. Its location across from the Boston World Trade Center makes it a busy headquarters for trade shows and exhibitions. The catering department each year keeps up with more than 1,200 breakfast buffets, banquets, and other special events. Aura (see page 116) is the hotel's full-service restaurant.

The well-versed Richard Rayment leads the Seaport Hotel's culinary team. He started his career as a teenager by selling fish-and-chips on the streets of his native London, and worked his way into hotel kitchens in England, Bermuda, and San Francisco. He came to Boston to be executive chef at the Ritz-Carlton. At the Seaport Hotel his staff plans functions ranging from a coffee break for ten to a martini bar for a hundred. This brunch recipe combines two classics—French toast and pralines. Because it's baked as a casserole, it comes together more easily than individually pan-fried slices of toast. Plan ahead, because the bread needs to soak overnight in the custard mixture. To serve a smaller group, cut the recipe in half and bake it in an 8×8-inch pan.

# BAKED FRENCH TOAST WITH MAPLE SYRUP AND PECAN PRALINE

[SERVES 8-10]

**BREAD:**

1 French baguette (13–16 ounces)
8 large eggs
2 cups half-and-half
1 cup heavy cream
2 tablespoons sugar
1 teaspoon vanilla extract
¼ teaspoon ground cinnamon
¼ teaspoon ground nutmeg
Dash of salt

1. Cut the French bread into 1-inch-thick slices. Butter a 9x13-inch baking dish. Arrange the bread slices in the prepared dish, overlapping with a shingle effect (each slice overlapping the edge of the one beneath it by about 1 inch) as necessary.

2. In a large bowl, combine the eggs, half-and-half, cream, sugar, vanilla, cinnamon, nutmeg, and salt and beat until blended but not too bubbly. Pour the mixture over the bread, making sure all slices are covered evenly. Spoon some of the mixture between the slices. Cover and refrigerate overnight.

**PRALINE TOPPING:**

1 cup (2 sticks) butter
1 cup packed light brown sugar
1 cup chopped pecans
2 tablespoons light corn syrup
½ teaspoon ground cinnamon
½ teaspoon ground nutmeg

Combine all the ingredients in a bowl and blend well.

**FINAL PREPARATION AND SERVING:**

Preheat the oven to 350 degrees. Spread the praline topping over the bread and bake for 40 minutes, until puffed and lightly golden. Serve with maple syrup.

## TREMONT 647

647 Tremont Street
Boston (South End)
(617) 266–4600, www.tremont647.com

**Chef-owner | Andy Husbands**

A hostess in a red bathrobe and flannel pants, her hair straggling out of a ponytail, greets those who arrive for brunch at Tremont 647. Behind her other flannel-clad servers glide through the narrow dining room, carrying trays of coffee and breakfast martinis. Andy Husbands, an apron tied over his red plaid pajamas, directs cooks in the open kitchen at the center of the room. Welcome to Pajama Brunch, a comical way for the mostly young South End crowd to ease into Saturday or Sunday.

Not any old egg and bacon dishes will do for Husbands, the high-energy chef who also owns Sister Sorel restaurant next door and co-authored *The Fearless Chef* cookbook. Out come plates of griddled ham steak with spoon bread and maple-poached green apples, or perhaps lobster omelets with charred tomato sauce. The smoked salmon is wrapped around grilled bread, to be dunked in poached eggs with hollandaise sauce.

Husbands admits that the idea of the Pajama Brunch is goofy, but it caught on and has been going now for nearly ten years. "It started because we had to go from working nights, then getting up and working again the next day. We thought it would be more fun for the staff if everyone could come to work in their pajamas." Dinner is equally fun, though regular attire is the norm. The boldly flavored dinner menu ranges from Tibetan-style momo dumplings and "Too Stinky" cheese plate to a Chilean sea bass with hoisin barbecue sauce.

One day, when Husbands had some extra base for a frozen lemon mousse, he began to scheme about possible accompaniments for it. Somehow the mix of spices in gingerbread seemed right. "I fantasize about what sounds good and then I make it," he says. The pancakes look dense enough to come from a health food restaurant, but their texture is actually light, and the flavors of the spices are brought out by the warm serving temperature. The citrusy lemon curd—and fresh raspberries or sliced strawberries—add color as well as complementary flavors.

# GINGERBREAD PANCAKES WITH LEMON CURD

[MAKES ABOUT 12 (4-INCH) PANCAKES]

**LEMON CURD:**

MAKES ABOUT 1 CUP

¼ cup freshly squeezed lemon juice (from about 2 lemons)
½ cup sugar
2 egg yolks
1 egg
¼ cup (½ stick) cold butter, diced

Place all the ingredients in a heavy-bottomed saucepan over medium heat. Stir constantly until the butter has melted and the curd has thickened, about 5 minutes. Pour into a pitcher or serving dish and keep warm until you're ready to serve.

**PANCAKES:**

1½ cups all-purpose flour
2 tablespoons cornmeal
1 teaspoon baking powder
½ teaspoon baking soda
1 tablespoon powdered ginger
1 teaspoon ground cinnamon
¼ teaspoon powdered cloves
½ teaspoon salt
1½ cups milk
3 tablespoons butter, melted
3 tablespoons molasses
2 eggs
½ teaspoon vanilla extract
Fresh berries, for garnish

1. In a large mixing bowl, mix together the flour, cornmeal, baking powder, baking soda, ginger, cinnamon, cloves, and salt.

2. In a separate bowl, mix together the milk, butter, molasses, eggs, and vanilla.

3. Add the milk mixture to the flour mixture and stir until combined.

4. Lightly grease a griddle or large frying pan with butter, oil, or nonstick cooking spray and heat it on the stove (or to 350 degrees if using an electric griddle). Pour the batter about 2 tablespoons at a time onto the griddle, spacing so the pancakes have room to spread. Cook the pancakes until bubbles appear and pop, about 2 to 3 minutes. Flip and cook for 2 minutes more. Serve hot with Lemon Curd and garnish with fresh berries.

## VICKI LEE'S

105 Trapelo Road
Belmont
(617) 489–5007, www.vickilees.com

**Chef-owner | Vicki Lee Boyajian**

For twenty-five years the cakes made by Vicki Lee Boyajian generated a buzz at weddings and birthday parties around Boston. No design was too outlandish for her to try—not even a series of square cakes frosted with purple and magenta fondant, the request of an artsy bride. She has also spent hours hand-painting and attaching to other cakes thumbnail-size flowers made from royal (egg white and sugar) icing.

At the shops Boyajian owned in Arlington, Westwood, and Needham, she sold baked goods to Neiman Marcus and local restaurants, as well as walk-in customers. After a five-year hiatus, Boyajian, whose thin frame makes her look more like a dancer than a baker, is back in business at a shop with bright yellow awnings. Taking a break from a seemingly nonstop pace in the kitchen, she surveys the sun-splashed tables where delivery people, clerks in nearby retail shops, and suburban women are taking a coffee and pastry break, and says with appreciation, "It's great to be back. I thought I was going to get out of the business for good, but I really missed it." Once again she turns out hand-rolled Danish, banana-caramel tarts, ANZAC (oatmeal-coconut) cookies, and other favorites. These can be enjoyed in the cafe, along with Armenian-style sandwiches on cracker bread, risotto cakes, chicken piccata, and other savory dishes.

On Sunday chef de cuisine Nora Martin Buchanan's "strata"—a layered casserole that's something like a savory bread pudding—delivers a hearty balance of eggs, cheese, and sausage. Its base of stale bread sounds unpromising until it is soaked in custard and baked, which transforms into a soft foundation for all the savory flavors that surround it. One slice is likely to keep you going for the entire day. Start making it the night before: The bread needs to soak for several hours before it is baked.

# SAUSAGE, MUSHROOM, AND GRUYÈRE STRATA

[SERVES 6]

8 ounces French or Italian bread, sliced ½ inch thick
(about 10 slices)
¼ cup (½ stick) butter
8 ounces sausage (any type), casings removed
½ cup chopped onion
8 ounces medium white mushrooms, sliced
1 tablespoon minced fresh rosemary
Salt and pepper, to taste
8 ounces Gruyère cheese, grated
6 large eggs
2 cups light cream
Pinch of fresh nutmeg

1. Place the bread slices on a flat surface, such as a countertop, and leave them out overnight to dry. Butter each slice on one side, using 2 tablespoons of the butter.

2. Generously butter an 8-inch-square baking dish.

3. In a skillet over medium heat, sauté the sausage until cooked through, breaking up clumps with the back of a spoon, about 5 minutes. Using a slotted spoon, transfer the sausage to paper towels to drain. Wipe out the skillet, leaving a little of the drippings.

4. In the same skillet, melt the remaining 2 tablespoons of butter. Sauté the onion until softened. Add the mushrooms and continue to cook until the mushroom liquid is absorbed, about 5 minutes. Add the cooked sausage and rosemary and season with salt and pepper. Transfer to a mixing bowl.

5. Place half of the bread in single layer, butter-side up, in the prepared baking dish. Layer half of the sausage-mushroom mixture, then half of the grated cheese, on top. Repeat with the remaining bread, sausage-mushroom mixture, and cheese.

6. Using an electric mixer or a whisk, beat together the eggs, light cream, nutmeg, salt, and pepper. Pour evenly over the prepared dish. Cover with plastic wrap and refrigerate for at least 4 hours or overnight.

7. Preheat the oven to 350 degrees. Bake the strata, uncovered, until it's puffed and golden brown, approximately 45 to 50 minutes. Transfer to a wire rack and cool for 5 minutes before serving.

## HALEY HOUSE BAKERY CAFE

12 Dade Street
Roxbury (Dudley Square)
(617) 445–0900, www.haleyhouse.org

**Executive chef | Didi Emmons**

After thirty years of serving meals to the homeless in Boston's South End, Haley House began offering baking lessons to its clientele in 1996. Bread from class projects was sold right from Haley House. As the program evolved into job training and a wholesale bakery, the retail enterprise increased its visibility by opening a cafe in Roxbury's Dudley Square in 2005. Didi Emmons, author of the *Vegetarian Planet* cookbook and co-owner of the Veggie Planet eatery in Harvard Square, decided to take on the challenge of starting up a cafe (which does serve meat) and overseeing the wholesale operation. "Most of the food around here is fast food, and that's what people are used to. We're trying to make healthier food," she says. The menu also reflects the African American and Caribbean flavors familiar in the neighborhood—jerk chicken, grits, collard greens, sweet potato pie. The sunny room, with exposed-brick walls and hanging plants, is a comfortable spot to pick out a book from the communal bookshelf and munch a slice of corn bread, or sip mango iced tea.

This flan, a Saturday brunch special, is good for entertaining because it can be served warm or at room temperature. Instead of a crust, a layer of baked potatoes lines the bottom of the baking pan. The starchy potatoes contrast nicely with the greens and tangy goat cheese. Each slice is also pretty; you can see the different textures and colors of the vegetables. "It's a handy make-ahead dish since it improves in the fridge after a day or two," says Emmons. The recipe calls for greens from dandelions—the pesky weeds cursed by gardeners, but edible and packed with vitamins A and C. You can pick them yourself, as long as your lawn is free from pesticides. The early leaves (before the dandelions flower) are the most tender. Some markets also sell dandelion greens, especially in spring. Fresh spinach leaves can be substituted. If you have it, drizzle some white truffle oil on the flan right before serving to make it what Emmons terms "a little slice of heaven."

## GOAT CHEESE AND DANDELION GREEN FLAN

[SERVES 6]

5 small (about ¾ pound total) unpeeled potatoes,
      such as Yukon Gold, red, or Yellow Finn, scrubbed
1 tablespoon olive oil
10 ounces dandelion greens (or spinach), tough bottom
      half of stems discarded, leaves left whole, about 8 cups
3 cloves garlic, minced
1 plum tomato, diced
4 large eggs
1 cup milk
½ teaspoon salt
5 ounces creamy goat cheese
Freshly ground pepper, to taste (optional)

1. Preheat the oven to 350 degrees. Either bake or microwave the potatoes until they are tender. Coat the inside of a 9x9-inch baking pan with vegetable spray. When they're cool enough to handle, slice the potatoes about ½ inch thick.

2. In a large skillet over medium heat, heat the olive oil. Add the dandelion greens or spinach and cook, stirring often, for 4 minutes. Add the minced garlic and plum tomato and stir for 1 more minute. Let cool.

3. In a medium bowl, whisk together the eggs, milk, and salt.

4. Assemble the flan: In the bottom of the prepared pan, lay the potatoes in a single layer if possible (you can layer them if you need to). Then add a single layer of the dandelion greens. Then, using a teaspoon or crumbling with your fingers, distribute the goat cheese over the top of the greens. Season with pepper if desired. Pour the egg-milk mixture over the goat cheese. Cover the baking pan with foil.

5. Bake for 45 to 50 minutes, removing the foil during the last 5 minutes of baking so the top browns. A knife inserted into the middle of the flan should come out clean. Let cool for 5 minutes before serving.

## UNION BAR AND GRILLE

1357 Washington Street
Boston (South End)
(617) 423-0555, www.unionrestaurant.com

**Chef | Stephen Sherman**

Don't roll out of bed and pull on a sweatshirt to eat brunch at Union. The dining room, outfitted with black leather upholstery and yellow orchids on each table, reflects the stylishness of this up-and-coming urban neighborhood. The owners also own Aquitaine (see page 48) in the more established part of the South End. Right down the street from Union, art galleries and furniture stores have been reclaimed from warehouses once in the shadow of elevated train tracks. A jazz soundtrack sets the mood for the crowd of casual yet fashionable twenty- and thirty-somethings. A bracing start to the day is the Eye Opener: chilled espresso mixed with coffee and chocolate liqueurs. Not far behind are cinnamon swirl sour cream coffee cake, spinach goat cheese omelets, and French toast with orange marmalade.

Stephen Sherman paid attention to each step when developing the recipe for these Banana Nut Muffins. "I slice the bananas instead of mashing them, because I like the textural component of large pieces of banana," he says. "As long as the bananas are ripe enough, they do get slightly mashed when folded into the muffin batter. And I really like lots of big pieces of walnuts for the crunch." Banana extract can be found at a well-stocked grocery store—and is worth the trouble, because it really boosts the flavor. If you're making the muffins for a small group, cut the recipe in half, or freeze leftovers to serve another time.

## BANANA NUT MUFFINS

[MAKES 2 DOZEN]

11 ounces (2¾ sticks) butter
3⅓ cups sugar
1¼ teaspoons salt
5 eggs
3 egg yolks
5⅓ cups all-purpose flour
2 tablespoons baking powder
1⅓ cups buttermilk
½ teaspoon banana extract (see note)
3 cups sliced ripe bananas
3 cups chopped toasted walnuts
Coarse sugar, for sprinkling on top of muffins

1. Have all ingredients at room temperature. Generously spray 24 muffin cups with nonstick cooking spray, or use paper liners for 24 muffins. Preheat the oven to 375 degrees.

2. In a mixing bowl using an electric mixer, cream the butter, sugar, and salt. Beat in the eggs, egg yolks, and banana extract.

3. In a separate bowl, mix together the flour and baking powder. Stir the dry ingredients into the batter, alternating with the buttermilk, until almost incorporated. There should still be some lumps of dry flour.

4. Add the sliced bananas and toasted walnuts and fold gently to combine. When the fruit and nuts are well distributed, the batter should just come together. Do not overmix.

5. Spoon the batter into the prepared muffin tins. The batter should just come up to the top of each tin. Sprinkle the tops of the muffins generously with coarse sugar. Bake for 25 to 30 minutes, until well risen and deep golden. Cool the muffins in the pan, remove, and serve.

:: **Note:** If you can't find banana extract, substitute ½ teaspoon vanilla extract and add ¼ to ½ teaspoon grated nutmeg to the batter.

# METRIC CONVERSION TABLES

## APPROXIMATE U.S. – METRIC EQUIVALENTS

### LIQUID INGREDIENTS

| U.S. MEASURES | METRIC | U.S. MEASURES | METRIC |
|---|---|---|---|
| ¼ tsp. | 1.23 ml | 2 Tbsp. | 29.57 ml |
| ½ tsp. | 2.36 ml | 3 Tbsp. | 44.36 ml |
| ¾ tsp. | 3.70 ml | ¼ cup | 59.15 ml |
| 1 tsp. | 4.93 ml | ½ cup | 118.30 ml |
| 1¼ tsp. | 6.16 ml | 1 cup | 236.59 ml |
| 1½ tsp. | 7.39 ml | 2 cups or 1 pt. | 473.18 ml |
| 1¾ tsp. | 8.63 ml | 3 cups | 709.77 ml |
| 2 tsp. | 9.86 ml | 4 cups or 1 qt. | 946.36 ml |
| 1 Tbsp. | 14.79 ml | 4 qts. or 1 gal. | 3.79 lt |

### DRY INGREDIENTS

| U.S. MEASURES | | METRIC | U.S. MEASURES | METRIC |
|---|---|---|---|---|
| 17³/₅ oz. | 1 livre | 500 g | 2 oz. | 60 (56.6) g |
| 16 oz. | 1 lb. | 454 g | 1¾ oz. | 50 g |
| 8⅞ oz. | | 250 g | 1 oz. | 30 (28.3) g |
| 5¼ oz. | | 150 g | ⅞ oz. | 25 g |
| 4½ oz. | | 125 g | ¾ oz. | 21 (21.3) g |
| 4 oz. | | 115 (113.2) g | ½ oz. | 15 (14.2) g |
| 3½ oz. | | 100 g | ¼ oz. | 7 (7.1) g |
| 3 oz. | | 85 (84.9) g | ⅛ oz. | 3½ (3.5) g |
| 2⅘ oz. | | 80 g | 1/16 oz. | 2 (1.8) g |

# Glossary

Below are a few key ingredients and cooking terms that the chefs in this book commonly use in their recipes. For more extensive information, consult a food reference book.

**Amaretti:** crunchy, almond-flavored Italian macaroons

**Au gratin potatoes:** sliced potatoes topped with cheese sauce, then baked or broiled until brown

**Blanch:** to briefly immerse in boiling water

**Braise:** a meat, fish, or vegetable cooked in a small amount of liquid in a pan with a tight-fitting lid, so that the steam also helps do the cooking

**Brine:** to soak in a salty solution

**Caramelize:** to slowly heat a food until it releases its natural sugars, which turn brown. Sugar can be caramelized by heating it in a pan, stirring constantly, until it becomes liquid and its color deepens.

**Chiffonade:** to cut a leafy ingredient into thin strips

**Chinois:** a fine strainer

**Chipotle chile peppers:** see sidebar, page 59

**Clarified butter:** the clear liquid that floats to the top when butter is melted. (The layer that sinks to the bottom is the milk solids.) This clear liquid, skimmed off to make clarified butter, burns less easily and keeps longer than regular butter.

**Coarse sugar:** also called decorating sugar, a large form of sugar crystals, about the size of the coarse salt sprinkled on hot pretzels

**Cream** (verb): a basic baking step of mixing together butter and sugar until smooth

**Crème fraîche:** a thick, French-style cream that's similar to sour cream but has a milder flavor. It does not curdle when added to boiling sauces and soups.

**Crusty bread:** European-style bread with a well-baked, brown exterior and a softer interior, such as French baguettes or Italian pane

**Deglaze:** to add liquid to the ingredients in a hot pan, which loosens the brown bits in the bottom and adds their flavor to the liquid

**Demi-glace:** a rich, brown sauce made with beef stock and Madeira

**Flambé:** the dramatic-looking technique of dousing food with liquor and igniting it with a match to let the alcohol burn off

**Focaccia:** a flat Italian bread (often round in shape) flavored with olive oil and herbs

**Foie gras:** a specially enlarged goose or duck liver with a smooth, rich texture, considered a French delicacy

**Fromage blanc:** a creamy, French-style cheese similar to sour cream, typically eaten with fruit as a dessert

**Ganache:** a chocolate-cream mixture often used as cake frosting

**Hearts of palm:** the pale green stalk of a young cabbage palm tree, usually about ½ to 1 inch in diameter, packaged in cans or jars outside of the tropical areas where it grows

**Immersion beater:** a handheld blender that can go right into a pot of soup or another liquid and puree the contents

**Kosher salt:** coarse salt

**Mandoline:** a specialty slicer that works well for cutting extremely thin pieces

**Mascarpone:** a creamy Italian cheese that's often used in desserts

**Mesclun greens:** a mix of small salad greens that might include arugula, oak leaf lettuce, baby spinach, and radicchio

**Micro greens:** miniature (approximately finger-nail length) leaves, such as arugula and basil, typically used for garnish

**Mirin:** Sweet Japanese rice wine

**Nonreactive container:** glass, ceramic, or stainless steel. Metals including aluminum, copper, and cast iron can interact badly with acidic ingredients (especially citrus juice and vinegar) and give an off taste or color to the food.

**Panko bread crumbs:** coarse, Japanese-style crumbs that are lighter and crunchier than American-style bread crumbs

**Parchment paper:** heat-resistant, nonstick paper commonly used to line baking pans or keep dough from sticking to a countertop. It is usually sold in rolls like aluminum foil.

**Pastry bag:** a reusable bag for frosting, dough, whipped cream, or thick batter. The contents are squeezed out through a tip. The width and shape of the tip varies according to the desired effect, such as a decorative border or a frosting flower.

**Prosciutto:** Italian ham that has been cured with salt and spices, but not smoked. It is often served in extremely thin slices.

**Ramekin:** a baking dish, usually 3 or 4 inches in diameter, used for baking individual portions of food, especially crème brûlée

**Reduce:** to let a liquid simmer until some of it boils off, concentrating the flavors of what's left in the pot. A reduction is a sauce made by this process.

**Ribbons:** when eggs and sugar that are beaten together become thick enough to fall off a beater in strands that look like ribbons. These ribbons rest on top of the batter before they sink down.

**Sake:** Japanese rice wine

**Scrod:** a small cod or haddock fillet, not, as many believe, a specific fish

**Toothpick test:** a method for testing a cake to see if it is done. A toothpick (or cake tester or skewer) is inserted in the center. If it comes out clean (without batter still clinging to it), the cake is done.

**Wasabi:** Japanese horseradish, typically mixed into a pungent, light-green condiment served with sushi. It also comes in powdered form.

**Water bath (also bain-marie):** this technique for evenly cooking custards and puddings involves placing the baking dish containing the food inside another, larger dish. The larger dish is then filled with enough warm water to come halfway up the sides of the first baking dish. Both dishes are placed in the oven. The water from the larger dish is discarded when the baking is finished.

**White pepper:** a paler, milder version of black pepper, made from a peppercorn whose skin has been removed. It is mostly used in light-colored foods, where its appearance blends in better than black pepper.

**Wok:** a Chinese pan with a concave shape, typically used for stir-frying

**Zest:** the aromatic outer skin of a citrus fruit, excluding the white pith underneath

# Index

## About the Author

**Clara Silverstein** is a former food writer at the *Boston Herald* who edited the *Here's How* column for readers to request recipes from their favorite New England restaurants. *The Boston Chef's Table* grew out of her interest in working with local chefs. She is a founding member of the Ladies Who Lunch networking and social group for Boston food writers.

She has contributed articles to the *Boston Globe* and *The Oxford Encyclopedia of Food and Drink in America* and is the co-author, with chef Marjorie Druker, of the forthcoming *New England Soup Factory Cookbook* (Rutledge Hill Press). Her first book is the memoir *White Girl: A Story of School Desegregation* (University of Georgia Press). She is Program Director of the Writers' Center at Chautauqua in western New York. She lives near Boston with her husband and two children.